LIGHT YEARS

LIGHT YEARS

Augustus Young

London Magazine Editions

First published in Great Britain 2002
by London Magazine Editions
in association with
Enitharmon Press
26 Caversham Road, London NW5 2DU
Copyright © 2001 Augustus Young
ISBN 0-904388-91-3
Set in Monotype Ehrhardt by
Rowland Phototypesetting Ltd
Printed in Great Britain by
St Edmundsbury Press Ltd
both of Bury St Edmunds, Suffolk

A CIP catalogue record for this book
is available from the British Library

CONTENTS

PART ONE
LIVING IN ENGLAND
Tales from the Sixties

'London is beautiful if you have only one eye without too many beams in it.'
Vincent Van Gogh, *Letters*

'At last one morning I came on deck, and they told me Ireland was in sight: a foreign country actually visible! I peered hard, but could see nothing but a bluish, cloud-like spot to the North East. Was that Ireland? Why, there was nothing remarkable about that, nothing startling . . . I might as well have stayed at home.'
Herman Melville, *Redburn*

PROLOGUE:
THE IRISH SEA, JULY 1967

I left Cork at the age of twenty three in an aeroplane, not a boat. The plane was a status symbol for emigrants, signifying a job waiting. I checked in two lumbering suitcases and an umbrella. This was my first trip abroad and I wasn't taking any chances. I knew from the novels of Henry Green that a black brolly was a required protective in London. When folded it was a decent weapon. Unfurled it made a hat unnecessary. I had never had an umbrella before, despite Cork being the capital city of persistent drizzle.

One suitcase was crammed full of important books I had not read. The other contained all my clothes, including two outsized pullovers (Texaco blue, wild salmon) knitted by my mother. Five strong pairs of shoes completed my wardrobe. At Mass the previous Sunday the epistle from Ecclesiastes was discouraging. 'The labour of the foolish wearieth everyone because he knoweth not how to go to the city.' Nevertheless, boarding the plane I was composing a verse in my head. 'A refugee from my roots/ On my own for the first time/ Carrying cases tied with twine/ Bursting with sweaters and boots.' I scribbled it down on the back of my ticket before strapping my arms in the safety belt like a straightjacket. The twine was a cummerbund.

It was a muggy morning in early July. I cannot recall who drove me to the airport. But it certainly was not my mother. The family did not expect that I would last long abroad, and made no fuss about what was regarded as a trip for me and a welcome respite for them. My mother must have been glad to see the back of me. My college days had been protracted by exam failures, and the last year was something of a penalty shoot-out between us.

She always scored the last exasperating goal. 'James, you're no good, no good at all.' I netted my last chance with a hopeless 'I am what you made me'. All the same, shame drove me eventually to scrape a degree. This qualification would have been useless, but an eccentric external examiner (a lady professor who liked my mother) noted my dogged refusal to acknowledge the obvious and recommended me for a trainee research post in an Essex hospital.

Saying goodbye, my mother was not her usual straightforward self. After all, despite everything, I was her eldest son, and all partings are a foretaste of something more permanent. But there were no tears or embraces. Large families inhibit physical demonstrations of affection. Room cannot be found where, of necessity, territorial lines have been drawn. But the hurt look in her eyes told me she was seeing the event in larger terms. She was also appealing to me to spare her shame by not returning in a week. The long and the short views were conflicting, and I sensed that not coming to the airport was not a mark of indifference. Her pragmatic advice at the door came as a relief. 'Don't be afraid of an overdraft, and for God's sake take out a Life Insurance.' I sorely needed guidance on money matters. I didn't know yet how to write a cheque.

I was wearing my only suit, a green check tweed outfit with tight pants and shoulder pads. I left the house with its scraggy hedges, where tall palms once reigned, wanting for the first time in years to stay. I made up my mind not to look back as the car took me off. I raised my arm for form's sake like a defeated diplomat being chauffeured to his execution, and caught a glimpse of my mother's brave wave at the gate.

The tiny airport on the hill welcomed me 'a hundred thousand times'. The 'Cead Mile Failte' sign was, of course, for the benefit of tourists and businessmen, the predominant users. The greeting meant something different to me. It welcomed a hundred thousand escapes. I suppose it was my more successful younger brother who drove me to the airport because all traces of sentiment had evaporated. I was in a let's go mood, and took in the pocket terminal building, the Viscount forty-seater and the lone airstrip like Gary Cooper casing his chances of escape from a Last Hope saloon. The route to freedom looked clear.

I looked back at the town below. Down there in a slight haze it was crouched like a begging dog in the lap of the estuary's maternal mantle. It appeared more like a sepia-tinted heritage postcard than a place I knew off by heart. I could tell with my eyes shut every uneven stone and redundant tram track in its streets, from years of cycling. The sludgy river, dividing the town into three sunken heavily housed islands, was crossed by nine bridges. I could feel them like my own rib cage. Now that the living disorder contained within this complex frame no longer included me, it nicely distanced itself into a neat map. Even so, I knew I could fill in its details. Where all the trees, statues and corner-boys were standing at this moment. What churches were hearing confessions on a weekday noon. I could have made a litany of the public houses and categorised them into sawdust or plush, good talk or brawls, literary or philosophical. I knew too much about this lowly town. It was time to go.

The take off was a flight into the unknown. But it was a charted one, unlike the modern turbo jet which backfires a Jumbo into the great beyond. The Viscount explained its ascent to the interested passenger. It seemed like a car with its engine and wheels, but with the addition of powerful propellers to levitate its bulk. There was no mystery. The rise from ground to clouds was gradual, more arrow from a bow than bullet from a gun, and the cultured flier had sufficient time to estimate the Pegasian horsepower of the machine against the likely compound weight of fellow passengers and crew. As the plane was half full and the cockpit door open this calculation proved easy and reassuring. This was my first flight and I was alert to everything. The Viscount plateaued off at four thousand feet. I looked down through the wispy racing cloudlets and saw the Lee estuary below. Soon I could witness my beloved delta widening into the Irish Sea. The sight made me forget the craft's uneasy rocking in the wind. So far my departure from home was fairly matter of fact. Now I felt emotion. Being alone in the clouds I found I could give in to it.

Unlike the town the estuary changed every day, and no two days were the same in any given month. It was the self-renewing swamp in which I grew up. Here my father took his evening walks. I accompanied him when my mother was indisposed. We talked of higher things, at least he did. In return for the company I was rewarded with a bar of Fry's chocolate cream. Essentially I was there to prevent people thinking my father was talking to himself. I was not expected to understand a word he said. This, no doubt, gave him free reign for some soul searching in preparation for his philosophy lectures at the university. I made my manners at moments of silence by pointing out a kittiwake in the dunes or a tramp in the bushes, nothing too substantial.

Just occasionally he would surprise me with a question, not to test my listening powers, but to acknowledge my presence. 'How high can you jump?' It was important not to reply immediately because that was to devalue the question. The answer would be subjected to his scholastic scrutiny. 'I'm not a jumper, I'm a runner.' Such a reply would be taken in and approved by no further questions. He would continue with his discourse. As though boys' matters had been dealt their due. On one walk he dropped a remark which I understood (therefore intended for me). My father's eyes twinkled as he dryly confided, 'It would be strange if when we died it turned out we had been fooled by the theologians.' From an academic who in his later years sought the Papal imprimatur before publishing, this was indeed a momentous confidence. And my crew cut shot up by an inch.

The friendly Aer Lingus hostesses in Kelly green fussed around me, replenishing my coffee and brandy. How they kept their balance as the Viscount tacked against the crosswinds was beyond me. I watched their lovely lurch from – widely spaced – passenger to passenger. Coffee and brandy. This was heaven. I recognised both girls from my ill spent youth holding up the steps of the Savoy Cinema. Schoolgirls came out in giggling flocks to parade through Patrick Street for the titillation of the boys. It was know as 'doing Pana'.

We hung round the cinema's entrance smoking and smirking, and squinting sideways to 'assay the talent'. Posing in school uniforms was restrictive. But we pocketed our peaked caps once out of school and swaggered to our observation station, hips to the fore. There we stood displaying our manly, rugby-playing physiques as best we could (I was convinced I was possessed of a tiny head, a gargantuan bottom, and fat fleshy lips which I kept biting to bring down the swelling). The sight of our posing and our perception of it must have been two very different things, but the girls were a delight. How we looked forward to the long summer months when the strictures of term time were lifted, and boy could meet girl without the whole town knowing, in seaside places at the mouth of the estuary. Anything could happen (and rarely did). The names of these trysting points were wonderful to me – Fountainstown, Myrtleville, the lower class and sensually seedy Graballbay. My friend Fergus would have dismissed my two hostesses as 'pretty but not clever'. I was not so sure.

The estuary was my pleasure garden and my wilderness. We went back a long time together. Probably as far as my amniotic origins. And further. How many of the sons of Cork were conceived on the banks of this estuary? I did not know or care to speculate. Once, as a baby, a cousin let slip my pram and I rolled down the grassy bank into the Atlantic pond, a modest artificial lake siphoned from the river for family outings. My baby carriage stayed upright and the daughter of the local policeman, Mandy Dent, waded out with her voluminous underwear afloat to rescue me. I was still sleeping when a horde of screaming children brought me home triumphantly. This was my main contribution as an infant to family legend.

Several years later at the time of the Kon Tiki expedition the pram was used to transport a raft down to the Atlantic pond. Our homemade craft sank into the silt. Angry swans waded on to the bank and flapped us away. My sister and brother retreated back up the hill, to the hoots of the village cabal. The pram was recovered, dismantled and became their toboggan. Down the grass bank face front they sledged. Watching from a Japanese cherry tree in the garden, we saw our parents strolling by the pond. My mother would have recognised the sleigh, but nothing was said. My father stood, head back, amused by the reckless manoeuvres of the village boys.

Their leader was Morgy Fox, bigger and rougher than the others, and newly arrived from Wales. His age was a mystery. Morgy broke up the unwieldy conglomerate that comprised the village boys. A new tolerance was extended to sissies from fee-paying schools like myself, more likely to have access to cake tins and loose change at home. I latched on to Morgy's gang, paying my dues with fruit from our orchard and pinches of tobacco from my father's tin. Apart from the odd sideswipe to let me know I was only there on his sufferance, I was accepted. Old enemies grudgingly allowed me to tag along.

The boys congregated where the estuary narrowed into the town. The Marina was a tree-lined river walk not unlike, in its modest way, a certain Monet painting. A gigantic pylon and a disused bandstand were the landmarks that defined our territory. Boys idling from the city gave it a wide berth. Morgy and the pylon were edifices to avoid. Both sparked when touched. We spent long summer afternoons on the grassy banks or in the bandstand when it rained, talking big and thinking small, watching the boats and the birds on the water.

There were three boat clubs with bright-striped wooden pavilions beside the marina. The rowing boats carried upside down by headless crews on to the river were like prehistoric beetles, transformed into elongated crayfish as they whirled away, oar-blades dripping. The rowers looked like gods on the water. But back on dry land we knew them all, bandy-legged workers with sloping shoulders from Ford's or Dunlop's.

The cormorants we called billy divers. Their plunging prowess gave rise to a betting game. We put halfpennies on birds fancied to stay down longest. These jet black lozenge-like fowl were capable of disappearing for minutes on end. Morgy's stopwatch was used to time them. Nicknames were given to favourites. Esther Williams stayed submerged for three minutes and twenty seconds. More gob-stoppers than it would take to dam the Lee river were won on the strength of Esther's lungs. Sometimes a billy diver spoilt the book by failing to resurface. This made us thoughtful. All to a man were still altar boys. Talk about eternal things usually ended with fierce wrestling tussles on the grass. On one such occasion I found a ten shilling note under a seat in the bandstand. It was a blistering hot day and we marched into town in formation and bought blocks of water ice in the Cold Storage Company on the Grand Parade. I can recall thinking 'I will remember this', as my slab melted faster than I could lick.

The river widened into the estuary proper at Blackrock Castle, built by a nineteenth-century Cork merchant, a mock baroque eyesore that demarcated the dividing line between the haphazard but immutable taste of humans and the consistent but ever-changing imperatives of nature. The town was stuck with this folly. Dinghies from the Yacht Club behind the Castle butterflied at the foot of the estuary, light-wind dilettantes compared to the battered trawlers that staggered into the harbour, having eluded the gales that whipped around the Fasnet Rock. I well remember three days in the 1950s, glued to the radio, listening out beyond the estuary to the Irish Sea in full storm, to reports of a small ship, the Flying Enterprise, sinking. Brave Captain Dancey was my hero, leaping back on board for reasons I can't recall. I experienced that titanic struggle between sea and sailors as vividly as though I had been winched down as part of the rescue.

One bright, bitterly cold Sunday in early winter when I was twelve I watched an upturned dinghy drift into the delta. I was not alone. Half the village came out for the afternoon to see the distant shell-like craft being sucked into the crosscurrents and tossed around until it sank. We were entertained, not knowing that Peter Dent, Amanda's brother, was clinging to its hull. The funeral of Peter Dent was an occasion for the collective guilt of Blackrock village to be assuaged. We were not helpless witnesses, but uncomprehending ones. It was my first drowning and I did not realise it.

Trying to conjure up what Peter Dent was like when alive (popular with the girls, good at school), I looked around the plane for inspiration. Several rows behind was a classmate from school, now an aspiring actor. I disappeared into my seat. Eamon, a notorious wit, doyen of the Literary and Philosophic Debating Society, was to be avoided at all costs. Like many witty Irish people he lacked a sense of humour and a true sense of himself. I would be assaulted by anecdotage if he spotted me. My flight reverie would be grounded.

Lakelands, where the river road gave way to fields, was where I last saw Peter Dent, walking with a girl from St Angela's. Each carried a book under an outer arm, their adjacent arms linked. They were sauntering along the open shore. Across the bay lay

Little Island where Peter's body was washed up a few months later. Brown hares darted along this rocky stretch. Few people came here during weekdays. The lone man with a dog was perhaps sneak-previewing hare scents for coursing on Sunday. Blood sports then were taken for granted. I did not bat an eyelid at a game hare being torn to pieces by a tongue-load of prize dogs. It was part and parcel of life in the fields of Lakelands. One afternoon I watched a cow calving on her own, not a farmhand in sight. The sloughing of the placenta, a great glob of saliva, made me want to retch. But I recovered to wonder as the cow, still on her haunches, licked the bloody birth fluids off the nascent calf.

The brandy in my head made me feel the plane would loop the loop. I was upside down and so were the two air hostesses. Pulling myself together, I readjusted my perspective. Sound was still faster than air flight and the voice of the past caught up on me, pleading to be heard. It was probably the propellers or the engine, identified on the wings as a Rolls Royce. Whatever it was, it was insistent. Hindsight propelled me forwards like the exhaust of a jet.

The past twenty years or so I had lived as though in a glider. At the wind's mercy, I was wafted forward, more or less, by the rocking commotion. The forces of circumstance controlled my destiny and were with and against me at the same time. I had drifted somewhere. Probably here. I had no idea of what to expect of my newly propelled and engineered life. So there was no point in thinking ahead. But now I had a past I might as well reflect on it.

I thought of recent summers grounded by exams. I spent my days in Lakelands, taking a short cut from the Atlantic pond along a disused railway line. In a well-worn duffle bag I carried lecture notes, doorsteps crammed with cheese, a plastic mac, swimming things, one of my father's pipes with a pouch full of cheap shag tobacco, and some books for diversion.

A couple of miles down the ghost line a defunct railway bridge crossed a creek from the estuary and I was in the peninsula of

Lakelands. Under the defunct bridge the waters swirled with currents. At high tide good swimmers dived in for their daily plunge. Here the estuary broke into an archipelago of inlets and pools. The overgrown banks down to the water were thick with honeysuckle, brambles and wild roses. After the frequent showers of summer rain the fragrance was swoon-inducing. I did not trust myself to lie down, but drank some water from a cress-covered spring nearby to clear my head. The heaviness of low-lying Cork in summer was a hazard to students and intellectuals.

Ambling on, it was possible most days to survey the bay – Little Island, the golfer's paradise, across the water, and Monkstown languishing a mile or two seawards, once a prosperous shipbuilding village, tucked in neatly. I always stopped here. Once or twice each summer I glimpsed a kingfisher skimming the sides of the inlet, a blur of blue and green, perhaps highlighted by a sunspot.

Then skirting an abandoned orchard, I made for my favourite field. It opened on to the shore, and featured a copse of monkey-puzzles, some monumental boulders, a ruined farmhouse. The orchard was a temptation. I sneaked in to pocket some choice crab apples or gnarled plums. Belonging to Bessborough convent, which sequestered unmarried mothers and disowned orphans, the orchard was utterly neglected. Moulding apple trees draped to thrice a man's height with tumbleweed and wild lily-like flowers. When feeling virtuous (not hungry) I tiptoed past the wall, respectfully, observing the husks of cars dumped from the steep river road that dissected my path.

My field was a meadow of clover, cowslips and cowpats. Amiable herds of cattle occasionally strayed in to graze on the succulent verdure. It had not been cultivated for many years. Gates had been removed, as had the roof of the farmhouse. The owners had probably long left for England. Boatloads of emigrants, mostly hanging out of steerage, could be seen departing in the late evening. The mail boat sailed twice a week. But that was another story. A story of the depopulation in the 1950s of the small farms and slum districts. The owners of this large, solid-looking ruin undoubtedly travelled by plane or luxury class. Maybe they just went to Dublin, a prosperous enough city, though it did for me carry a burden of guilt. Ireland was a wasted island with a lolling big-headed capital city and a self-centred Third Economic Programme.

I was well out of it. The Just Society was not here. Although the tired government of thirty years was slouching into the modern world, it was at the expense of the poor and dispossessed, and driven by greed. England, it seemed to me, was different. Having put its past behind, the shrinking empire was paying off its indemnity, welcoming its colonial victims and providing its own poor with proper health and education. I was a great admirer of the postwar remedy for eliminating the Five Giants – Ignorance, Idleness, Squalor, Poverty and Sickness. I would play a small but honourable part in slaying these Miltonic monsters. Not for Ireland, of course, but I consoled myself there were five million Irish people there. We were flying over Wales now, and my thoughts returned to Lakelands for a last time. The plane was descending.

I used my lecture notes mainly to prop up my book, lying face down on the scrub-grass facing the water. In this position I experienced inch by inch the estuary changing in a few hours from sluggish mudflats to a bouffant high tide. I swam most days in complicity with the moon. At full tide the estuary was awash with seawater. For five minutes each side of high tide, the murky water became clear and full of life. This not only made it healthy to bathe in, but warmer, like a spa, and of course I could find my depth. I learned to follow the tides around the clock, an hour later each day. It had the exhilaration of the arrival of summertime. I swam in the morning chill, the dew making the grass slippery, and as the darkness descended (always the sweetest swim). But the Grand Opera of all swims was when there was a spring tide, and the distance between where I undressed and where I leapt in was a thrilling few seconds. Then I embraced the estuary so fully that had I stood up in the water it would have clung to me.

My desultory reading was likely to be something like Turgenev's *Sportsman's Sketches*, or one of Mauriac's painful little novellas of provincial life, *The Desert of Love* or *The Knot of Vipers*. His chic essay of Continental Catholic Despair, *The Stumbling Block*, figured then as my bible. Irish Catholicism was full of optimistic hollerings which I could not abide. Here, lying on my back, I scribbled *bon mots* (half thoughts, half-borrowed – 'Life is death in moderation', 'He loved others and sweet cakes', 'A clever young man is one who uses the word numinous quite a lot').

Improving my memory was a task I set myself. Each day I learned by heart a verse from Palgrave's *Golden Treasury*, choosing stanzas that sounded ludicrous in terms of everyday life. For example, Ralph Waldo Emerson's 'Far and forget to me is near' and Walter Savage Landor's 'Rose Aylmer, whom these wakeful eyes/ May weep but never see'. In Ireland the myths are often more tedious than the reality they are attempting to transcend. I knew this somehow and basked in the hyperbole. But the lines I loved most to bellow into the wilderness were from W. H. Davies. The poem began with promising bathos. 'A glass of cider and a pipe/ In summer under a shady tree.' But climaxed with 'Let me be free to wear my dreams/ Like weeds in some mad maiden's hair'. That made me jump up and leap around. There was nobody behind the bushes to watch my dionysian revel, thank God.

I read with half an ear and an eye to the estuary. The incoming tide was my guide. Fingers of surging water were pushing mud through the ebbing channels. I read slowly, the tide was slow. Nothing much seemed to be happening. But it was working furtively as the pages turned faster. I was getting into the book. Landmarks of wrack and rock flooded over, the mud flats disappeared. It was a race between the tide and the end of my book. I was reading the tide in. Sudden surges, then apparent withdrawals. Moments of stasis allowed me to read on in panicky snatches. Approaching full tide, choppy little waves nibbled audibly at my concentration. If a ship passed by they swelled into real breakers, shifting more than pebbles. I had to put down my book. I dog-leaved the page and went to the water's edge for an exact reading. When the tide began to leave a wet lip of frothing shingle on the shore I knew the estuary was telling me, 'The tide is turning, time to swim.' I was already in my togs and leaping.

The buoyancy of my reception (brine meets blood) made me forget my book, and I sang out something silly. It might have been a snatch from Fats or Edmund Waller. 'When my baby kisses me/ on my rosy cheeks/ I let those kisses be./ Don't wash my face for weeks', or 'The Seas are quiet, when the Winds give o'er/ So calm are we, when Passions are no more/ The Soul's dark Cottage, batter'd and decay'd/ Lets in new Light thro' chinks that time made/ Leaving the Old, both Worlds at once they view/ That stand upon the Threshold of the New'.

When the downpours came the mushrooms appeared. This was usually the last week of August, just before the exams. I spent long voluptuous hours scouring the field in my plastic mac. These off-white wonders, large as cowpats, sprouted overnight where sheep cropped the grass. Luminous in the gloom of rain clouds. Finding a choice morning mushroom, a pink blush in its brown under-blades, was indeed a pleasure. I put it in the hood of my mac for my mother. It would crown one of her giant omelettes.

Most of my pleasures were made more interesting by guilt. These mushroom hunts were tainted by the thought my earthy relish had something to do with D. H. Lawrence. As an antidote to E. M. Forster I had been reading Lawrence, in particular the sickly seductive poems about deflowering figs and sucking sorb-apples. The alternative was Virginia Woolf, but that was out of the question. *To the Lighthouse* lost me. I turned to D. H. as the lesser of two evils, never a good idea. My epiphanies with mushrooms, I feared, were a poor man's version of rolling naked in the long wet grass. What my mother no doubt viewed as an innocent pleasure was perhaps a debauch among plumose anemones.

Captain Rushbrooke announced we were now flying over 'England's green and pleasant land'. His cackle was not soothing. It was not just his Cork accent. I looked to the girls in Kelly green and was reassured they were still pretty if not clever. The one called Olive waved a miniature brandy and pointed at it and then at me in exaggerated mime. I shook my head like a cured lush.

I remembered my penultimate swim in the estuary. This day last week. When the tide turned I tore off my clothes. I had forgotten my togs. I stood there naked and in despair. Then thought of D. H. Lawrence. He would know what to do. But the contrast between my swarthy bronzed limbs and chest and my bleached private parts made me hesitate. They were two different things, and contradictory too. The body I knew, the rest could only be guessed at. I grabbed my underpants from inside my shorts, and plunged in like an anchorite.

I swam out into the bay with long ungainly strokes. There was nothing American about my crawl. But unlike my father who was vain about his white mane I dunked my head in the swell and thought of the opposite shore. It was a mile across and I knew I would never reach it. Turning around to survey my field I saw a straggle of orphans from Bessborough pucing their faces on a heavily fruited blackberry bush. A rare invasion of my sanctuary. Had they escaped? I decided to stay out longer than usual. But restrained myself from engaging the midstream currents, although they looked benign as raindrops today. I did not feel like resisting them. It would take all my bodily strength. And to be swept out to sea in my underpants was a sight to sink the ocean liners. I floated on my back and took in the sky.

The estuary was no longer enough for me. It changed throughout the day but its patterns were predictable. Beyond it was the

Irish Sea and the Atlantic Ocean. Worlds for me that were un-patterned and unpredictable. I would be going out there soon. I backstroked thoughtfully to the shore, my local world where only moods really changed. The orphans were gone. I returned home with the wet underpants in my pocket.

I considered flights from Ireland – The Flight of the Earls, The Flight of the Wild Geese, and *The Flight to Africa* by Austin Clarke. There were no famous flights to England, only boats – The Boat to England, a sorry fate for the poor. Of course there were migrant birds. The estuary was their sanctuary. Low tide brought out the oystercatchers, sandpipers and bitterns. When storms were augured they were joined by herring gulls and guillemots. I knew the names of birds but not of flowers. At spring tide the swans were swept down river.

In town there were thousands of swans. Their territorial jostlings were beyond me, or how they got on with the grey mullet that infested the Lee. When these powerful creatures took to the air the bell beat of their wings could have been harking a plague in the city. The swans of Cork were not heraldic. Outside the Mercy Hospital was one of their hosting spots. Hundreds of them below the weir. I recalled wondering why they were there in the stinking lower reaches of the river, the day my mother and myself visited my father and took him home to die. The Sisters of Mercy were swans.

Oil slick from the new refinery at the mouth of the harbour was seeping up the river that summer. Blackened swans, tearing with their beaks wings that could not spread, became a sad feature of the riverbank. There were three pubs in town called after the swans, one The Black Swan. The autumn variety show in the Opera House that year was titled *The Swans of Cork*.

The migrant birds knew the world beyond, but they told me nothing. The swans who never ventured much further than Blackrock Castle told me more. But herons I knew from walks with my father were the wisest of all birds and expressed their wisdom by staying still. Still-lifes standing in slipstreams, drawing silence into themselves. They were a silent reproof to the chatter of lesser species. Twig legs criss-crossed like a footballer just before taking a crucial penalty. But they did not shoot. Herons wait, and take the fish as they come. I threw stones at a heron once as a boy.

Now descending into Heathrow, the flight was almost in the past with its own memories. I had watched the tattered coastline of Ireland recede like a map being torn up. From the estuary to the coast I believed I could identify people in the tidy patchwork of fields. Static dots unmoved by my departure. The beasts in the fields were more distinct. More like maggots. I opened the book I had brought for the flight. It was a red velvet covered volume of Shelley. My father's copy, his favourite poet. 'As the bird within the wind/ As the fish within the wave.' These were the lines that came to eye. I was moved to spill my brandy.

The hate I felt festering in Ireland was receding too. Stickers had recently appeared on all the garbage containers in Patrick Street. 'Honour Ireland Dead' (*sic*). A moderate politician was asked on *The Late Late Show* to revise his views. 'I'll sleep on it', he said. An extremist rival cut in, 'You won't sleep.' A New Ireland businessman in a Cromby coat emerged from the toilet, buttoning himself up. We were circling London. It seemed an age. I closed my Shelley. This was his country. I would need to keep him in mind.

The descent into Heathrow was something of a come down.

[1]

THE QUEEN'S ARMS, JULY 1967

I arrived in London with twenty English pounds, more than enough to keep me going until I started work in Romford in two weeks. The mint-fresh notes gave substance to a brand new wallet, my first. I tried out various places on my person to keep it. The tartan pouch sat most snugly in the back pocket of my trousers. Reunited with my suitcases in the baggage hall at Heathrow, I was not surprised to find the one with the books about to burst open. The cummerbund was sagging and I secured its obesity with my trouser belt. Hip-huggers, the trousers stayed up.

A classmate who graduated some months ahead had given me the phone number of his brother in Highbury. Edward Kenny was not particularly a friend. But I needed a stop-off place before plunging into a life abroad, and Eddie's brother was my sole contact. I bought an evening paper for change to phone him. The front page headline read 'COLOUR COMES TO BRITAIN'. It referred to the arrival of colour television.

I was surprised how easy it was to use the airport phone. I suppose I thought that because the official money was different the instructions would be in some strange language. Mr Kenny answered. He unhesitatingly offered to pick me up in his car. I took this for granted, although it was a twenty mile return journey

17

in the rush hour and he did not know me. By the time I had bought a box of Black Magic for his wife and children, Denis Kenny, brusque building contractor, was bundling my battered cases into a station wagon.

Denis crunched my hand in a brisk shake, and zig-zagged off through the evening traffic with brutal skill. I did not know this man and he had nothing to say to me. It was like being party to a kidnapping and I was the kid. I clung on to one fact. Denis identified me with two words, 'Ned's friend?' Edward was Ned in the world of his family. The one thing Edward and myself had in common was rugby. I babbled on about rugby, bluffing, as double concussion had sidelined me early in the season. Desperately (and hopelessly) I built up Ned – always Ned – and myself as best buddies on and off the field. My invention was far too specific. An inter-faculty match against Agricultural Science in the college quarry during which Ned felled the referee. An end of season game against Schull fire brigade during which an arson attack burnt down half the town.

Denis could have checked out these fictions easily enough. But worse, I had forgotten that Ned had missed most of the season with groin strain. Denis would have been aware of that. But this tough, taciturn block of a man did not raise an eyebrow, and stoically put up with my hysterical lies. I can't say I was happy with myself. Here was I on my first day out of Ireland conning a fellow countryman in order to cadge a bed. The only excuse was that I could not see beyond his windscreen. The dazzle of the oncoming traffic and the darkness all round seemed to suggest the bubble I was in was bursting.

The arrival at the Kenny house happened suddenly. Denis pulled into the gravelled drive of a modest semi and cut me short in mid-mendacity with an emergency stop. I lugged my incontinent cases on to the porch without accident. Denis opened his mouth for the second time, calling 'Ned's friend' as he unlocked the door. Mrs Kenny and three children who should have been in bed appeared and unburdened me of the luggage. Denis disappeared upstairs. I did not see him again that night.

Daisy Kenny's cordial effusiveness alarmed me as much as Denis's efficient impersonality. But as the children totteringly shouldered my battered suitcase like a coffin in a cortège she barked out a brisk 'Nuf' and they dropped it. Books tumbled down the staircase. Hefty green and gold Irish Texts Society hardbacks, handy Everyman editions of Goethe, Plato, Henri Barbusse and St Francis's *Flowers* avalanched down to crush a flimsy art edition of Thoreau's *Walden*. Everybody helped reassemble my portable library. Next day one of the children handed me a torn copy of Albert Camus's *The Myth of Sisyphus*.

The Black Magic was opened and I explained to the lady of the house who I was. Daisy made sure I got the walnut whirl and told me things about her life I was embarrassed to hear. Seven years ago Denis, a third cousin she barely knew, effectively abducted her in Ballincollig and brought her back to England. This was looked on by the family as an elopement but she was not so sure. It had worked out alright in its way. Denis was a good provider and well regarded in the Irish community. Although his business was thriving he still found time to help emigrants from the parish to settle. She told me what she really liked was her flower garden. But being pregnant most of the past six years – there were two miscarriages – bending down was difficult and her patch sadly neglected.

Denis, she sighed, was not an easy man to get to know. A dark side was hinted at. He worked too hard and so much business now was done in the pub. Something from classical mythology came to my mind. I couldn't quite make the connection, then I remembered. Denis and Daisy's story was like the Classic Comic version of Hades and Persephone. At present she was wintering with the dark but helpful Hades, even though the month was now July. I laughed out loud at this conceit and Daisy gave me a strange look. A silence fell between us and my embarrassment became hers. Exchanging confidences with a stranger is foolish unless circumstance disappears the unsolicited ear immediately, and I was here to stay. Shrugging her shoulders, Daisy broke the silence with forced animation. 'You must be exhausted. Off to bed with you.'

The Kennys did not stand on ceremony with guests. They were from a small town in County Cork where hospitality was still a matter of pride. The tradition had survived their transplantation. Some folk responsibility (the Gaelic *geis*) required the Kennys to house and feed a continuous stream of people in transit from Ireland. The obligation did not obey the demands of bourgeois etiquette. Visitors were honorary family, the nomad branch. Nobody played up to them. Pot luck was not even mentioned. It was possible to feel at home because it was not personal.

Once Denis Kenny handed me over to his wife he ignored me completely, as he did his children. I took my cue from them. The little ones did not need his attention. Not that they avoided it. Far from being afraid of their father, they were amused. Denis was a performance they attended in the wings, an event rather than a person. He bounded through the front door, the Master Builder himself. If a head was in the way he patted it. If a hand was stretched out he put a coin in the palm. Exit daddy out the back door trailing clouds of cigarette smoke and largesse. His stage-manager was Daisy Kenny. Her barked 'Nufs' to any child who tried to detain him were peremptory. This no-nonsense mother and spouse knew something the audience didn't. 'Nuf', I knew, was 'Fun' spelt backwards.

Mrs Kenny tried to draw me out with the big questions. 'How old are you?', 'Are your parents alive?', 'Have you a girl friend?', 'Why are you in England?' I answered warily, giving my name, as it were, but not my number. Still my politeness must have been wearying, particularly when her openness on the first evening was considered. I was even polite with the children. I overheard arguments on whether I was a Protestant or not. One of them asked me straight out. In a cantor's monotone I replied, 'I'm a Cork Jew.' They were terrified. Daisy undercut my performance. 'Don't listen to him. He is just a college boy.'

On weekdays the Kennys retired early. Country people are early risers. For some reason that pleased me. The only time my father went on a camping trip he greeted the dawn after a rough first night and declaimed, 'I must do this more often.' The next night we booked into the Great Southern Hotel. Anxiety over insomnia ruled. He was never to see the day break over Skellig rock.

I went to Sunday Mass with the family. The celebrant was rather more balletic in his officiation than would have been the case in Cork. His gaunt expressive hands were manicured. Excursions into plain chant surprised me, it being a Low Mass. His tall effete demeanour hinted at spoilt High Anglican, I decided. Back in Ireland parish priests were of the people. Mumbo-jumbo was kept to the minimum. Their personal cleanliness was commensurate with Bachelor Status rather than Godliness. Vestments would be immaculate, but everyday garments underneath showed a certain indifference to laundry. Hands obtruding out of frayed cuffs were likely to betray signs of human weakness (smoking stains, nails chewed, the odd tremor). Apart from the sermon, which though disorganised carried practical clout, the ceremony was dispatched as fast as possible.

Here it was the other way round. The liturgical obsequies were lovingly languorous, every gesture symbolically acted out as though an Oscar was on offer. The homily was brief and to the ecclesiastical point, delivered with embarrassment rather than hellfire relish. I missed the raw realism of Mass at home. But I was interested in the difference. Here where priests had little temporal power they presented themselves as superior beings. Back in

Ireland where priestly power was an everyday reality they could afford a certain vulgarity.

The priest ended his announcements with something which made me look around. 'And no Irish florins in the collection plate this week.' It was said with artificial jocularity. The congregation could have been transplanted from any rural parish in Ireland. Rigid in their starched Sunday Best, they were not amused. Hard-working women in scarves, blouses and thick skirts, each regimenting a tidy line of obedient children. Menfolk at the back of the church, high-coloured, big-featured, and uneasy in blue or grey suits. An undertow of scarcely concealed anger wound its way through from the back, seeping away before it reached the pious front pews. I found my blood rising and wondered whether my race showed in my complexion.

After Mass, Daisy Kenny barked 'Nuf' to the children and dragged them home. She had a Sunday dinner to prepare. Denis took me to the pub. The Queen's Arms, perched on a hill, was a Victorian palace in red brick with a brightly painted black and gold façade. It dominated a non-descript council estate that skirted its matronly buttresses. The houses, though newly built, were already sinking into grey decrepitude. It was a hot sticky day and my first view of London down below was hazed over like a veiled monster. 'Hell is a city much like London/ A populous and smoky city/ Where many people are done, and undone/ Small mercy and still less pity.' Shelley was my guide. I reluctantly turned my back on the smoggy pit and followed Denis into the public house.

Dante saw steamy rain rising from Hell's circle for heavy drinkers. Here it was billows of blue cigarette smoke. Drinking in the atmosphere of this barn-like expanse damaged more than the fabric of my suit. It was a gigantic shebeen. Covens of heavy, hard-looking men, sweating in suits, sat at little round tables. Mostly from the building trade, I gathered. If the church was a little bit of Ireland, this he-harem was a lot of it. Samuel Johnson entering the door of a tavern 'experienced an oblivion of care'. In here there was certainly oblivion.

Denis Kenny was obviously a doyen of the construction business in the locality. He accepted acknowledgements of this (arm salutes and the odd 'How do, Denis') from each and every table as he made for a snug where a dozen men crouched. His non-chalance and dignity impressed me. Not a word was exchanged. But his body language bespoke authority and ease. The expression 'a well-liked man' could have been tailor-made for him.

It was customary for the men to affiliate with fellows from their parish back home. Each table represented a place in Ireland. Tuam, Inch, Ballyneety, Muckross, Garryspittle or even Bruff. Navvies and bosses from the trade sat together with hangers-on and left-behinds. Deference to wealth or importance was temporarily suspended. All grown men were equal in the rigorous ritual. Rounds were the metronome that tapped out the drinking session and determined how long it lasted. Their rotation was rapid as butter churning just before it sets. Each participant was ordered a short (whiskey) and a half (beer). These arrived and were downed with dispatch. There was no question of missing out a round. Although exempt from buying ('Not yet in work', Denis interjected) I would be expected to drink eleven shorts and halves in swift succession.

Nothing in my student bashes had prepared me for this. I looked around the drinking den for an escape. It was shaped not unlike the map of Ireland. The main body, open plan, took the form of a shaggy dog begging. Nooks and crannies for snugs, juke-boxes and phone booths outlined the dog's coastal cragginess. But The Queen's Arms was not like an Ordinance Survey of the United Parishes of Eire in any other way. The detail was wrong.

The individual tables with their parish gatherings indeed repre-sented place names. But their scatter did not match Sir George Petrie's (the Survey's first topographer) precise locations. If they had, the West and South of the shaggy dog (the limbs and rump respectively) would have been overcrowded, the East (the dog's back) empty enough for ballroom dancing, and the North (the dog's head) enigmatic with discrete settlements signposted 'No-go' (that catchphrase and its onlie begetter Civil Rights were not yet abroad). An accurate map would have mirrored sad reality: congested poor places, the rich Pale for the privileged and the fortress headland of divided Ulster.

A far cry from the Golden Age map of Ireland – an evenly populated and peaceful island, I thought. Looking around, a dioramic distortion of this ideal reared its ugly head. The pub was in fact evenly populated. Every corner of this drunken island was packed with people. But its uproar was not at peace with itself. Unlike the island of the Golden Age where free movement was a given grace, this one was crammed and chaotic, and difficult to get out of.

I learned from a stooped, knuckle-nosed old man sitting next to me that most of the men at the table were working on the Underground. The new Victoria Line was being built. Old Knuckle-nose talked close to my face as though not wishing to be seen. But he looked younger by the second as he spoke. His eyes with their alert hunted look were veined and murky, but the keenly focused irises burnt like the sun on glass. Weather-beaten skin like old shoe leather and white hair raked and sparse, nevertheless he could have been in his forties.

Knuckle-nose told me that labour in the Underground was well paid, being back-breaking and dangerous. It was all overtime. Twelve hours a day, six days a week down in the tunnel's dusty, gaseous, blowlamp-lit dark, workers quarried by hand what dynamite couldn't. It sounded like a cross between the popular song 'I Am a Mole and I Live in a Hole' and one of those charcoal drawings by the young Van Gogh of subterranean Dutch miners at the unforgiving rock-face.

Two years at it, he said, aged a man twenty years. None of the men here intended staying that long. Each had a chosen piece of land in Ballincollig parish which this purgatory would buy. And affably he confided that working together for a year in extreme circumstances would do wonders. Litigation over land would perhaps be a thing of the past in County Cork. 'The New Ireland', I remarked. And we both laughed. He at the unlikelihood of the benign Brehon Laws being restored to the Old Sod, and me at having managed a joke. I saw over his crouched shoulder a half a dozen bold warriors of the Underground sinking whiskeys and beers as though their life depended on it, and wondered briefly how many of these men would make it to their home village in health and prosperity.

The obligation to eat or drink the local stew or brew tests the good faith of the outsider who falls amongst a closed tribe. I was failing my test, tipping shorts into halves and allowing the fortified beer to accumulate. Four full glasses stood before me as a reproof. I concentrated my mind to avoid a blackout, listening intently to Knuckle-nose's informative drone. My heartfelt wish was that he would vary his intonation more in order to keep me awake. I must have been looking at my eloquent friend like a madman would at his last hope. But he was too close to notice.

Russian novels had taught me that at vodka gatherings the serious drinkers are all right until they stand. Menservants were then called in to sort out the bodies. So I sat tight. The strapping shoulders of the Underground workers had begun to slump. I was not sure they would be able to pick me up. My best hope indeed was Knuckle-nose. He still made sense, though not to me. Denis acknowledged one of his sallies with a slap on the shoulder. 'Sound man.'

In a limited way I could think clearly. For instance, I counted the knots on Knuckle-nose's string tie. Noting his scarce white hair and burning eyes, I remembered from school Virgil's description of Charon, Hell's ferryman. He would ferry me out of this. Of course I had got the journey's trajectory the wrong way round. Suddenly Denis (now definitely Charon in my mind) leapt up. 'We're off home to listen to the match.' Something on radio, a Munster football final maybe. I will never know. The moment of truth had arrived earlier than expected. By my calculation there were two more rounds to go. I resisted the moment with a lopsided shrug. Denis hauled me up. I stood, swaying for a tenuous second, and stayed standing. I could not move.

Knuckle-nose was on his feet too. His stoop disguised a lanky rake of a man who had hit rock with his loy many a time and lived to tell the furrow. Denis and my Charon, alert to my state, supported me. Not too conspicuously, like two thoughtful policemen escorting a felon through a public thoroughfare in handcuffs. A sea of bodies glued together blocked the passage out. Playing pass the parcel with me, my guardians eased our way out more by suction than anything else.

Once out in the air I finally collapsed. Hands hoisted me into the station wagon and I woke up in the Kenny spare room. I dunked my head under the tap and came down to tea. My calibre as a drinking man was at stake. Knuckle-nose was still there and still talking. He had come round to where our conversation started. 'Underground workers', 'land litigation', 'a return to the Brehon Laws'. I interjected my weak joke about the New Ireland. Nobody laughed. 'Who won the match?' I asked Denis. 'Cork lost.' His usual brusqueness softened by despair. He looked at me as though I was the Cork team. My failure in drinking with the men and theirs on the playing field went to his heart, and we were forgiven.

I spent the next three days living the life of the Kennys. On the third day at supper Daisy suggested I ring my mother ('She will be getting worried'). I explained my mother did not like surprise long-distance calls, and in any case I had nothing to tell her. Knuckle-nose, who was still around and reduced to talking to Daisy and the children, gave me a sly look. 'Are you sure?' It occurred to me I probably should be seeing the sights of London and arranging digs in Romford. My job began in nine days. As though reading my mind Daisy told me she knew some young people from her home town who lived in Romford. They were chiropodists and had a house. If I wanted she could fix me up with them while I was looking around.

I lay in bed that night thinking that I could profitably stay on here in Highbury for a few more days. I knew I had not come to England to shelter in an Irish ghetto. A little Ireland in exile struck me as a particularly ignominious form of satellite captivity (a sentiment often proclaimed as a student). But here with the Kennys I was learning more about Ireland than twenty or so years living there. Moreover I was putting off as long as possible the day when I would have to face the outside world on my own.

It was a stuffy night and I left the door of my bedroom open. Anyway I felt at home with the Kennys. I could hear their voices in the master bedroom across the landing. To distract myself I took out a sheaf of poems and laid them on the bed before me. I was putting together a slim volume to be called *Ruined Stones*. Their voices were almost audible. Denis to my surprise was talking more than Daisy. His flat Ballincollig gutturals were distinct enough for me to catch sporadic phrases as though he was talking into a crosswind. Daisy's lilting voice fluted up and down like an arpeggio or petals falling and being swooped up by the gusts. Fancifully I conjured up a picture of the scene in their bedroom, painted by nineteenth century Cork's own Daniel Maclise, entitled 'Hades and Persephone in the Dark Talking on a Stormy Night'.

Their voices were raised not in anger, but in dispute. Phrases began to cohere into sentences. Despite myself I was all ears. It gradually dawned that they were talking about me. 'There is something wrong with that fellow. Where on earth did Ned pick him up?' I was stunned. 'Jim is all right . . . just young . . . beginning to loosen up . . . At the Arms he showed willing.' It was Denis who was standing up for me. Daisy continued. 'You know very well he's hopeless. Ned said he fails exams and writes poetry. How long will he hang around? I can't stand him. Get rid of him or I'll do it myself.' I was not upset by what she said. But my safe haven had become personal. This devastated me.

I heard the door of the master bedroom open and before I could hide my poems there was Daisy standing before me in a fuzzy pink nightgown. She was about to speak. I knew what was coming, but it didn't come. 'Excuse me', Daisy fluted and made for the wardrobe. 'I need to get something.' Picking a flowery frock from a hanger, she added coquettishly, 'Now don't you be looking. That's a good boy', and scuttled back out the door. I heard Denis's gruff 'Did you tell him?' and Daisy's dulcet 'I think so'.

I looked out the window into the late evening sky. An amber heat cloud was mounting up. There would be thunder and lightening tonight. An evocative school smell rose to my nostrils. Looking down at my feet I saw my socks were still on. Something of an oversight in this heat. I cheered up. I had done nothing and nothing much had really happened that was not inevitable. Real life had merely obtruded on my solipsism. I could hardly be resentful of that. What Daisy said could not be taken personally. The tenor of her remarks (which were roughly right) had not been followed through to the threatened conclusion. She had not thrown me out point-blank.

Denis's surprising support – though half-hearted – was something of a compliment. I had become part of the family. But I had made up my mind. I would move tomorrow. I reflected with nefarious satisfaction that since coming to England I had only broken one of the twenty pound notes in my new wallet.

[2]

SIR FRANCIS CHICHESTER'S MAP

It was all fixed up. Daisy left a note on the kitchen table instructing me to meet Ossie Osmond, one of the chiropodists, that evening at The Bunch of Grapes off Carnaby Street. I was already packed to leave, the broken suitcase now strapped with a belt borrowed from Denis. I decided to make a day of it and see the sights.

I sneaked off without breakfast to avoid farewells, leaving a thank-you note. Waddling down the driveway with two hefty suitcases and an umbrella under my arm, I felt like an ocean liner being escorted out of harbour by two tugs. My cumbersome manoeuvres unlatching the gate were observed by the children at an upstairs window. They waved to me. I saw Daisy standing behind them in curlers, laughing.

The half-mile expedition to the station called for organisation. I could manage my burden for forty paces at a time if I trotted along at a slight tilt. The bags were like wings and the umbrella a tail but the wings were useless for flight and the tail a nuisance. I chugged along, more like a prehistoric monster than a liner. I suspected that dinosaurs failed in evolution because they did not adapt their appurtenances to their ambulatory needs. At least my two bags were equally heavy, and this gave my forward lunges ballast.

Two regrets engaged my mind as I progressed. The wild waves

from the children made me realise I had given them scant attention. And then there was my thank-you note. I reconstructed it word for word and by the time I reached Highbury I was red-faced with the realisation that it was too flowery, even poetical. My only hope was that Daisy threw it way before Denis saw it. But I knew she was too good a wife to deny him the pleasure. I could never go back to the Kennys.

Tourists are counselled to encompass London, then the third largest city in the world, by the Tube. What is the Tube? I asked myself. Preconception answered: an automated scorpion eating its way circularly with a cat's-cradle of criss-crosses under the bowels of the city. I could not wait to be sucked in. But where was it? What passed through Highbury station were, to me, manifestly trains. Not as steamy and as grossly caparisoned as back home. But still trains.

And this Underground station was, incongruously, above ground. Ornately formal, it only lacked Paddington Bear and a jolly stationmaster. But it was hardly a haven of affable aplomb. The ticket official in his pokey cage was apathetic and abstracted. The travelling public were lost souls that he looked through, unseeing. I was surprised to find the waiting room locked and the platform littered and unswept. I had expected a suburban station in England to be kempt and orderly.

What made me imagine it was like a junction in a children's book? Apart from the dinky design, the passengers were stereotypes. City gents in pinstripes with the salmon-coloured *Financial Times* tucked under their arms, brisk but bored by the routine journey to the office, schoolgirls in abbreviated uniforms, schoolboys in scruffy ones. All typically Enid Blyton. The bullet-like trains riding low on narrow tracks raised electric sparks as they came and went by the minute. Their frequency amazed me. The flow of City gents and schoolchildren was consistent but sparse, and the trains almost empty.

A far cry from the stations back home where accumulating crowds of people foregathered for hours, waiting in crude and chaotic conditions for the main event of the day: the rare arrival of a train. Passengers piled in excitedly until the train was packed. Then the guards began a hopeless operation to cram in the live-stock and parcels labeled 'fragile'. In Highbury things ran smoothly if to no great purpose. The only guard idled in his regu-lation uniform, smoking (railway officials were never seen smoking back home). He was not needed.

I studied the network map on the station wall. So many of the names were familiar to me from Monopoly: Chancery Lane, Blackfriars, Notting Hill, St Paul's, London Bridge, Trafalgar Square, Tower Hill. They were all there except the Old Kent Road. All I knew about them was their property values. But the litany of these place names seemed more real to me than that of the honorific listing of the Blessed Virgin's attributes (ending with 'Mystical Vessel of Devotion') which I learnt at my mother's knee. Sir Francis Chichester's lifetime ambition was to redesign the classic map of the Underground. All his attempts failed. Instead this doughty pensioner had recently circumnavigated the globe in a tiny yacht, single-handed. I wondered how I would ever negotiate my way around this maze.

I lugged my bags to the edge of the platform, pushed them into the next locomotive (sleek and sooty from going through tunnels) and jumped in. The inside was like the interior of an earthworm. The roof and walls of the carriage rounded off, enclosing me in what could only be described as a Tube. I was in it. My day in London town had begun. I took the pound notes from my wallet and put them in a pocket convenient for spending, and chose the centre point in the map to come up for air.

Piccadilly Circus was a spinning top of traffic in the morning rush. Bouquets of young hairy people in sleeping bags garlanded the statue of Eros. The God of Love danced on one leg in the middle of a dry fountain. More Unknown Boy Up The Chimney than Cupid Incarnate, he was not a pretty sight. Pigeon droppings stood out like spilt tippex on his grimy flanks. The arrows he shafted to symbolise carnal liberation were broken. He looked in pain. In the trough of the fountain I spotted some hypodermic syringes. Fixations and fixes. Love and pain. Operatic rather than courtly. The working-class experience transmuted by the middle class into entertainment for the idle rich. Such were my thoughts. I wrote them down in my imaginary notebook.

I lugged my burden to the Burlington Arcade, an elegant shopping passage between the fleshpots of Piccadilly and the world of private art galleries. Cork had a canopied English market. This was its original. Certainly the Cork market had lost something in translation. Not merely the opulent ornamentation of the arches. Here the shops sold luxury products, fine art scented for upmarket tourists and jewellery for chaps and their fiancées. Back home it was the produce of the soil and abattoir. What they had in common was flower and tobacco shops. The flowers were the same. But the Burlington tobacco shops displayed heaps of hand-blended mixtures without brand names or prices. They gave off a powerful whiff of distant colonies dedicated to their cultivation.

The lure of freshly-ground coffee drew me to a little café in Cork Street. The aged waitress fussed about my luggage as though it was part of my body, and served me a small earthenware pot and Danish pastries. I had not asked for the latter, but gobbled them down. I was already sweating from my haul through the Arcade, though the full heat of the July day was yet to come. Still I was happy with my lot. Loose in London with money in my pocket and fancy-free. I looked out of the café window at the elite art galleries. I had arrived, but nobody had told me about left luggage deposit. I was destined to carry my unwieldy wings and tail everywhere that day. It proved to be quite an accomplishment.

Leaving my inattentive waitress to sleepwalk standing, I looked into the gallery next door, window-shopping the kinetic art inside. Alexander Calder. Delicate diddery objects playing cat's-cradle with reality. Tingaly. World War One infantry carts creaking eerily. The door was open but I did not dare to enter. Looking through windows always made me feel I was in a movie. Today it had subtitles, the names of the artists written on the pane. Reflected in the glass was my waitress across the road in the café, a jam tart abstractly in her hand.

I filled my Meerschaum pipe with Cork shag and contemplated the august facade of the Museum of Mankind. It loomed large and whale-like at the end of the street. The idea of a Museum of Mankind struck me as redundant, a zoo for the dead. Cemeteries surely served that purpose. A museum dedicated to the Future of Mankind I could countenance. I would not be troubling the doorman with my luggage there.

I fingered the sharp edge of my sideburns with satisfaction and turned to the street. Although mid-morning, the thoroughfare between Oxford Street and Piccadilly seemed less populous than the Grand Parade or Patrick Street in Cork. This I conceded was a matter of space. London had room for everybody. But the people had a haunted pallor from Underground travel and their energy was sapped from walking between stops. If this was the enemy I would shortly have to parley with, they looked dispirited. I lit my pipe and puffed smoke signals to myself.

Recharged, I resumed my odyssey. A preponderance of ugly heavy buildings encouraged me to increase my trotting quota to sixty or more steps at a time. My pauses between trots grew shorter. The streets were paved with uncollected garbage. A strike of dustbin men? Sweat glued my tight trousers to loose body hair like elastoplast, the palms of my hands were inflamed. Blisters could be expected, but I was ready for anything. My expedition into the jungle of the city was never going to be easy.

I caught a roofless tourist bus to cover the obligatory sights. The

Stock Exchange, St Paul's Cathedral, the Tower of London and the Post Office Tower. I gloried in the red-blooded Byronic Blackfriars rather than the soulless Westminster Bridge of Wordsworth. Then back past Buckingham Palace. Broken glass topping the walls could not deflect the eyes of subjects, but the Queen was nowhere to be seen. The great muscular arm of the Thames held the splendours together. Cleopatra's Needle was stuck in it, and Battersea Power Station fuelled its onward flow. Scotland Yard eyed Whitehall suspiciously. And Whitehall infiltrated the gaudy gothic of the Houses of Parliament, a nervous sprawl. The civil servants had the politicians well in hand. Big Ben tolled as we got off the bus. The tourists clapped.

I entered Westminster Abbey. Leaving my bags with the vendor or verger at the holy picture kiosk, I stood on T. S. Eliot's floor plaque in Writers' Corner ('The earth his bones, the heavens possess his ghost'). A vagrant smoked a roll-up and stamped it out on poor T. S. The young Eliot would not have disapproved. This sacred barn garnered dead bones: Chaucer, Spencer, Dryden but not Papist Pope. Still for me Shelley, Byron, Emily Brontë, parts of Hopkins and even Kipling lived on, in the flesh of their work. I made a sign of the cross over James MacPherson, plagiarist of Ossian, with my pipe. Sam Johnson nearby tut-tutted. Then the myriad forgotten writers paving the floor moved me to drop my mocking stance. I raised my right hand to them. I felt a poem coming on.

At every street-corner peaches were being sold. It was like a city with a one-crop economy. What Marvell called 'the curious peach' was a luxury back in Cork. I basked in their succulent presence, resplendent on the stalls in circus red and yellow. The glut lowered their price. They were almost free. But ripening apace in the heat of the day. I envisaged a collective explosion of overblown peaches splattering London with sticky juice and lethal stones, and bought a bag before the rot set in.

At the foot of Nelson's lions I ate a couple. The juice sweetened the sweat on my clothes and hair. Saliva flowed once more. The mid-day sun had dried me out. I opened my poetry jotter and scribbled the next lines of the verse I started in the plane. 'In the city round me sing/ Cauldrons of unholy loves./ Feeding peaches to the doves/ I feel free to stroke a wing./ Pigeons panic in my hand/ And fly off, O Pentecost./ At traffic lights there I am,/ The green man who beckons "cross".'

The steps of St Martin in the Fields was a hippie spike. Pastoral resonance and Palladian pillars drew these vague creatures, their presence an unspoken protest against asphalt, the pillars maypoles for hide and seek with cannabis. Inside the church I longed to lay myself out in its morgue – or anywhere cool. But a lunch-time recital was in progress: a Polish organist poured out his overheated soul in Scriabin's 'Vers de Flamme', the organ a victim of too much pedal. Rushes of baleful sounds out-howled one another. The vertigo of his crazed cadenzas made me feel faint. I sat down at the back and finished my peaches. The confusion of overlapping emotions and sustained aural attack shocked me to alertness.

The organ echoed Charing Cross Road's unrelenting waves of heavy traffic: thrown into constant uncertainty by injections from side roads, the industry of Chinese laundries and strip-joints feeding slipstreams into mainstream. The peaches like miraculous bleeding hearts seeped juice that made the walls weep and congealed the Pole's fingers on the keyboard, his hands hammering down as fists not fingers. I prayed for a Pompeii moment to still him mid-ecstasy in an avalanche of slavering lava. I too was overwrought by excessive exertion. Was it possible I would boil alive in my own skin?

Then something disastrous hit me like a blow from behind. I had left my bags in Westminster Abbey. Freedom is illusory. For an hour or so I had felt free, but from what I did not know. It was merely freedom from my absent baggage. There was a taxi outside and I jumped in. Ten minutes, the longest ten minutes of the day, and I was dancing before the verger disjointedly demanding back my burden. He smiled and bowed towards the kiosk. My suitcases stood there in dolmen formation like dispossessed gods. I pressed a pound note in his hand. 'For the Abbey.' The guardian angel of my luggage chose a postcard from his display. It showed Big Ben. We shook hands, equally pleased. Definitely an old soldier, probably an unsung war hero, I decreed. Big Ben tolled four. I still had time for the National Gallery.

My burden made me free. I peeled off my short-coat, and in ten minutes (the shortest that day) I was in the National Gallery. The cloakroom attendant relieved me of my load. I went straight to the Rembrandt room, a banquet hall with no natural light. Blinded by the contrast between the harsh glare outside and this magnificent gloom I lost myself in the Great Master's shadowy world. His work I knew from prints. Now I was in the presence.

I had just seen Alexander Korda's classic biopic *Rembrandt* at the college film society. Charles Laughton brought to life the self-portraits, particularly the later ones. Here was a man, I thought, desperately striving to make a humane life for himself and the people around him. He wanted to simplify things but thick torrents of paint would not let him. Now the 'Old Man as Saint Paul' sat there before me all hands and trepidation, utterly out of character with the part he posed.

The silhouetted 'Man in the Room' was crossed with a shaft of light. The 'Woman Taken in Adultery' and the 'Woman Bathing in the Stream' were one and the same woman. Both so kindly painted, their contrasting stories did not matter. The lapping water caressed the bather, the judging crowd the sinner. The titles made no sense, but the pictures did. I saw the two women grow old and become 'Margarita Trip', honest woman and mother of twelve. 'Belshazzar's Feast' explained how this could be so, but not clearly. The gold-lettered writing on the wall above the revellers

refracted on the high ceiling of the Rembrandt room. Four mysterious words suspended their meaning above the table like fireflies,
brilliance shivering into darkness. Nothing was explained. I was
not disappointed.

At six o clock I was the last visitor to leave. The cloakroom girl
called me 'Sir' and I felt truly knighted. But reunion with my luggage brought me back to the mundane world and blisters. Out in
the streets the heat had the presence of an animal hunting down
and enveloping all before it. It breathed its swelter down my neck,
pressing up against me and threatening to melt me to a pool of
sweat. Hungry and exhausted, in Leicester Square I made for a
neon sign, 'The Golden Hind'. In the hold of this glittery ship-
shaped eating-house I wolfed down a mixed grill and a double
helping of apple crumble with clotted cream. Over two pots of tea
I took in the crowds milling around outside, as though slowly
stirred in a cauldron. Above them in the thickly foliaged trees that
crowned the square birds sang deafeningly. This conspiracy of
sparrows and starlings drowned out the roar of traffic from the
surrounding streets.

A Hispanic dwarf was standing over me. 'Your bill. Pay!' I must
have fallen asleep. It was dark outside but I could see rain falling
across the square's festival of neon. A queue stood at the door,
watching me. Unsticking two crumpled notes from my trousers I
paid the waiter. As I struggled out into the thunderstorm with the
cases there was a rush for my table.

The clock in the square told me it was nearly eight. Not too late
to meet Ossie, the chiropodist. Illuminated signs pursued me as
I tumbrilled through the crowds. The first and last letter of the
Odeon cinema had blacked out, leaving 'DEO'. I thought of
sheltering in the gateway of an embassy, but a large luminous command confronted me. 'SOUND YOUR HORN. GO SLOW.' I
put up my umbrella.

To free a hand to hold it I girdled my arm around the right-hand suitcase. This lopsided me. But I could make progress and fence the rain off by walking sideways. Entering Carnaby Street I must have looked like some strange Chinese skiff. The downpour stopped and a turquoise cloud hung above this Mecca of psyche-delia. The detritus of the day's trading was anything but trendy. Black men with pink plastic brushes swept sodden junk and crêpe streamers into the gutter.

The Bunch of Grapes was just around the corner. I could already see its ensign, a vermilion cornucopia. The remains of the poem in my head needed writing down. Sitting on my cases I jotted, 'Taxis flow by me in fleets./ Still don't stop, though the pain/ Of my blisters brings on rain./ I shelter in the back-streets./ Banks give way to warehouses./ Bombsites where the watchdogs bark./ Sound your horn. Go slow. Carparks./ Towerblocks where the real world is./ "Deo" speaks the neon sign/ On the picture palace, closed/ To reality, God knows./ But at least my life is mine.' I knew my poem and reality were at odds. That was Art.

In The Bunch of Grapes I made for the toilet. A red-faced wraith in a shrunken green suit, hair matted as though sat on, greeted me in the mirror. I looked like white trash Robinson Crusoe dragged out of the swamp, stinking of muskrat and fear ('Walter Brennan in *The Southerner*'). I stenched of congealed sweat and self-doubt.

The pub was full of carousing middle-class Irishmen casually dressed in modish styles. No doubt one of them was Ossie. Perhaps the fellow who remarked as I wrenched my way through, using the cases as a battering ram, 'What have you in there, the Crown Jewels?' Or his friend, 'Nah! It's probably the chest of drawers from back home.' I could not face meeting him and escaped through the back door. I had Ossie's address in Romford from Daisy's note.

It was midnight when I arrived. A Jerry Lee Lewis record was blaring out the open window of an upstairs room. Something to do with 'Who's my Baby' and 'Bebop-a-loola'. During the next few days I was to hear the complete works of Jerry Lee Lewis and develop diplomatic lockjaw from agreeing with Ossie's hip gloss on their finer points. The fact that Jerry Lee played the piano with his feet must have impressed him professionally.

I was given a student's welcome – cordial in its casualness. The barrel had already been rolled out. It was the last day of term (all except Ossie were, in fact, teachers) and beer was flowing. Nobody asked me who I was or where I came from. In their cups they reverted to college days and I was a fellow student prepared to see the dawn up in a drunken stupor. Ossie was the chief reveller though he had never been to college, obtaining his diploma by correspondence.

The mood of the gathering was playfully pretentious. *At Swim Two Birds* has a lot to answer for. The relative merits of Gene Vincent and Buddy Holly plumbed in depth. Arcangelo Corelli was invoked. The left hooks of Cassius Clay and Benvenuto Cellini were compared, scholarly niceties and mock profundities entertained or dismissed without rancour.

As a university veteran I stood in good stead: the serious or solemn were to be avoided. The main thing was to bond with the moment and preserve the netting of the time warp all felt safe in. Empathy eased into the amicably maudlin. Towards dawn we fell into the old standby of hollering 'Guinness' and 'Venus' in French accents to make them rhyme. Eternal friendship was assured, blackguard gibes and bull-dancing followed.

The student spree lasted two days. The others paid for everything ('Not in work') and I subsisted on the loose change from my day on the town. We talked in pubs, heckled at movies, picked up carry-outs and left them half-eaten. Beer kept us going. And conversation. The initial facetiousness relaxed into youthful heart to hearts, as though we were people, not students. One of the teachers let drop he wrote plays. 'Kitchen comedies', he grimly disclosed. I did not mention my poetry.

When the teachers departed for their summer in Ireland, Ossie and myself wearily resumed our conversation on Jerry Lee Lewis and then fell silent. The silence was wonderful and we both enjoyed it to the full. We were silent in pubs, silent at the cinema, and silently left carry-outs half-eaten. Almost like friends. I sank happily enough into the familiar round. It made me feel good, but at the back of my mind I was uneasy.

That evening I rang my mother, determined to tell her how well I was doing. Her voice was defiantly loud and clear on the phone as though she did not trust this means of communication. She spoke my name with a disconcerting mixture of relief and concern. Relief at finally having made contact. Concern at something I knew I would not want to hear. 'Are you all right?' I knew I was not. I was about to bluster an amusing account of my encounter with the Kennys and the vagaries of London town when she pre-empted me. Two days ago my future employer Dr Forth's assistant rang Cork. A wallet had been found in the Tube and sent on to him. Mine, with Dr Forth's business card tucked inside. My mother worried that without money I was probably sleeping rough. I hastened to reassure her, explaining my neophyte distrust of wallets. Her 'Oh! James, you haven't changed' came with half a laugh. The other half contained in purée form a sad reflection on my prolonged childhood of careless irresponsibility.

I was not laughing. Worrying my mother yet again was only to be expected. I regretted it. But she would enjoy telling my brothers and sisters about James's latest foolishness and how he extricated himself through a primitive distrust of wallets. I was not laughing. I was furious. This was my introduction to Dr Forth and my new life as a serious person. Daisy was wrong. It would have been better if I hadn't phoned my mother.

[3]

DEVALUATION IN ROMFORD

I put the crease back in my trousers by sleeping on them. My hair, washed in soap and water and brushed back, made me look like a Transylvanian count in a Hammer film. As the morning wore on the hair would go frizzy, and the crease collapse into crinkles.

The kitchen table was a mess of cornflake bowls. An evil-looking cat roamed from one to another. The creature leapt from the table taking a bowl or two with him. A patina of food droppings overlaid the lino. I knew from my student days that it would be an unpardonable sin to clean up the mess. I kicked the larger chunks of crockery into the corner and fled the squalor. The cat followed, scratching at my heels. I kicked him aside, but the bloody creature clawed back. Leaving the door on the latch – no key – I left the house with the cat attached to my trouser-ends like a clubfoot. It was time to find myself a place of my own.

This was Romford. Once a tidy market town, now disintegrating into the conurban sprawl. The present was suspended in dust and mortar. The terraced houses on Western Road were up for demolition. A prevailing air of insecurity veiled the fog of imminent dynamite. This was the place to be, I decided. On the cutting edge of tomorrow. I resigned myself to the cat.

Something living flitted from the dusty undergrowth of bulldozers and chainsaws. A brown squirrel, skidding across the road, free-skating on air. A dull thud was followed by the scream of car brakes. What looked like an old moth-eaten glove clenching itself landed at my feet. The cat released my foot and tore into its entrails. I made my escape.

Miss Frost of the local bedsit bureau was sorting papers with half an eye. The other half looked me up and down. She was a prototype secretary from the Rank movies of the period. Hollywood had vamp blondes to scare the pants off young men looking for a place or a position. Rank had dainty dragons of a certain age in twinset mother-of-pearl, permanent wave and sensible shoes with a clack in them. 'Mrs Beveridge' would 'suit' and was 'reasonable'. Miss Frost's spot attribution meant Mrs B's lodging house for single men, a haven for the white-collared. Her hiss was polite but peremptory. '38 Western Road – you can't miss it.'

I bear-marched my tattered suitcase towards the designated digs. There was an almighty bang from the demolition site. I was thrown in a heap and the case burst open. Debris rose in the air like a nuclear test in the Nevada desert. I watched from a bunker improvised from clothes and papers. A human voice called from above. 'Do you want a hand?' It was Mrs Beveridge, her squat form elongated to colossus status by my worm's eye view. The helmet of closely curled, rust-coloured hair made her seem like a Valkyrie caught in a sunspot. Gathering up what I could of my scattered belongings, I was helped by Mrs B into her lodging house.

38 Western Road was a dirty red-bricked mock baroque semi, three storeys high. Mrs B, brushing dust from my lapels and wiping her hands on a permanent apron, offered me an attic room ('Five pounds, all-in'). An attic appealed to my artistic pretensions but it was her smile that made me forget to look at the room before accepting it. The Beveridge smile was a sudden sweetness in an honest slab of suet pudding. It transformed her for an instant into not so much a swan maiden (Valkyries did that) as a Bow Belle

coquette. In time I learned to appreciate the honest pudding more than the throwback smile. But they went together.

Five of Mrs B's lodgers were there for life. They were all Ind Coope brewery clerks (one retired). Single men, irrevocably bound to Mrs B by her gravitational pull of comfort and convenience. Only divine intervention or a job transfer could move them on. The house had room for two more lodgers. These were the temporaries who served as free electrons in the molecule of the Beveridge ménage. Their ionic role was to couple the five fixtures with the outside world. I was the sole electron, currently. Someone unmentionable had just left.

Mrs B called her lodgers 'my boys', and indeed she looked after them like a mother. It was a real family. The double bind was both emotional and economic. 'Five pounds, all-in' meant bed and board, washing, and that sweet smile from time to time. The two meals a day were punctually served and lavish, though the ingredients were bargain buys. Everything a boy might need was purveyed by Mrs B's suet pudding self. Her pride in this and in her boys was touching and true, but they were hardly boys.

Mrs Beveridge ruled the roost with a repertoire of all-purpose phrases. Their limited range would have encouraged a student of English as a Foreign Language, but the student would have been misled. The stock phrases were Mrs B's signature tunes, not intended to make direct sense. Her surname, for example, was used both as a noun and a verb to euphemise the unmentionable. Her dog 'did a Bev', her errant son-in-law 'Beveridged' a salesgirl.

She had a *mot juste* for every occasion. The plu-punctual evening meal invariably started with Mrs B's version of Grace. 'My boys are never late.' This signified displeasure if someone was not on time, or pleasure if everyone was present. Her intonation in either case was the same. The expressed meaning was imparted by circumstance.

Absence from the evening meal was only tolerated if negotiated

43

twenty four hours in advance. Even then, *bona fide* truants returning late were confronted by a pile of sandwiches. The filling comprised the cold remains of the main course. Greasy bacon sweating
into chutney on slices of Mother's Pride served as a reproof to be
swallowed and digested.

Consuming the untimely collation was the only way to appease
this Brunnhilde of Romford. Mrs B would rave about like one possessed if it was left ignored on the kitchen table. But disposing of
the body in the dustbin or wrapped in a newspaper in the wastepaper basket was risky – Mrs B had a keen nose for her late night
tributes. The simplest method was to eat the stuff.

Mrs B celebrated the main meal from the side rather than on
high, officiating from a hatch behind which her invisible daughter
laboured. Once the overflowing plates were dispensed she sat
down on the corner chair to watch her boys eat. Conversation
at this stage was incomprehensible to an outsider. The boys and
Mrs B seemed to be exchanging snippets of nursery argot. In fact it
was the verbal version of a chain letter. One of the boys would
throw a bouquet of words on the table. While profound mastica-
tory homage was being paid to the Beveridge cuisine, the posy was
ping-ponged back with trimmings.

I took it to be free association and avidly applied myself to
Freudian interpretation. I got nowhere until I realised that
between the marathon munchings and the banter something quite
harmless was being put together by several hands in harmony. It
could be the lyric from a musical, such as *Easter Parade* ('We're a
couple of swells,/ We stay in the best hotels') or a coded gibe at
a showy shirt someone was wearing.

Mrs B oversaw relative appetites and this game of incon-
sequences with earthy gusto. She would josh her boys with teasing
observations like, 'Who has been at the cake tin? Alan, I'm disappointed in you.' Or, 'Fred Astaire, now there's a man I could
dance with!' Jolly remarks designed to inspire cheeky retorts. And

she was rarely disappointed. 'What cake? When last did we have an edible cake around here?' Or, 'You're hardly Judy Garland, my dear.' It was Pippin's song. All was right in the Beveridge world.

When pudding was served Mrs B withdrew ('I leave you boys to it'). Like a class without a teacher or a herd without a stag, the lodgers were unleashed to improvise their own hierarchy. The talk changed from the elliptical to the explicit, volume turned up. A marked competitive edge became apparent, but a code of conduct prevailed. Though the sniping between the five fixtures could be sharp and even hurtful at times, each lodger had an exclusion zone that was never quite crossed. However a temporary lodger foolish enough to take sides between two fixtures would be scragged unmercifully by all five. I learnt to keep quiet, suspecting temps were merely game-fodder fed by Mrs B to satiate her boys' blood instincts. The chase united them.

Pudding topics were mostly political. The personal was avoided as far as possible. When disagreements threatened to go beyond robust banter the retired clerk was drawn in as the designated arbiter. He usually brokered a cessation of hostilities. The fixtures accepted his superior knowledge (he read the papers) and wisdom (he had a tan from sitting thinking in the sun). The Judgement of Barry was delivered amiably, and received accordingly.

Those days everybody was more or less a socialist. The boys went with the consensus, but uneasily. Roused, they revealed the angry underbelly of dispossessed conservatism (with a small c). Barry was his own man, a highly organised anarchist by conviction, and a mild-mannered pacifist by nature. Still, his political views were healingly similar to Richmal Crompton's William. Conservatives want to make things better by keeping them the same, Liberals by altering them a little bit but not so anyone would notice, Labour by taking everyone's money off them, and Communists by killing everyone except themselves ('I want to be one of them', said Ginger).

45

The Judgement of Barry – more Haydon than Titian – was glorious to behold. When sniping sessions threatened to get out of hand, Mrs B returned to watch. She did not sit down but stood at the door like an usher in the House of Lords, proudly observing her boys at debate. The sweet smile intimated that all was right with the world, or rather it was time Barry put a stop to the nonsense.

Mrs B was indeed proud of her boys, but the boys were not so sure of her. Valkyrie that she was, they sensed she had control over their dinner and destiny. And could devour them. Familiar with Wagner and the admission fee to Valhalla feasts, and Brunnhilde's dominion over battle outcomes and the fate of the warriors, I also knew about her vulnerability when transformed into a swan maiden: the man who stole her plumage would have her in his power. Retiring after pudding to the TV room for a half-cock at the box before bed and sleep, the boys would drop their guard and exchange unkindly gossip about Mrs B. I was shocked at first by this treachery, but soon recognised it was boyish bravado, not real subversion. Members of most families are rarely wholly happy with one another, or able to do anything about it. The family like the herd has its instincts, and knows that occasional disloyalty is a psychological holiday, a respite from the eternal burden of belonging.

Hiding behind my high-piled plate at meal times made me a dead loss as game-fodder for the boys. Mrs B took on another temporary lodger, a blond Tasmanian backpacker. Damien ('Call me Day') was a dead ringer for Bazza the Aussie Abroad in the sixties cartoon. This bushwalker in gumboots was shooting through Europe's beer festivals and bullfights and needed to slow down. Why he chose Romford with its breweries to dry out remains a mystery. The Wild Colonial Boy sported a rug of unruly hair, and made me feel urbane and knowing. That he had not a clue about pommy culture was evident in his 'Good on yas' and

'G'days'. My first blarney with him was a lesson in outback dialect. 'Howda, sport, this dump gives me the Jimmy Britts. What's the oil on the nightlife?' I told him there was a cemetery in Dagenham. He seemed interested.

But Day was no fall guy when it came to the boys. Although behind his back they referred to him as 'the convict' or 'G'day' (his usual jaunty greeting to all), they were flummoxed by his outsized presence. Day lived by Rafferty's Rules. 'No worries' was his credo, 'Anything goes' his *modus operandi*. It wasn't that he was no respecter of custom. He didn't notice it. 'Playing possum' is an Oz expression for feigning ignorant. Day was not playing anything. He behaved as he was, a misplaced Tassie lout with a big heart and mouth. When he skittered on about wild times with stray Aussies met up with in Rome, Lyons and Bavaria his muscular frame dilated and the dinner table disgorged the chunder of good times.

He elbowed the boys to nudge a point (they squirmed). Matey confidings of surfing prowess back home were met coldly with ineffectual sarcasms ('Is that so', 'Well, I never'). Day ignored irony completely, and the boys reverted to podgy yellow stares intended to scald. Waves of disapproval at the Beveridge dinner table rolled towards and over him. But worst of all Day blatantly flirted with Mrs B ('Sheilas! They're all the same') until the honest suet pudding turned into the sweet-smiling swan maiden. Mrs B was chuffed by his gormless gallantries, and fluttered her mop-like plumage. This was the last straw for the boys. They had bandied double-meaning jokes with Mrs B for years without her catching on. Now the woman was blushing, almost.

All this did me no harm. The inner circle in its helpless indignation was expanding its circumference, occasionally enough to include me. I wondered about this. I felt uneasy.

Watching ice floes cracking up in an Arctic river is exciting. Each crack is like a gunshot. No-one can be prepared for the kickback. So the effect is always shocking. Observing hidebound tradition disintegrate – and the cracks were certainly showing in the Beveridge ménage – is exciting and shocking. Day's ace card was not turning up till halfway through pudding time. Waiting for his arrival had the boys on edge, and they squabbled with one another. Barry's happy resolutions became rarer, and Mrs B's sweet smile froze into a fixed grin stuck together with molasses. By the time Day bounced in, the unrest at table was beyond redemption. Nothing he said, and he said anything and everything, was pinned down by the boys. Day was getting away with it. Mrs B's grin softened, and the sweet smile was reinstated. The boys could not handle this. Day could. He took the liberty of making personal remarks about the boys' get-up ('duds') or mood ('snaky'). Mrs B left the room, smirking. Fixtures began to use flyting comments made by Day to score off one another. The herd was turning on itself.

One fateful evening Day sauntered in just as the boys were about to retire to the TV room. The blond buffalo was carrying a crate of beer (Australian) and plonked it down on the table, scattering the pudding plates, and declared gleefully, 'Pommies, I've just cracked the jackeroo. I'm in the money. Tinnies from the Bottle Shop! It's buck night. Joy yourself. Pot screamers may leave.' He sat himself between two of the boys with an oafish arm around each. 'It's the cambio from Canberra', Day hollered. 'Tasmaniac', one of the boys retorted, and the others took up the chant. The well-tanked tourist took this as a willingness to revel, and he leapt up and unzipped cans with myriad hands, passing around the foaming tubes with gay abandon. It appeared for a few minutes that Day had found himself suitable mates for an all night grog session. The boys were united around him, all aggravation forgotten. Barry even accepted a can, and began to sing 'Night and Day, You Are the One' (with the emphasis on the 'one').

Suddenly Mrs B appeared from the kitchen, bearing a feather duster. The fixed grin was back with a vengeance, all jaw, no eyes, and the jaw was locked. 'What is this?' she snapped. 'A wedding?' Alan and Derek were dancing to Barry's Cole Porter. Ian was leering at Day. Hubert Buckle was Doing His Own Thing. The bacchanalia, a beat behind Mrs B's inopportune entry, stopped in its tracks. All except for Day who buckleapt towards her, grabbed the feather duster, and jiggered obscenely before her, singing 'She wears red feathers and a hula hula skirt'. Mrs B clobbered him on the neck with two hands knitted into a claymore. And the drunken fellow fell down on the kitchen floor. 'Explain yourself, young man', she howled. 'This is no way to behave. And in my house.' Barry was the first to recover. He slapped a thigh and stood up. 'Christ', he said, in wonderment. 'It's the Devaluation. I read about in the papers.' Day guffawed and picked himself up. 'Honest dinkum, that's what it's called. De-val-u-a-shun. Done wonders today for exchanging Oz dosh. Called for a celebration.' The boys left one by one, off to their rooms. One of them muttered, 'And in foreign beer.' Mrs B shooed them along as they exited. She turned to the defeated reveller. 'I'll see you, Day, in your room later.' The embattled feather duster was moulting in her hands. 'You might as well have it.' She thrust it at him and fled, confusion apparent in her gamey flounce.

I remained on out of pity for the puzzled Day. 'Might as well have a pot', I remarked (now slick with the lingo), grabbing a can and sipping the sweet fizzy beer. He belched and opened another. 'How much is it?' I tried again. 'What?' he blurped. 'The Devaluation, I mean.' Day did not answer. He was sucking a beer tube and scratching somewhere intimate. I decided it was a shilling in the pound, and was working out how much extra I would need for a half-planned visit to Bayreuth that summer. My sums suggested I would have to wait until it all blew over. Damn you Harold Wilson, I thought, and I left my Bacchus to drink himself senseless on his own.

Back in my attic, I pottered half-heartedly with some poems, but gave up. I thought I could hear Day's dingo bays pitching themselves hopelessly against the mute house. Britannia Ruled, indeed, in deadly silence. Next morning the Tassie went walk-about and did not return. His skittles went with him, but the beer remained. It was thrown out with the garbage by one of the boys. Life resumed, but not quite as before, in the Beveridge lodging house. Day's name was not mentioned again.

[4]

PARTY POLITICS

The next temp appeared almost immediately. Mrs B wanted to obliterate the memory of the infamous Day. Curiously enough, his successor's name was Knight. Richard was a Cambridge graduate, a Roman Catholic, and like me in his first job. He had the perfect reason for being in Romford. The construction company he worked for was demolishing the town.

Richard was the first coeval I met who spent serious money on his own clothes. He was the very model of the modern swinger in leather trousers which cost a week's wages. But I was more impressed by his explanation. A chap has to dress up to get invited to parties in town, or to be invited to stay with friends.

He lived for the weekends, when the fruits of his sacrifices to sartorial fashion flowered into trendy socialising. I was fascinated, not having entrée to sophisticated London Youth and its sensual opportunities. When he paraded his latest buys, I was struck by the sorry contrast between their Carnaby Street foppishness and his manly physique. I did not let on, of course, and we shared confidences. He mentioned girls. South Kensington had the highest density of confident beauties anywhere. They flocked there like rare birds to a sanctuary. It was heaven. Richard was breathless with adoration. Their confidence particularly delighted him. This was expressed in the shortness of their dresses.

He was elusive when I tried to elicit precise information on his weekend jaunts. One Sunday night in the kitchen, tired and rumpled, Mrs B's sandwich pile untouched before him, Richard's guard dropped. He hinted at disappointments. I was told that the sisters of friends were the best bet, but that was difficult because of personal loyalties. Then he changed the subject, laughing loudly as he told me that really his driving ambition was to qualify for the next Olympics in the long jump ('Just two feet more and I would be the third choice'). But he found training runs tiresome. I offered to come with him on weekday evenings.

Being a foot shorter than Richard, my pace-making was frenetic, but at least it got him out on the road. Once we reached the sports club where there was a sandpit to practise leaps, I was not invited in. Emboldened by our heart-to-hearts, I had let drop, ever so vaguely, that I wrote 'published poems'. I accepted that this exclusion was due to a proper recognition of our differing ambitions, his in a field sport, mine in the Elysian Fields.

I returned to my attic to make verses about the joys of running and jumping. But made a point of joining the nightcapping Richard in the kitchen when he returned. I became the sounding board for tactics to control run ups, increase spring and stretch landings. He was inching forward towards a magical flag on the Olympian sands. But his weekends were a worry. On most Mondays his jumps were well short of the two-foot target.

Richard showed no eagerness to see my poems. It suited my shyness about them and towards him. But I would have dearly loved to make myself sufficiently interesting to be invited to one of his parties. It never happened. Once I carelessly revealed my current passion for Wallace Stevens and he gave me a strange look. Henceforth I blamed Wallace Stevens for my exclusion from fashionable London.

Nevertheless we found a common interest which talk could not exhaust. Richard was intrigued by the Beveridge household and we lingered late into the night discussing its vagaries. This created a happy complicity. The recent changes made it easier to understand where Mrs B and her boys were at. It was like the Old and New Testament: Before Day, After Day became points of reference. Richard with his Catholic background appreciated the dichotomy.

The victory – through passive resistance – over Day had been achieved by the forces of chauvinism uniting in adversity. It was a last stand. Around this time Bertrand Russell harangued an anti-war rally with the shibboleth 'Change is indubitable, progress is controversial'. The controversy was over, change was in. The boys must have realised that their victory was pyrrhic. The real enemy of pound sterling and the tottering Empire was within. They had turned in on themselves.

Herd *mores* flounder with introspection. Individualism had poked through the floorboards of 38 Western Road and found itself in the kitchen. The boys were becoming more themselves. Finickiness with food was the first precise expression of the New Order. Alan went vegetarian, Ian asked for less salt, and Hubert Buckle gave up puddings. Mrs B amazingly responded by making concessions to choice. She did not, however go as far as to offer an evening menu. Her sweet smile at pudding time was saying, 'My boys are individuals.'

The emergence of distinct identities made it easier to cogitate with Richard on the characteristics of the Beveridge family. One could conjure up a name, relay a history and relate it to a real person who sat at table. In anticipation of eavesdroppers, each was given an alias. Mrs B of course was called the Queen B. Derek, a plump little Tony Hancock with a nasty tongue, became the Chancellor. He was the arch-sniper. His politic style was to disconcert and then appease. He might bitch out, 'Paddy, my boy, why don't you go home? There's enough Micks here to keep us laughing into the next century.' Then, savouring my rising anger, would add, 'Don't mind me. I'm just a bluff Yorkshireman who says what he thinks and takes the consequences.' My anger felt absurd.

Derek's friend was Alan, a quiet curate-like fellow from Doncaster. He was christened the Diplomat. Alan's apologetic mildness was the perfect foil to Derek's rude aggression. The Chancellor liked to give the impression that he was protecting his gentle, ineffectual friend. But it was the other way round. In Derek's loud, hollow world Alan was his more acceptable echo. When the bluff Yorkshireman gave offence, Alan took it away. His friendly smile to the victim intercepted a hasty response. And the bully's peace warbles were prompted by the Diplomat, whose aim in life was pacification. Latching on to Derek gave him ample opportunities to exercise this aspiration. They had adjacent rooms and their friendship was a double act. Richard at first called them Darby and Joan, but I thought that cheapened their social synchrony. He agreed.

Then there was Ian, dubbed the Nondescript, and Barry the Judge (already introduced). Hubert Buckle, the court clown, was called Hubert Buckle. These were the five boys and Richard and myself relished their individual (After Day) and collective (Before Day) peculiarities. My friend's background was officer class, and mine was middle-class professional, as far up as class went in Ireland. But Mrs B's boys did not see us as peers. They respected Richard, and he laughingly put them down when they went for me. I took Derek's teasing to heart, something Richard found uproarious. When amused, he found it difficult to contain himself. Most people limit laughter to the muscles of the mouth, with occasional excursions to the ears and neck ligaments. Richard laughed with his whole body, his delight in it released a rippling energy that scattered plates and spoons. I sometimes thought this profusion of merriment would be better put to use in the long jump.

If Mrs B's husband has not been mentioned before it is because Fred Bev was unobtrusive, almost to invisibility. Twenty years older than his stout spouse, he was teetering on the brink of senility. Mostly she ignored him, occasionally letting fly in his direction a rich vein of what sounded like Cockney invective. Fred Bev, as she called him, said nothing, not because he was stupid (he was a dab hand at the Pools), but because he had no teeth and there was no point. Nobody would understand him, and if they did who would listen?

Fred was the house handyman, and an unnoticeable one (therefore probably good at it) as he trawled the house mending things more or less continuously. As Richard and myself sat in the kitchen exchanging house gossip in the small hours, we became aware of this skinny Haile Selassie of a man working his way along the skirtings, patiently rooting out electric wires and skilfully winding fresh insulation tape around them. His most distinguishing feature was a smouldering butt stuck with congealed saliva to his quivering, unsupported lower lip. Talking to him was a waste of time. He just smiled, and the butt did a little dance but stayed stuck. It was always the same rictus smile. Was he deaf? People treated him as though he was, talking over and about him. But a wrench or a screwdriver in his hand was well treated. He had a house to fix.

The Beveridge daughter was perhaps providentially hidden behind the kitchen hatch. Lankily stooped, dowdily smocked, blondish hair bleached and greased with a lifetime of concocting big meals for her mother's boys, this was one unpleasant sight, and woman. Mrs B called her Bevette. The boys called her Bevvy. Her husband, Trevor (Trev Bev to Mrs B), called her nothing one could repeat.

He was a balding spiv, as shifty as the sands of Araby. Bevette was the brains and ran a day nursery, more a baby farm, in a portacabin behind 38, where the couple lived and fought. The nursery, I gathered, did not have a proper licence, and it was run more in fear of officialdom than care for its tiny clients. If the Beveridges were Bow Bellers, Trev Bev was a beau for the belles, with Flash Harry suits, string tie and roving eye. He wasn't around much, having a station wagon, the only car in the household. Mrs B liked her Trev Bev, flirting with him in the style of Margaret Dumont. He did not reciprocate.

Trevor even gave Derek the creeps. His lean look of unrequited crime, as though he was up to something and had forgotten what it was, made one tremble for the tinies in his wife's charge. 'Councilmen', 'Inspectorate' were the longest words in the Bs' lexicon and only deployed in a hushed undertone. Worse horrors were not mentioned. But they were suggested by his very presence. Richard was not alone in speculating that Trevor's wagon was chock full of stolen goods or dead babies. Bevette and Trev Bev, however, had a four year old boy of their own, beloved only by his wayward father. The Kid (no Beveridge connection acknowledged?) was fed perpetual candy to keep his runny nose running and to occupy his drool. This veritable nougat of sticky, spoilt infancy would not have been missed in a massacre of the innocents, except by Trev Bev and possibly Fred.

And finally there was Bev the Dog – flat, matlike, barely animate. His encrusted white coat and clumsy rhino shape carried misery, nowhere. Bev the Dog was dying on his haunches. Everyone knew it except Mrs B. His most energetic activity was incontinence. The mat before the kitchen stove was invariably fouled by the couchant creature. The boys were used to the stench. But even this was changing. It was not excrement any more but the smell of death and decay. Nobody wanted to touch him. Except Mrs B. She cheerfully cleaned up after Bev the Dog. With love. I knew it was love because it was selfish. Mrs B would never admit the dog was in pain and wanted to go. The word 'vet' almost rhymes with death. It was forbidden in the Beveridge house. Even Derek would not dare utter it in her presence.

Richard's training began to fall by the wayside, and our nightcap chats grew rarer. Once hearing me scratch out the melodic line in Bach's concerto for two violins in my attic room, he dropped in all excited. He had learned the violin himself and knew the piece. Next time he was home in Kent he would bring back his fiddle. It never happened, but our talks together deepened. They took place occasionally in my room. I learnt that Richard was 'probably in love'. He spoke in generalities. There was much soul-searching ('Was it the real thing?') and breast beating ('Was he missing out by focusing on one girl?'). Lapsing on the long jump bothered him too. Not having any experience in the matter I listened, dying for details. They never came.

The new love-sick Richard was given to silences with sighs. I tried to fill them by diverting him with poetry. He was much taken by my favourite Shelley ('I love all waste/ and solitary places, where we taste/ the pleasures of believing what we see/ is bound-less, as we wish our souls to be'). He asked me to write it out for him and went off clutching the piece of paper. I reread the lines when he had gone and sadly decided they had more to do with Romford and me than love, a foreign country that one day I would visit.

Despite myself I was getting closer to the boys. After Day it was not uncommon to come across one or other of them alone in the kitchen or front parlour. I found a chastening thought in Pascal's *Pensées*, my bible at the time. 'The greater intellect one has, the more originality one finds in others. Ordinary people find no difference in men.' I stayed to talk.

The boys believed I knew all Richard's secrets. Annoyed that I didn't, I felt no disloyalty in elaborating on the little I knew. I fed them tales of romantic and athletic yearnings and pratfalls. Their interest was inexhaustible and I was inspired by flattery to tell all.

57

Each of the lodgers in their different way seemed relieved that the officer class did not have everything their own way. Not from malice, as it did not spin over into table teasing when Richard dropped his food on the plate and sighed or left to read a letter, probably for the tenth time. Even Mrs B held her counsel. I had no doubt that Derek had filled her in, with embellishments. My reputation with the boys was enhanced. Mrs B included me in her sweet smile. Derek stopped contradicting everything I said. All the same, I didn't get too close.

I learned to sit quietly in my room listening to the strains of Judy Garland or Duke Ellington wafting up through the floorboards from Derek's radiogram. Brewery clerks and slushy music, I accepted, had more to them than I had thought hitherto. The superior beings I conversed with in Penguin Classics or empathised with in art-house movies were not the sole repository of human subtleties. My fellow lodgers and their tastes were not just flotsam to snigger at.

One evening after supper the boys told me about Fred's Pools prowess and the Beveridges' foray abroad. After a lifetime filling in weekly forms Fred Bev made a killing. It financed the Beveridges' first package tour. Previously working-class people only went overseas with war in mind. They were the fodder. Mrs B and Fred went in peace with Romford Tours. It was the Crusade in reverse. The heathens were on a flight to Rome. God intervened, a rogue strike in the Holy City, but Romford Tours had His measure and rearranged the Roman Holiday to Corfu. Fred being deaf, Mrs B did not bother to explain. So Fred spent two weeks in Greece, the cradle of civilisation, thinking it was Italy, its playpen.

Someone unkind, undoubtedly Derek, on their return tried to disenchant him. But Fred, unable to accept the golden days downing fish and rice dinners were somewhere other than the Eternal City, assumed it was a joke. Good-naturedly he joined in the laughter, all the while shaking his head. Periodically the matter was raised but Fred was not to be dissuaded. He flexed his wiry hands, wanting to get his fingers on some electrical fault, and waited till the laughter had subsided. Then he slipped out of the room, confirmed in his belief. Two great civilisations had been interchanged by this modest man and ace fixer of things. (The world, indeed, is a strange place.)

The retired Barry, who spent his days with the ducks in Romford Park and had a Costa Brava tan, was the only one of the boys that I hadn't had a heart-to-heart with. One sweltering evening, with the smell of rotting summer in the air, we met in the kitchen. I had been to *Red Desert*, a film by Antonioni, at the local Polytech. He was sitting at the table like a cardboard cutout. I would have liked to talk to someone about the movie. I casually addressed the table. 'I've just been to an Italian picture and the star came from Cork.' (Richard Harris was in fact from Limerick. But I knew that people sojourning in a foreign country must endeavour to make themselves interesting.) Barry looked at me and said, 'I am in the kitchen of Mrs Beveridge and I too come from Cork.' I was astonished, particularly with myself for not catching his accent. It was indeed a Barracks Street brogue. But the soft gutturals had lost their local lilt. Out of courtesy to people abroad, Barry enunciated each word slowly and clearly.

Forty years delivering words with precise care gave his speech a certain authority. It was the first time I had heard him speak about himself. Barry told me that the past was his business, the present was others'. He lived in the present to be with others. He would never be lonely. If asked he would answer about where he came from, but it rarely happened. Barry was a listener. This was difficult because it was not easy to understand exactly what people were saying. So he had got into the habit of summing up as precisely as possible what the other was going on about. Called the Judge, he should perhaps have been styled the Editor.

He told me this, and then I was the recipient of a classic Barry summary. 'It's Saturday night. You've been to a movie. With subtitles. Alone. You are young and still have a chance to find someone to share your life. Don't miss that chance by keeping a cautious distance from others. Books and fancy films are fine. But there are plenty of nice girls out there waiting for a fellow. You should be getting yourself a girlfriend. You're not bad looking. You have a job. There must be someone. We think backwards and live forwards. You should live more and think less of living.' Barry relaxed his upright seating position for a moment, almost into a slump. 'I would have liked to get married myself. Don't miss your chance.'

I felt privileged, even a little humbled, to be party to Barry's confidence. This shy, dignified man who had effaced his past so successfully, and not for any untoward reason, was the exemplary man abroad. I could not ever hope to emulate such strength of character and true sophistication. We never spoke together like this again.

One Sunday evening in the late autumn the Beveridge household was thrown into confusion by the arrival of girls. I was in my attic composing a Larkinesque sonnet when I heard shrill, eager voices downstairs. The lodgers were in their rooms as usual. Returning from a solitary stroll through the desolate streets of downtown Romford, I had noticed the lights under their doors. All except Richard's and I knew he had two sisters, one at art college and the other at school. I still harboured hopes of being introduced. Richard had often spoken warmly of them. How clever they were, and pretty. I dreamed that his closeness with his clever, pretty sisters would extend itself to me. After all, I was their brother's educated friend in his Romford exile. I tossed my poetry jotter on the table facing the attic window, put my feet up and waited. I looked around my orderly garret (Mrs B insisted on tidiness) and wondered what they would think. Some creative disorder would impress them, I decided, and took my violin out of its case and put it on the bed. It was my most beautiful possession.

I heard Richard lead his sisters up the stairs. He paused outside each lodger's door and whispered quite audibly chortle-worthy details of their lives. The girls laughed with pretty, clever voices. I distinctly heard the words 'exquisite' and 'can this be real?' uttered with delight. I felt a twinge of regret that my friend should be displaying the boys so nakedly to his smart sisters. And that my confidences could be freely shared not only with his sisters but with the whole household. When the party reached my door I heard Richard's strident whisper. 'That's the Irishman who says he writes poetry.' The girls laughed, pretty and clever as ever. I had the strange feeling that they could see me through the door and I was being scrutinised with opera glasses by white ladies slumming. One of the girls was heard to say in a clear alto, 'That dog. We must see the dog. Mustn't miss that.' The party moved down to the kitchen, talking and laughing.

Then it happened. Bev the Dog barked. He never barked. It was more a croak, an excavated memory from the past when Bev the Dog was a virile watchdog. The baleful bark amplified into a hopeless, hollow howl which drowned out the gaiety in the kitchen. It was a dreadful sound, half-brewery horn, half-swansong. The house resounded with a shocked silence.

The baying of Bev the Dog continued, like a burglar alarm with rundown batteries and an inaccessible switch. A voice from on high shouted down, 'Quiet down there. Leave Bev alone.' It was Mrs B from her bedroom. I heard the front door being closed with exaggerated care, and Richard and his sisters failing to suppress their laughter once out in the street. A car drove off with a getaway scream of tyres. Mrs B thumped down the stairs and carried the whimpering dog up to her room.

The house was quiet as the grave again. The invasion was over. Mrs B's lodgers were safe, and I was one of them.

[5]

ROMANCE AND RHYTHM: A JOB

The job that brought me to Romford was not poetry but bio-medical research. As a student I came across Virchow's Law. 'Medicine is a social science, and politics nothing else but medicine on a large scale.' Faith comes before reason. Without under-standing him, I really believed this nineteenth century sage. The writings of C. P. Snow on the Two Cultures, and Ivan Illich and Chekhov on the centrality of health in a civilised society, came as some sort of explanation.

My bemused attempt to juggle medicine with poetry was not foolish. I knew what Ezra Pound's Mr Nixon advised ('And give up verse my son/ there's nothing in it') and decided there might be a life in poetry, but not a living. I also curtailed my medical career before it became an all-consuming vocation. Bachelors of medical science were wanted in research laboratories and I became one. Poetry's night calls would not have to clash with their doctorly equivalents.

The post went with a generous Medical Research Council grant. Romford Hospital pocketed most of this and paid me a pittance. I was without experience, resources or guidance (Dr Forth, the Medical Director, was away in America, I was told, head-hunting and fund-raising). I was allocated a workbench in a portacabin behind the private wing of the hospital. Miss Reid, a tough old laboratory technician with World War Two decorations on her white coat, handed me a blank sheet of paper. 'This is your project. Make what you can of it. You don't have a budget. So you will need to steal if you want anything. Don't expect any help from anyone. Keep out my hair and you'll face the firing squad in good health. Any questions, no. Well, get on with it.' She obviously ran the place. There was no one else around. Elisabeth, her dogsbody, was 'off sick as usual'. It was clear to me that any real research would have to wait till Dr Forth returned.

I liked Miss Reid, with her over-the-top sergeant major act and brutal honesty. Beneath a rough exterior a soft-hearted soul lurked, I decided, and was quite wrong. My substitute boss was a pragmatist driven to cynicism by her experience in a hopelessly impractical world. My offer to help until I knew what I was doing and Elisabeth came back was immediately accepted. Though her raised eyebrow informed me in no uncertain terms that I was unlikely to be much use. I considered her acceptance as sensible (the bank of little bottles waiting for testing was intimidating) and her judgement of me as sound. I resolved to get on the right side of this wise woman as best I could and as soon as possible.

The laboratory, I soon gathered, was a glorified pregnancy-testing centre. A two-tier system prevailed – private ('Get it done today') and NHS ('Tomorrow will do'). Not knowing where to begin with my official project, I devised with Miss Reid another one to pass the time until Dr Forth came back. I would classify the names of clients into ethnic groups and compare their results. Miss Reid showed me how to carry out the tests. Confidentiality was strictly observed for the private ones. Nevertheless it proved possible to perform a sub-analysis comparing the ethnic origins of NHS and private subjects. Over the nine months I laboured in this conception factory I carried out thousands of tests. I had no time to contemplate the pride and anxiety that the results doubtless engendered. Regretfully, I couldn't follow up their consequences as happy births or TOPs (Miss Reid's acronym for the unwanted). But I did discover that Irish Catholic names were more likely to go private than any other group, particularly in Dagenham. I was not sure whether it was a matter for pride or shame, but positive results were significantly higher among the Irish, and that despite a sizeable Italian ghetto in Ilford.

The portacabin was a lonely place. Although Miss Reid was like two people, she didn't encourage one to get to know either. Apart from Clive, the specimens deliveryman, there was only Elisabeth. 'Only', I should say, because of her frequent absences. When at work E, as Clive liked to call her, lightened up my day. She was twenty years of age and from New Zealand. At first sight her appearance was a disappointment. Surrounded by urine samples and pipettes, I could have done with a dollybird or something flashy to distract me from the grim facts of life. E was a healthy girl despite her sickness record. Long beribboned chestnut hair, pinafore frocks with frilly tops, sky blue eyes devoid of mascara, and an attentive eagerness that could have fooled me. When I recite the word 'salubrious' it conjures up Elisabeth.

Days that E was in at work were seven hours short. Side by side at the bench we worked through the tests. It was possible to talk. Miss Reid must have noticed the phalanxes of samples marched along briskly to the fife and drum of my chatter and E's giggles. She said nothing. We were an effective team. The talk at first was about the Beveridge household. I suppose I should have observed that E said little about her own digs. But I didn't suppose anything could compete with my lodging house. It was a subject that was never quite exhausted but I did move on, encouraged by E's attentiveness, to reveal more about myself than was perhaps decent. If that was to get E to talk more about herself, it failed. I hardly noticed my failure. Until she was off sick again and then I wondered who was this Elisabeth, and the work suffered. Miss Reid noticed. 'Pining, young man, for your little companion?'

I did not like Clive, the specimens man. His bland egalitarian air and open-necked shirt with medallions hanging out seemed inappropriate for a delivery job. But worse still, he always brought the news about E's sickness. Clive knew her landlady, apparently. What bothered me most was the way Clive went into intimate detail about E's latest ailment. Even though I suspected that it was pure invention and intended to annoy Miss Reid and myself, it made me oddly jealous. He had rights over her body which seemed wrong. When Miss Reid invariably stopped him short with a 'That's enough. When will she be back?', I shared her annoyance, but with a personal twist. We both knew that productivity suffered when E was away. I was not thinking of productivity. I had begun to depend on Elisabeth's presence to make a dull day in the laboratory burst into sunlight.

Miss Reid set testing quotas. When these were not achieved, she gave me the portacabin key and said, 'Young man, you'll be burning the midnight pipette tonight. Make sure you lock up properly.' I found it peaceful in the cabin. It was surrounded by trees which reminded me of home. As streetlights came on, the branches hovering over the roof performed shadow dances on the vacant lot, reclaiming it from the developers. Nightfall is associated with the dulling of the day and silence. Not here in my tree-hut. Overhanging branches came alive with the dry strokes and vibes of a jazz timpanist. Blackbirds pretended to be nightingales. Cats and squirrels caterwauling with one another in the undergrowth. All inhuman life was abroad in the night. Romford beyond was just a low moan in the sleep of the conurbs.

I forgot my pipettes and quota and gave thought to a French film that had recently disturbed me. Called *The Lost Domain*, it was an artful fantasy of pubescent neurosis set in a wild garden peopled by beautiful young things wearing gossamer. Its vacuous absolutes made me angry at being drawn in. I distrusted the merely beautiful. I wanted to contemplate instead the really important things that had happened in my life so far.

My father's death four years before. The association between trees and that event was, however, suddenly infuriating. I spent the summer he died cutting down a colonnade of withering trees in our garden at home. The smell of bark resins and ineffectual medicines were mixed up forever in my blighted senses. I had experienced my father's death only with my nose. I could have cut it off to spite it.

I thought of E too and wondered about her importance. At least to me. I spent most evenings completing quotas now because even when she was in, the work had begun to suffer. I talked less and looked at her more, as though learning her presence off by heart. When she was off sick I would be able to remember her.

E left promptly at five – she had a regular lift from Clive. My lonely vigils gave me ample time to consider her importance to me and what I should do about it. I was averse to the preliminaries of courtship. A provincial upbringing had bored me with the notion of conventional good times as a prelude to true love. Instead I was bent on making myself fascinating enough for her eyes to brighten when she met mine. A spontaneous combustion of mutual passion in the portacabin was inevitable. But so far it had only happened when E was laughing, and she invariably looked away. I was not encouraged.

Miss Reid could not but register my state of nerves and the cause. She spoke to me twice. Each time with an equal and opposite impact. I was told that 'mooning over a colleague is quite unprofessional'. Miss Reid's first intervention only served to increase my resolve to wait for E to come running. I was crazed with the conceit of youth and, moreover, finding my evenings fulfilling in other ways. I was writing what was to be my first book of poems, *Survival*. Two main strands entwined that first fine rapture – poems about chopping down trees (the end of child-hood), and poems about a disintegrating market town (the end of adolescence?). Strangely, E did not figure at all in my Romford poems.

This was certainly not because E was stubbornly resisting my fascination. In her presence I increasingly attained the condition of a jelly baby in a heatwave. I couldn't avoid noticing she was show-ing signs of irritation with me, moving her work at the slightest chance to another bench. Once I followed her and petulance mani-fested itself ('Following me around, now, are you'). I did not repeat the pursuit.

The days of her girlish goodfellowship were over. She looked tired, and not just of me. Hair a mess, bags under eyes. She could have been twenty-five. I even suggested kindly she should go off sick. This did not go down well. My attentiveness became furtive. Years later, reading Proust, I recognised a mite of myself and E in Swann and Odette, the superior being smitten by the interesting elusive one. On reflection E was closer to Swann perhaps, and myself to Odette.

The absent E, though, still lured me to daring indiscretions. I knew she lived in Dagenham and on Sundays I took a bus there and scoured its dreary streets, willing a chance encounter. The dreariness of Dagenham outflanked Romford (which at least was undergoing change). This wasteland of identical terraced houses and symmetrical streets was a monument to Lego. Even the locals must have been hard put to find their way around the banality of murky red brick and piebald 'Portland' stone.

I hunted through the streets of Dagenham with a thoroughness that belied my frame of mind, which was indeed desperate. I even haunted the vast cemetery, surely the most woeful eternal resting place this side of Belsen with its mass-produced plaster angels and jugs, in vague hope of a sighting. I never did meet E in Dagen-ham. I doubt if it would have been a happy confluence – her eyes brightening as she met mine, me talking with the carefree air of an accident about to happen. I think I saw Clive once and ran. I recalled my father's words of warning many years before when I was lazy at school. 'You'll end up in Dagenham with a little suitcase.' During the War the unskilled of Cork City emigrated in droves to the ammunition factories in Dagenham. At least I hadn't a little suitcase.

I came to dread going in to work. Not merely because E avoided me. My survey of tests continued, but the results were boringly predictable. I could have done with the odd virgin birth or at least an occasional mix up. Miss Reid, in response to a recent health circular, had reorganised the confidentiality of specimens. Names did not appear on the labels, not even for NHS clients. Samples came to me as numbers, pre-coded for ethnic group. It was no longer possible to take a sporting interest in how the O'Reillys compared with the Pirellis.

There had been talk of being trained in research techniques. Since the lab was exclusively for pregnancy tests, I had nothing more to learn. When I finally met Dr Forth – at the hospital Christmas party – there was no mention of starting my 'serious' research. Instead, he asked me what I intended to do with my career, and did not wait to hear my answer. This master fundraiser wore a three-piece suit with so many pockets in it that he didn't know what to do with his hands. He took one look at my pullover and faded flannels and saw at once I was a loser in the world of grants and trial by sherry. He had also got wind of my ethnic survey and had dismissed it as too politically sensitive to publish. My prospects were clearly at a dead end. The daily grind was leading me nowhere, except up the wall. Later, I caught a glimpse of Dr Forth talking suavely to an eagerly attentive E. A moment of jealousy passed when I considered his podgy form bursting through an undone button in his waistcoat. Against E's grace he was a poor thing.

Miss Reid didn't bother me anymore. As long as the quotas were achieved civility could be maintained. Brusque put-downs were a thing of the past. She had given up on me. I felt like a shadow on the skirtings and behaved like one, unobtrusive, temporary, preparing the portacabin for a disappearance without trace.

Passivity towards E improved our relationship. Tetchiness gave way to a tolerance that allowed her to talk to me quite spontaneously. She told me a few things about her life. A show up town that she went to, something from home. She was the eldest of three in a Wellington family, very close. Her father sold radios, her mother was a doctor's receptionist. I said nothing. Listened with apparent attention. Avoided her eyes. Concentrated on the nape of her neck. I decided if I could touch it without upsetting her I would be requited.

One lunch break, Miss Reid plonked her metal lunch box down on my workbench, drew up a high stool and sat by my side staring out the window. We were to have a talk. Conscious I would know through whom the reports on my performance had filtered to Forth, she was not her usual forthright self. She hadn't come to explain, but to justify the disappearance of my job. I could have spared her, for I essentially agreed with the Forth conclusion, but for opposite reasons. The problem was not me.

It was that Romford Hospital's research department was insufficiently organised to accommodate a poetry-writing rookie without experience or the faintest notion of what was expected of him. I was pretty sure Miss Reid and Dr Forth could not possibly know the right reason for freezing me out. I forgave them as long as I did not have to explain. At least Miss Reid. She was a brick, although in this case through my window of opportunity. Forth was a swine who picked up money like muck for bogus projects, swilled from the tender carcasses of guileless youths.

This was to be the second occasion the doughty Reid spoke personally to my situation. I was ready, but not for what followed. 'I am not sure, young man, you quite fit in here in England. Maybe you should give serious consideration to returning home to Ireland where you would understand things better, and be better understood.' Her metal lunch box remained unopened. Miss Reid did not break bread with an alien.

A new darkness entered the hurt pores of my innermost being. It was anger, and I liked its chiaroscuro. Its smouldering hardened the raw portals and released a cloud that, in the time it takes to hold in the breath without discomfort, purified into a clear sky, a cold one. I studied Miss Reid's unease and resolved that my shadow in the skirtings would turn into a phantasmagoria to haunt Dr Forth and his jury of ignorance with magic lantern tricks, before disappearing into a nothingness to be feared. I knew my Sartre, or some of it ('Freedom is the apparition of nothingness in the world'). I got up and walked around the portacabin once. Then returned to my bench. I was a new mouse. I would surprise Elisabeth yet.

Nothing changed in the laboratory. Except me, and that was inside. Nobody need notice. Small changes, however, are the enemy of big ones. For instance, Clive no longer brought E to work. He delivered the day's samples at eight sharp. She arrived late-ish, apologising for the bus. Miss Reid cast a blind eye. At least E was in. I was already halfway through the day's job-lot (my speed at carrying out the tests had doubled since my chat with Miss Reid) and E would throw me a grateful look. This I treasured. It spurred me on to new heights of meticulous swiftness. The quota was reached mid-afternoon. So E and myself enjoyed a leisurely wind-down of the day's work. My grateful friend and colleague became accustomed to talk during this happy hour. I half-listened and concentrated on her nape which was now almost within my touch.

One morning in Clive's delivery I spotted an uncoded sample. I tested it (negative) and put it on E's desk with a note. 'Give it two zeros and an Irish code or better still speak to Clive.' Later that day in the happy hour I saw E remove the numberless sample from the batch and slip it into her handbag. I caught her eye in the act and she threw me such a winning smile I was in high heaven. We both laughed, happy together, and she said thanks. For saving Clive's ass, I thought, but did not dwell on it. I was so pleased to find E in such spirited form and to be able to share a little conspiracy with her. She was near enough to touch. I leant towards E and tweaked behind her left ear the exact spot where her nape met the hairline, a place in her person I had long contemplated. She took it as a joke, and laughed some more. Then we both sat there doing nothing. Suddenly serious.

Next day I invited her out to lunch. Just like that. She accepted as though it was the most natural thing in the world. In the gloom of a heavily brocaded Romford pub we seemed quite alone together. E did the talking. This was a relief, and what she told me was a sort of relief too. I was informed that I was her only friend in Romford, an ordinary friend but a good one. I listened to her. She could talk to me. I did not make demands. She was so unhappy.

Elisabeth's story emerged through a gauze of lacy handkerchiefs and pauses for sympathy. She had a boyfriend, at least up to a few weeks ago. She was so upset, let down, didn't know what to do. I gathered he was an older man who lived in the same house as Elisabeth in Dagenham. A sort of cousin. They had met in New Zealand. He was on holiday. He was her reason for coming to England. It had been a horrible mistake. It had been alright at first, but now his wife was back. And it was all over. Her tears told me something I had not suspected. Elisabeth did wear make-up. And being upset made her closer to my age, at least twenty-two, I decided. I approved of her tears. I gave them my benediction. An older man. A cousin. A married man. Passion in a Dagenham semi. After a holiday romance. Of course that should end in tears.

71

I was thrilled to be drying the tears of a wronged woman. The next best thing to having an affair. I looked around. This Free House in Romford of all places would hardly be the setting I would have ideally chosen. But it would do. At least it was not done over in the sixties spare-rib style. It was a voluptuous old trout of a pub with cubicles for secrets shared. I was sharing Elisabeth's. Surveying the scene I glimpsed Clive, the specimens man, propping up the bar. Catching sight of E and myself, he threw us a blank look that unnervingly denied recognition. Then downed his pint hurriedly and slunk off. I looked at Elisabeth with wonder. She didn't seem surprised. Her look told what I should have guessed. Clive was the older man.

Elisabeth was no longer upset. 'Thank God, I'm finished with him.' This said with a hard edge of bitterness. My anger was now the real thing. Elisabeth looked at me with alarm. I stopped myself rushing out to confront the cad, but only at the expense of terrifying Elisabeth. I tried to calm down, using a technique I learned as a child. I closed my eyes and attempted to disappear into myself. In a way I did. I was quite clear about my rage. It was not wholly on behalf of Elisabeth, the wronged woman. It was the rage of humiliation – mine. Clive was not handsome. He dressed in the cheapjack foppish style of the period with overgrown hair, probably dirty. He was at least thirty-four, earned less than me, didn't write published poetry, was definitely lower class. Worst of all, he had made me waste valuable time trying to fascinate Elisabeth by twisting her life up into a hopeless knot. I woke up, opened my eyes, and informed Elisabeth that my anger was all used up, and that I was now just miserable. She laughed, and put her hand on mine, and delivered the immortal words, 'Never mind, Augustus, we still have our pregnancy tests.'

It was spring and the weekend of the May uprising in Paris. Students not much older than me were holding de Gaulle and the French middle classes to ransom. And I was off to a Come to

Kiwiland Trade and Culture Exhibition at New Zealand House. I had no illusions, only intentions. I had made a fool of myself. But why brood and turn a banana skin tumble into a tragic dive? My rage with Clive had puttered into contempt. Elisabeth was exempt from judgement, being young and in a foreign country which she did not properly understand.

As an ex-rugby player I knew that anger dissipates if translated into action ('When under pressure expand the game') and Stendhal also helped ('Put fresh events between yourself and sorrow. Even if it means breaking a leg'). This robust support boosted my purposeful mood, and I strode into New Zealand House prepared to drink an All Black or two under the table.

Nobody asked for my pass to the exhibition. The invitation came courtesy of Elisabeth (she wasn't interested). I noticed it read 'Elisabeth Rayner and friend'. I was the friend. A brisk woman – perm, cravat, shirt, tidy gray suit – passed me in the lobby carrying a stuffed animal. I ran after her and on the trot she told me 'It's over'. Adding, as she disappeared into an office, 'But you may prowl round, if you like.' Her eyes indicated the exhibition hall with a diagonal tilt of her head and neck.

It was no party inside. Not a single famous rugby player in sight, unless the little old lady in plaid seated before a fish tank in the corner was in disguise. The bar was just a table and teetotal. I helped myself to a paper cup of kiwi juice, and looked around. The display was a dutiful tribute to antipodal kitsch. Maori knick-knacks, papier maché geysers, contour maps of earthquake zones, black and white photographs of rugby players dawnlighting as dustbin men, and a slide show (in colour) of natives dancing for the Queen against a backdrop of green hillocks and hot water springs. I examined the hieroglyphic script on the explanatory placards, and glazed over. Not much here, I thought, to make a Kiwi homesick. I noticed the tank gazer had not moved since I entered the hall, and wondered if she was a cardboard cutout – authentic Kiwi granny guarding the goldfish. I picked up a handful of leaflets and brochures on the way out.

I pored over the promotional literature in a nearby pub, memorising choice features such as the light collapsible housing characteristic of earthquake areas. Apparently nobody had ever died, except from natural causes, in a New Zealand earthquake. Healthiness, homeliness, family life, church communities, old-style schooling values, sporting prowess, hunting, shooting and fishing were the keynote words, recurring ad nauseam. The 1950s feel was daunting. Elisabeth could hardly miss this.

The following week my uncertain campaign to encourage home-sickness in Elisabeth complicated the happy hour. She was puzzled by my sudden interest and probably a bit wary ('Is he thinking of emigrating?'). But once I announced I had accepted a new job in Welwyn Garden City, she relaxed, and we talked about what it was like to live in Wellington. Geysers or earthquakes or Maoris, except as criminal types, were not mentioned. Good old traditional family values were to the fore. It was clear to me that Elisabeth was already deeply homesick and needed no encouragement. I was amazed.

E offered to type my letter of resignation. While she clattered away on the portacabin's ancient portable, I chattered on about the new job being a real research post this time, not a game of commercial roulette with nervous eggs. Miss Reid overheard us but merely remarked, 'I'm glad you took my advice.' I did not contradict her. Her remark was a concession.

Celebrating my imminent departure with a box of Black Magic and some bottles of Cidona, I crowed, 'Only one month more and I'm out of this.' Elisabeth voiced a heartfelt 'Lucky you'. I responded that there was nothing stopping her doing the same. She confided there was. Having only fifty pounds saved, it would take another three months at least to get the extra hundred for the fare home. I said nothing but noted the amount.

On my last day in the portacabin I wrote E a cheque for one

hundred and sixty five pounds, a quarter of my savings, and left it on her desk. Conveniently enough she was off sick. I never saw her again. Six months later I received a letter from New Zealand. It had been forwarded from Romford by Miss Reid (I recognised her military handwriting). E's was round and childish, the calligraphic equivalent of the Elisabeth I first met with her ribbons and pinafores. It was a nice enough letter, fulsomely expressed but a little heavy, I considered, on the commonplaces. Thanks for the cheque were included twice. At the beginning of the letter and as a PS. The PS thanks was followed by five Xs.

The extra money over and above the fare had allowed E to round off the trip home by sailing from Australia. She had met 'someone special' on the boat and marriage in the autumn was on the cards. She was happy, and her parents and sisters were glad to have her back. Nothing very much happened in Wellington, but that was how she liked it. Two pages of blue vellum dutifully completed. I had perhaps expected something more. But I was not really disappointed. I had almost forgotten Elisabeth. And when I thought of her it was only with vague satisfaction at having facili-tated with a modicum of grace her return home to New Zealand.

My new life in the Garden City had no room for regrets or fancies. All the same, receiving the letter reopened a hope, foolish no doubt and vain, that there was something more that Elisabeth had to say to me, something that couldn't be said face to face but might be allowed in a letter from the other side of the world. What it was I wanted I did not know. She wished me well for the future and my new job. It was hardly that. She would always remember me. That was getting closer. Written as a second PS. I had to be satisfied with that. I reread the letter. Tore it up slowly. And decided I was free.

[6]

LANDLADIES OF THE
GARDEN CITY

Now twenty-four years of age, I decided to settle down. I needed a steady place to live and work. Welwyn Garden City was my choice. From a through-train it looked like one of those playpen burial settlements described in Manzoni's *I Promessi Sposi*, a placid ghost town set in a boundless plain. I was to learn the town was ghostly because its citizens were too old or too motorised to be seen except at shopping centres, and the plain was only boundless because the M1 motorway cut through the flat terrain.

My callow conviction was that the Garden City would be my last resting place. Here I would settle down to live and work, away from the unsatisfactory temptations of the avant-garde with its beads and joss-sticks and dreadful food. Promethian thoughts of wild wanderings in pullovers and boots in mountain redoubts were put aside as a cop-out. I had had my share in youth of peasant cynics crouching behind scraggy hedges in the foothills of the Boggeragh or Knockmealdowns. Braver would it be to confront suburban bourgeois life in its comfortable smugness and live out my days as the enemy within.

Nearness to the cultural Mecca that was London would be a safety valve if escape at weekends became necessary. Though I told myself that I must appear to fit in, even if it meant joining in community life in my free time. I brought my violin and rugby boots to that end.

Ebenezer Howard's ideal town was now forty years old and cracks were showing in this worthy Valhalla. He laid out the Garden City like a socialist version of Los Angeles, spacious streets with discreet semi-detached houses, egalitarian in brick – the antithesis of the Aldgate East slums and cramped chaos that made a bus journey from Romford to Liverpool Street so depressing. The first citizens of the City had been transported in protesting trainloads from the insalubrious East End. Forty-foot gardens opened on grass-kerbed boulevards lined with cultured crab apple trees. All the houses, according to the grand plan, were notionally equal, but some were more equal than others.

Inevitably time and human aspirations had conspired to secrete that invisible ink which in England marks out class boundaries. Proximity to the coyly camouflaged factories – mainly manufacturing drugs – defined this. The further houses were from the industrial cluster, the better the class of people who lived in them. This was not immediately obvious to the outsider. But a saunter through the sparsely peopled streets identified tell-tale signs of what were less latent than blatant class distinctions.

The posher side had more fragrant street names – Azalea or Dahlia Drive, rather than Sparrow Road or Cowslip Walk. The posh tended to border on woodland walks, the common on motorway slipstreams. Nevertheless, in the late sixties the Garden City as a whole was affluent enough. The sweeping avenues were well swept, and social disadvantages were more a matter of etiquette than anything else. Weeds, feral animals, and gypsy encampments on the outskirts were yet to come.

I found myself lodgings in Acorn Mews off Beehive Lane, a medium posh area near the sports stadium which had an artificial ski slope made of brown high impact plastic. Digs for single young males were only obtainable from widows and widows were thick on the ground in this part of town. The Citizens' Advice Bureau told me that spare rooms to let in the City were hard to find. There were no landladies in the place, only widows. I was a quiet lodger but not an ideal one. The widows liked me at first – a lodger who kept to his room in the evenings and did not entertain friends was a godsend. But my loner ways also made them feel uneasy. Did they know what they wanted? I was polite but peremptory, always in a hurry in their presence, talking to them in a sort of shy riddling shorthand for a quick getaway. The widows of bank managers, army officers and hardware store owners expect more than cursory consideration.

Then there was my violin playing ('Up in the attic away from the din/ Someone is playing an old violin'). A harmless enough hobby, for I played *sotto voce* with a mute, tastefully adapting my repertoire to the surroundings so as not to disturb neighbours or cats. All the same, the Thousand Best Tunes soon began to pall on my widows ('Lovingly, soothingly, all the day long/ Just for the love of the music, that's all'). The music itself did not bother them, but it was symptomatic of something else, like being Schopenhauer's landlady. There was something they didn't like. Hard to put a finger on it. And then there was the wastepaper basket. Each morning it was full of crumpled foolscap and dead matches. I smoked my pipe – harmless enough in itself, even reassuring – but in the bedroom. The fitted carpet was occasionally smudged with dottle, even suspected of being singed. These details were examined and discussed with relatives and cronies. And I was no help around the house.

During the first year I changed lodgings and widows six times. In retrospect, I now realise what the problem was. It was not the fear of fire, or the fairy fiddling. What all the widows had in common was that each had an absent son, and the sons were war babies. I too was a war baby (though that was in a different country, and my mother was very much alive). If only I had submitted myself to a little sideline mothering all would have been well. Each change in widow was preceded by a surprise dénouement, a shocking display of subliminal passion. I was just settling in, getting my shorthand right, accommodating to the limitations of widow life, and beginning to smoke my pipe and play my violin with a modest degree of abandon, when the big moment came to shatter my peace and quiet.

The big moment was never the same. Sometimes it was Grand Opera, at other times it was subtle as poison in a pastoral play. Common politeness gave way to 'feelings', not usually presented directly, but unmistakably real, a crisis I at least had to confront. One rather demure widow communicated her feelings through her son-in-law, a solicitor. This otiose smoothie delivered her suit in the form of a casual remark. He arrived to feed the cat while the widow was away (some Bank Managers' Widows Convention, I was lead to believe). I was informed, as he coaxed food into the obese feline, that I was consuming an undue amount of honey at breakfast. Two jars a week to be precise. This was excessive. I could have defended myself – the widow's dainty little meals had driven me to coiling mounds of Safeways honey on etiolated slices of toast – but I didn't. I knew the game was up, and once the week's rent ran out I moved on to the next widow.

She was a nervous creature who wore woollen gloves with the fingers shorn off. Her fingernails were long and gnarled and yellow with nicotine, though I never saw her smoking. She wore a gray smock like a lay nun and never went out of the house. Groceries were delivered. I gathered that her son was recently dead. It was not clear from her incoherent keening whether it was a car accident or an overdose. One way or another she seemed to blame him. I felt sorry for him, but thought darkly he was well out of it, whatever it was.

She pottered around the immaculately clean house with a duster, muttering imprecations and droning out misericords of 'Stardust', out of key. Her conversation was wholly one-sided. Once she ventured beyond parrot politenesses ('Nice to see you', 'You're going out'), the next widow babbled in snatches, Cassandra-like vaticinations ('If you only knew'), interrupting herself before sense was made with an abrupt change of topic, usually an excuse to escape (merciful for me). One time she held up a Green Shield Stamp coupon and read the token quotation, 'He who does not live in some degree for others hardly lives for himself.' I contained my alarm by pretending all was as it should be, a grieving widow and mother finding consolation in amateur dramatics, a tragedy in two acts and a half. Until one night I woke up to find my hair being stroked by the widow seated by my bed.

My subsequent landlady was not in fact a widow. Miss Mumfy was a tweedy spinster with more seasoned knick-knacks per square foot in her baroque abode than the Victoria and Albert Museum. My box room was like a film set for Monsieur Hulot. It was impossible to pirouette without bringing down showers of memorabilia. I took to hiding away the Hummel and Dresden figurines of an evening, and putting them back in place when I went out next morning. Every Wednesday night the house rocked with classical music – Miss Mumfy lead a lively string quartet, amateur but unashamed, in mainly romantic works, Mendelssohn in particular.

In my room I hid my fiddle skills by playing with a double mute. But Miss Mumfy, like all true musicians, had hypersensitive hearing. Soon enough one Wednesday evening, I found myself making up a quintet with her gentleman friends, T. S. Eliot look-alikes to a man. It was a cruel and chastening experience. Miss Mumfy conducted the ensemble from the piano and, sight-reading never being my strong point, she gave me hell. The piece in practice was Brahms – almost Brahms. I kept repeating mistakes until the session ended up with me continuing to repeat them unaccompanied with Miss Mumfy, Lully-style, beating my music stand with a rolled up copy of the *Daily Telegraph*.

During the tea and small talk afterwards, the old boys' eagerness to override my embarrassment was touching ('Brahms has too many notes', one said). But it only made things worse. I consoled myself tacitly with unkind thoughts about being young and having all my life before me. Miss Mumfy regarded me from the piano stool with pity and contempt, too upset to savour the sweetcake.

I moved on to my fourth digs as soon as I decently could. This time it was a widow with a bothersome daughter about my own age. Linda was sullen and sluggish, probably a depressive. Her mother and her circle of friends were the backbone of the City's tennis club, a middle-aged cabal, almost exclusively female. Linda came into her own on court – that was the problem. Her mother and friends played a tidy baseline game. Lobs were allowed, but spin, drop shots and cuts only occurred by accident, and accidents were rare. This drove Linda to despair. Her game was a man's game and it was the time of Laver and whiplash forehand drives.

The unsporting savagery of the awkward daughter's game was a serious offence to the genteel members. Nobody wanted to play with her. I was dragged to the rescue, willingly I admit. Lacking proper training, I could just about manage a low hop thrash game of the unclubbable kind. I was truly Linda's dream opponent, a tennis knight in off-white T-shirt and rugby shorts. Members turned their backs and sipped Dubonnet and lemonade while Linda and myself belted it out. Our games were all deuces and advantages, with eternal sets so matches were never quite finished. We drew them out. Darkness did not stop us. Only the closing of the courts could curtail hostilities. This muscular blonde went brown-haired with sweat as we traded hits and smashes in the growing gloom, eyes acclimatised to the dimming light, limbs at full stretch. The world beyond the much-abused balls did not exist.

I came to spend most evenings in providing this exhausting therapy for Linda (now revitalised on court, still sulky off it). Her

81

mother must have thought it was limbering love – Linda, hitherto, had eschewed the lure of Cupid. Nothing could have been further from the truth. True, the prolonged physical congress did throw us together for long hours. But we only communicated through the ball, in the killing of it.

When finally separated by the disgruntled groundsman, we lurched, muscle-bound, back to the dimly lit pavilion to be plied with maternal Cidona. Her mother's gratefulness to me for sweating the nerves out of her difficult daughter was quite blatant, and her wistful hopes of something more was tragic and probably touching. It kept me on tennis duty beyond the call for several welt-filled weeks. Linda to me was limp and listless when not extended in brutal bouts of interminable tennis. I began to take this personally. In the last resultless marathon we played I resisted aiming a beamer at the insatiable Linda's brainpan – she would have hit it back – and fled damaged to the fifth and final widow. I knew I had let Linda's mother down, but my body could not take anymore.

The last widow was perfect in herself. I could have settled down with her. She was a gentle soul who minded her own business while not utterly ignoring mine. I was aware of being the object of her benign mirth and liked it. Self-conscious youth craves to be teased. But she was a Quaker and I was not looking for a quiet life. I was on my own abroad and lurked shyly after passion, adventure and licence. I needed a nightly dose of the devils. She threatened to deny me that. I suspected she included me in her prayers. No doubt this was worth something, but in some dark corner of my callow artistic self I felt her eye was on me. I was haunted by her putative prayers. I took exception to this, quite unreasonably, for I don't recall her mentioning prayers. I dreamt perhaps this good woman wanted to save me. I did not want to be saved by someone else.

After this vain skirmish with widows and orphans, I settled for minding a passing acquaintance's empty house. This suited me for a while. But after a few days running up and down the stairs in my rugby boots and raking my violin fortissimo without a mute, I longed, not so much for company, as for an audience or an official opposition. I was tempted to scour the streets for potential squatters. Community was becoming a fashionable concept at the time. I wanted to create my own personal commune. But where to find the community in the Garden City was something of a mystery to me.

The young disappeared off to London whenever they could, and the highways and byways were predominantly populated by the elderly on the gad to the many Old Friends clubs and bingo halls. I knew, of course, from my excursions to the shopping complex and the park areas punctuating the town that there were married folk with children. These discrete nuclei of real life, remote in their contentment, were undoubtedly the Garden City's one true community. I had to accept this and once I did, I set about breaking into their hermetically sealed world. It wouldn't be easy, I knew.

[7]

KEEPING HOUSE

Opportunism is the exploitation of the obvious. Why fall upon thorns when there is a featherbed waiting for you? Shamelessly trading on my ethnicity through contacts in my 'respectable' job, I latched on to two Irish dentists. It was like Denis and Daisy all over again, only this time it was a conscious decision rather than happenstance. Pat and Paddy were partners in a busy practice in Beehive Grove. Both were in their late twenties, had wives and children, and lots of friends (not exclusively Irish) with wives and children. It seemed to me that this extended family represented the local community (inherently a transient one, given its inner city origins) and they certainly were bastions. I joined in on the fringes of their lives with a will and a way – my will was to be a younger brother figure, and my way was to be useful (available at weekends).

Pat was a porcine fellow with a jovial appetite for blood-red meat and money. His wife and children, being neither edible flesh nor money-earners, appeared somewhat marginal to his driving affections. The wife was a quiet convent girl with a frail presence which would have graced a Rathgar drawing room or a minor Ibsen play. I suspected she was more tolerated than cherished, being once a source of capital. Pat would have been a great man for a dowry.

I had no evidence of this – Pat was unlikely to share such a confidence and Yvonne would never mention money. But youth is a great judger. I was young and I liked Yvonne better than Pat. He gave the impression of being unselfishly social, one of nature's politicians – a big, generous man with enough of himself to go round the town and offer second helpings on the lap of honour. In fact his bigly, kindly, hail-fellow-well-metness was only skin deep, though his skin was thick. Pat would have been good on television for an armchair electorate, and probably now is, somewhere in Ireland. I had reason to believe he did not appreciate my finer qualities. I certainly lacked the capacity to join in his Falstaffian sprees of belly laughs and gut reactions.

Paddy on the other hand was one of nature's gentlemen, lean and clerkly in mien, serious and slow about everything, a secure slowness, measured but not hesitant. The slow motion was also physical – weightlifting was his surprising hobby. Paddy was particularly slow to judge in matters moral or muscular. But I suspected that once mind or fist was made up, this unhurried man, bowed down with the weight of his considerations and a gray raincoat, would act decisively and knaves and cowards should make themselves scarce.

Indeed, as I got to know this gentle, thoughtful dentist I began to doubt his modesty. He had, it seemed, the true arrogance of the virtuous man who did not eschew the venial. He put up with human weakness but that was as far as he would go. His wife was unexpectedly light and airy for such a pensive fellow, a pretty petite dark-haired girl who was, I learned, not to be underestimated. Angela was Paddy's metronome and earth (she couldn't hope to keep him on time but at least she kept him moving), and the mother of three children straight out of a Quality Street chocolate box cover.

Paddy's relationship with the more ruthless Pat was a working one. He was a model of sensible restraint, holding the reins of his tearaway partner with a firm but light, almost invisible, hand. They shared the collection plate every Sunday in the Catholic church, and it was instructive to watch them work the pews together. Pat drew pound notes from the tight-fisted with his intrusive bluster. Paddy never looked at (or listened to) what was given.

I was pretty well a fully-fledged agnostic at the time, and attended Mass eager to mock the sermon's attempt to square the traditional sonorities with the recent Vatican Council's disturbances to blind faith. Afterwards, I heard out Pat's tirades against theological trendiness over a pint but was held back by Paddy's mute disquiet from reacting with easy cynicism. Possibly I was learning something but not from Pat. It was the year of assassinations (Martin Luther King, Robert Kennedy), the student sit ins and outs in Paris, the Papal 'no change' on contraception and the unfashionable Civil Rights protests that went wrong in Northern Ireland. Pat and Paddy were most moved by the latter. When the backlash burning of Catholic homes started they both agreed that something should be done.

A lightning campaign fronted by the irrepressible Pat got the City churches together to support charity work for 'civilian victims of the violence'. 'Dialogue', 'Peace and Reconciliation' were the slogans that united the diverse denominations into organising raffles, whist drives, sales of work and folk concerts. The vicar and parish priest played an exhibition round of golf. The Garden City became for several months a shining light of ecumenical example. I kept my distance, being a disciple of Tolstoy when it came to charity (it was irrelevant in the larger scheme of things, and made people feel better about matters they could do nothing about). But I did play my last rugby match for the campaign, disgracing myself by being cautioned for stamping the Protestant minister's son in a ruck. I had learned my rugby in the playing fields of Munster where the mud tends to travel on the stud to the eye on the blind side. I went up several notches in Pat's book and he recruited me for the Gaelic Football Match for Peace. Fortunately two full teams could not be rousted up for this game (Australian Rules without the rules) and much mayhem was spared the Garden City.

However Pat disappeared to Ireland a few days before the ill-fated match. He never returned. The explanation for this sudden departure was a sick father and a family farm and pub needing a managing hand. Rumour had it that the Inland Revenue had caught up with him at last. This was a gross calumny. Pat would never be so obvious as to be caught on the hop, and in any case his family stayed on in the Garden City.

The owner of the empty house where I was ensconced in mag-nificent isolation rang long distance. The stay abroad had been extended and house-minding was to be handed over to a security firm. I was shortly to be replaced by a flock of geese. So I moved on, this time into Pat's house (where the dental practice was an overlapping annex).

Baby-sitting duties were discussed but there was no mention of a rent. I was more than happy with this arrangement. Particularly as Pat was not around. This house was in fact the commune I had dreamt of – a large, rambling, chaotic ménage. Stray guests and gatecrashers came and went like ghosts in a farce. Various babies – strays and Pat's – crawled, bawled and toddled around, often in a state of nature. Meals were scavenging sessions, raids on an errati-cally supplied fridge and larder. I was at home here with my own room, answerable to no-one.

Pat's cousin, a dentist from Donegal, moved in with her husband, two children and an Italian au pair to compound the bourgeois bedlam in Beehive Grove. Nano was a wild, swarthy woman whose disorganisation, both professional and personal, was epic. She was to take over Pat's patients but her heart was not in the work. Wearing a white smock (was she expecting again, or was it the dentistry?) she blustered around between the surgery and the kitchen, loudly declaiming her scattiness, a snack in her hand, talking nonsense nineteen to the dozen.

The disconcerting thing about Nano was her insatiable friendliness to everyone, even her worst enemies, and she made enemies easily. She did not seem to notice the effect she was having on others as she merrily discarded a crust or a core or an intimate revelation to a passing baby or patient or dog (she came with an incontinent but amiable collie). Her husband was a calm, chubby fellow who was not around much. Second generation Irish, he worked for an oil company and was now back from a stint in the Far East. For good, according to Nano, always an optimist. His mildness was perhaps deceptive. I once heard him tell in riveting detail how a colleague had his throat cut in a Bangkok bar. Nano made him repeat this story on several other occasions, once in the presence of the local vicar.

But Nano and her roly-poly spouse were difficult to take seriously. She came from a small town on the Northern Ireland border and was given to dispensing potted Irish history lessons to all and sundry while he sat by, nodding soporific approval. Catchphrases from Carty's patriotic history (the required school text in fifties Ireland), such as 'Ireland's life blood' and 'Cromwell's leeching troops', tripped off her tongue with embarrassing ease. She spoke of Queen Victoria with disrespect (a safe bet in the England of the sixties) but there was something distasteful in her diatribes – tribal wisdoms launched unilaterally at unsuspecting guests, showing no concern for their likely feelings. It was as though she was merely talking to herself or to the converted. The shibboleths of unthinking republicanism struck me as hopelessly out of date, a manifestation of effete ignorance.

But it was all so simplistically expressed that I did not feel it necessary to argue with Nano, nor did anyone else in my hearing. Her father-in-law, an Irish navvy, was said to have made his fortune in the post-war building boom in England. His wife, a fierce little woman, came to visit one weekend. Nano's politics were naive but the mother-in-law listened to them noddingly like her son, and added some distinctly dangerous views in favour of 'the lads on the streets of Derry', at that time busy loosening paving stones and making petrol bombs. She drank Irish whiskey neat and 'prayed God the boys would reorganise' and was 'glad the Cause was still flourishing'.

The dinner table was silent, reverently silent, and I felt uneasy (who might be listening?). I thought of Shelley's poem to the Irish, 'Blood may fertilise the tree', which ends with 'Slow to peace and swift to blood'. The poet patriots of 1916 were much given to celebrating blood and horticulture ('I see the blood upon the rose': Joseph Mary Plunkett before his execution). I felt rage coming on but once again Shelley saved the day with an apt felicity. 'The cold hand gathers its scanty fruit/ Whose chillness struck a canker to its root.' But the subject changed. Easily done in Nano's distracted world. All the same, the mother-in-law contributed generously to the Victims of Violence fund.

The au pair, a good Catholic Southern Italian, and myself managed to hold the makeshift household arrangements together for a couple of months. Caterina was a tall, sinuous girl with great black eyes orbing out from a saffron complexion and ample wiry black hair sparking with electricity. When Pat's wife and waifs got the call and decamped to Ireland, Caterina effectively took over the running of the house. Nano and her spouse were hardly housetrained, let alone their children.

They favoured a Method school style of child-rearing, in as much as there was a method. The little ones were encouraged to express themselves as nature intended. The parents' attention span was short and erratic – the children performed in a vacuum most of the time, veering between the hyperactive (to gain attention) and the listless (when they failed to obtain it).

They were more or less the same size, though not twins, and only communicated with one another. We called them Romulus and Remus (their Gaelic names defeated Caterina) and found ourselves increasingly alone with them in the house. Nano made frequent trips to Donegal, something of a relief. Caterina's untried maternal instincts proved exceptional. While the parents were away she wiped Rom and Rem's runny noses and sang them funny little pic-a-pic-a-lino ditties. Hitherto the 'twins' had withdrawn when touched and avoided contact except in battle. Now they were beginning to manifest signs of infant affection, certainly moving perceptibly closer to Caterina. A hug without a frightened squeal was occasionally achieved. We watched over each and every stage like proud parents. But their development was slow and regressions frequent. 'Rome', Caterina joked, 'wasn't built in a day.'

Caterina, the eldest daughter of a policeman in Bari, was in London for a year to learn English. She did not attend college, so I suppose I was her language lesson. And we talked about everything, like young people do, but mostly about literature. It was a continuous conversation though I had the upper hand, English being my first tongue. Lists of famous books and authors were exchanged like a litany while out walking with the children or going to and from Mass (she was religious), or sitting at the kitchen table when Nano and her spouse had retired to bed leaving the kitchen like the abandoned trench of a defeated army.

Caterina was translating for me the Italian bits in Ezra Pound's *Cantos*. Comparing Dante and Ginsberg was a favourite topic. Her life in Bari may have been sheltered but she knew all about the Beats. Indeed her thesis on 'Howl' had been interrupted by endless student strikes. This was why she had come to London in the first place. As my ideas became turgid with tiredness, what vocabulary we shared ran out. I would wander off for a midnight stroll through the blossom-scented streets of the Garden City while she finished the wash up and scrubbed and tidied the kitchen. This was the time of 'swinging London', but women's liberation was still at the silly stage.

My interest in Caterina was uncertain and curiously clinical in turns. Women were only known to me from books, films, my sisters and Elisabeth. Of course there were girls back in Ireland, cautiously dealt with through conventional Cork mores. In London I had kept my distance. Caterina was as close as I had got so far to the opposite sex, and I was squinting fiercely in the nearness.

She was obviously a good girl, but by no means innocent. More than blossom emanated from her presence. There was a musky something between us which bothered me. And then there were her eyes, great black Southern pools encircled with dark tense skin. They were far too large and had moons in them that waxed and waned and made me wary. These were child's eyes but with a woman's knowledge (I had been reading Verga's *Sicilian Tales*), lookout posts with passion points in the irises. I was afraid of being drawn into them, lost in their moons. I was no doubt a hopeless idiot.

Our intimacy, at least on my side (Caterina did not reveal herself verbally on the subject) was literary and ludicrous. I felt I had leaped clean through the dangerous hoop of love and marriage and landed personally intact. Only to find myself a proxy parent with Caterina of Nano's sad brats. I saw myself as I strode through the town at night, not a person in sight, just an occasional car dipping its lights and speeding on, as a premature *pater familias* in a strange dream, burdened with responsibility.

Caterina was the homemaker, the coddler of children, the eager ear always willing to listen to weighty wisdoms. I wince at the memory. The poor girl must have wondered at this talkative young man who posed interesting dangers, but ended up merely posing. I hope she didn't read my mind. It was not made up. Mills and Boon would say I had not the courage to leap into the deep unknowns of her dark Ionian eyes.

She might reasonably have thrown Blossom Dearie at me ('If you don't like my peaches/ why did you shake my tree'). Still I rather doubt Mills and Boon or the Blues was where she was at.

Dramatising myself made me feel superior and above action. That rendered me harmless. She must have been a little relieved. I recall her look of affectionate concern changing to affectionate contempt. She had my number and was amused.

Returning to the house I found the kitchen light on, but Caterina had gone to bed. I locked up, not forgetting to put out the dog and the lights, and retired to Verga. I dreamt of Anna Magnani.

[8]

THE TRIUMPH OF LIFE

My day job in the Garden City was coming to an end. It was a research assistantship in the local hospital looking at intravenous injection techniques, shots in the arm so to speak, and how to make them easy. A new apparently non-addictive sedative was to be used as a passive agent. I was responsible for supervising the needle-sticks, and the project nurse and myself had an easy time. Our subjects were required to be young and healthy, and the volunteers we got were incredibly cooperative, rubbing up unusual veins, guiding in the needlepoint fearlessly. We wondered not a little at this, as the participation fee was peanuts.

The young people were, even in high summer, uniformly pale and interesting. It took several months for the project team to register that diazepam was not a harmless downer. The town junkies saw a free fix coming and we were it. The research came to a sudden stop. I was left to patch together the tattered data. A couple of years later it appeared as a 'short note' in a learned journal. No mention was made of the side effects of the passive agent.

The Garden City was soon to become a byword amongst the Hertfordshire young for its drug culture. The cosy little factories nestling under the motorway were manufacturing curious substances and the woods behind the posh quarter were fertile with psychedelic mushrooms for those who wanted their stuff organic. My contribution was small, but it was good while it lasted. I once more entertained the notion of escaping to somewhere more healthy. But knowing it would be less a matter of choice than a necessity made me want to resist it.

I discussed my future with Paddy. But he had other worries. Pat's flight and Nano's maelstrom arrival meant the dental practice hung heavy on his lean and honest hands. The patients were bemused, the books in a mess, and the Inland Revenue was rumoured to be parked outside. If Paddy had been slow before, he was 'forever' now. All the same, he heard out my stubborn assertions on remaining in England ('I can't give up now') but said nothing.

Meanwhile a chain of ominous occurrences disturbed the peace in the Garden City. Social unrest was abroad in the model town. Poor Ebenezer would have turned in his grave. An armed robbery took place in broad daylight at Rumbelows. The gunman was believed to be one of our research subjects and I was interviewed by the police. The town had its first mugging, or to be precise the first street robbery called a mugging. There was a riot in the local ABC cinema – seats were ripped out and a showing of *Easy Rider* discontinued. *The Sound of Music* replaced it but even though it was a new print, further rioting ensued. Ambulance sirens could be heard in Beehive Grove as children and pensioners were ferried to the Queen Elizabeth the Second (sometimes called Seconal) Hospital. Richard Nixon was elected President of the United States. My student brother dropped into town in transit from Prague to inform me, while downing two consecutive dinners in the Golden Goose Eatery, that Socialism with a Human Face was finished and he was getting out.

Angela took me aside after Sunday lunch and said Paddy thought persevering with England was a good idea ('You wouldn't want to go back yet'). I bristled to ask why, but said nothing. I knew it was true and felt sad. She picked up my mood and told me the Garden community was breaking up anyway. It wasn't much fun anymore being part of it. Paddy and herself were thinking of leaving. It was no place to bring up children. And she hinted, ever so darkly, that there was trouble coming. 'Not for you, of course, but you will be well out of it.'

I was shattered – things falling apart, centres not holding, chaos around the corner, an apocalypse in the Garden City. Angela's veiled augury, I thought, might have something to do with being Irish at a bad time politically. After entertaining (not without some perverse satisfaction) unlikely visions of pogroms for Paddys, I dismissed that idea. Even if the worst came to the worst, I knew I was immune, being a citizen of the world, not Irish merely, who proudly believed like Samuel Beckett that 'the man who stakes his whole being comes from nowhere'. I was like that in those days.

That night I dreamed vividly.

I am standing by a pool formed in the middle of a forest by a torrent. Surrounded by hanging rocks. On one side a waterfall perpetually dashing. Twisted mountain ash top the rocks. Above them giant chestnut trees. Their long pointed leaves pierce the deep blue sky. The water is transparent as air. So the stones and sand at the bottom seem to tremble in the noonday light. My custom is to undress and sit on the rocks reading a book. Something classical. So I can concentrate on a few sentences. Reading them over and over to learn by heart. In hot weather I leap from the edge. And once refreshed by the water I call out the classical wisdoms and understand them. But today it is cold and I do not have a book. I clamber up the moist crags with difficulty, receiving the spray all over my body.

I woke up in a sweat.

The troubles ahead surfaced soon enough. A garden party for the Victims of Violence was cancelled abruptly and the Northern Ireland Fund disbanded (a posse of charity workers was organised to take down posters). Paddy would not talk about it. Nobody would. I stopped pestering people when I recalled the rumours about the Inland Revenue snoopers (not being in PAYE myself I had so far eluded the system and kept quiet). A year later I was to learn that the Garden City Victims of Violence Fund was one of several paid directly into the IRA's coffers.

Caterina returned to Bari. Nano and her family did not come back from a long Irish holiday. Paddy and Angela were now investigating schooling in Dublin. Everybody was leaving. The first men on the moon, Armstrong and Aldrin, bounced like balloons on the lunar crust. Sad clowns in a vaudeville act. I wrote a poem entitled 'Limbo'. 'In the flicking of fingers/ the rain falls through my head./ The startle of nothing is greatly to be feared./ The trees are uneasy in their leaves./ It is too late to care or be careless./ What is needed is a stasis/ of the fresh, a photograph of fruit./ In the bowl there are polythene flowers –/ eternity – / and I tear them to pieces/ or melt them with a taper./ We have made the everlasting/ but not to last./ The present is felt/ crumbling in my fingers.'

It was the first week of July – exactly two years since I landed in England. I commemorated by taking a day off work. The sun was up early and I decided on a three mile hike to George Bernard Shaw's house in Ayot St Lawrence. The full glorious morning made my spirits soar. When I crossed the M1 footbridge, even diesel fumes and grit from the thundering juggernauts below could not earth them. Beyond this inconvenience shrunken hedgerows heavy with dust afforded vistas of wheaten fields, rolling not into hills but into more wheaten fields. The flatness of Hertfordshire was a prospect in itself.

Passing through the old stone village of Codicote I wondered why I had not noticed before the self-contained prettiness of rural England. Although familiar from childhood with the rollicking poems of Chesterton and, more recently, the darker celebrations of Cowper and John Clare, I had not made the link between Life and Art. My literary Welwyn was limited to a dutiful walk around the church where two hundred years ago Edward Young, the rector, composed 'Night Thoughts'.

A towpath took me through the gardens of a mock Elizabethan mansion. Latticed elaborately in black and white, it only lacked for peacocks. I was surprised at the free access. The gravid baronial bulk of Shaw's house beyond was built to prohibit entry. But a National Trust sign announced 'Open to the public. No charge or dogs'. This mausoleum of the second half of G. B.'s life preserved unchanged its trappings. Fifty years of furnishings and sedentary pursuits maintained in cold storage. Brocaded brown was the predominant material. And even the dust seemed polished.

A batch of heavies from the Russian Embassy in shiny Soviet suits huddled in the drawing room, hands in pocket, conversing in thick Slavonic undertones. I looked around to see who they were guarding, but I was the only other visitor in sight. Shaw (like Dorothy L. Sayers) I knew to be big in the USSR. They did not look like readers.

I escaped to the meadow garden where, a plaque informed me, Shaw's ashes had been scattered. I walked carefully. At the furthest corner from the house a wooden shack lightened up the gloom. Here G. B. wrote in summer. I looked in. On the table a vintage high-backed typewriter stood on its heels, begging to be thrown epigrammatic scraps. I could see a gaunt, bearded pylon of a man crouched over it, pounding out an explanatory preface to a perfectly explicable play. A trick of the light.

A hole in the hedge lead out into a field derelict with ragwort. Beyond in a dusky copse a pocket Palladian church glowed white. Reaching it in a gamboling sprint, I took out my pipe. Smoking a pipe requires settling in a specific place. Ideally at a street café table to stare, puffing, at the world around you. A pipe is an immobilising element. I sat on the steps.

There was nothing much to see except a few ancient headstones submerged in the scraggy grass. But my brain, buoyed up by the run, was like a snipe, darting in every direction. Shelley's last poem before he was swept out to sea was 'The Triumph of Life', composed like Dante's *Divine Comedy* in terza rima. The penultimate stanza is 'And some grew weary of the ghastly dance/ (mask after mask fell from their countenance)/ and fell, as I have fallen by the wayside'. In the final verse only one line was completed. 'Then, what is life, I cried.' The 'what' is blotted and could be 'that'.

The book in my pocket was *Redburn*, Melville's tough little tale of an abused cabin boy. It made me think of Rita Hayworth – fire, red swirling hair and a tempestuous voyage. A newspaper cutting my mother sent me told how after the Sunday night showing in Lisdoonvarna of *Fire Down Below*, a picture about a flame-haired stowaway, a farmer from Beala Clugga ambushed the Rank van and carried the film reel off to the Burren country, to keep her for himself.

I thought about James Joyce and the end of the *Portrait of the Artist as a Young Man*. Stephen D.'s famous invocation to himself 'to forge in the smithy of my soul the uncreated conscience of my race' always struck me as a bit much. I preferred his poor mother's counsel, 'to learn abroad, away from home and friends, what the heart is and what it feels.'

Some nights previously I had an impulse to ring home, but thought better of it. Though I craved to hear my mother say, as she always did, 'It's good to hear your voice.' On the steps of the Palladian church there was no phone. So I took out my notebook and started the first weekly letter telling her about my life in England. I sent these two page missives every week for twenty seven years, almost fourteen hundred letters.

I was homesick but knew I would have to learn to live with it.

PART TWO
THE BOHEMIAN LIFE
An Experiment, 1969

Dedicated to literary youth everywhere

'God is the perfect poet
Who in his person acts his own creations.'
Robert Browning

'Poetry is fun.'
Laura Riding

[1]

FINDING MY VOICE

The rain had stopped but my umbrella was still up. Carnaby Street was as bright as day. My eyes smarted with the shock of light. I heard a clean, crisp report, then rapid echoing cracks across the street. Something struck by a whip or lightning. I dropped my suitcase. Three men and their shadows sprinted into a side alley. Folding the umbrella, I considered what a poor weapon it was in a modern city. A police car and an ambulance arrived from Piccadilly. So promptly I could only conclude they were waiting for the shooting to happen. The floodlights above the lamp posts should have alerted me. I saw an insect man with a proboscis camera move in for the kill. I did not join the crowds gathering around the stricken actor. I had no wish to be an extra. The excitement of the moment was defunct.

Holed up in my attic room, I read what I had written. Events of less than a year ago were as history. Exultantly, I paused to read again. The second reading plunged me into doubt. What was I doing? An advanced avant-garde poet (and author of a play under consideration by the Abbey Theatre) thumping out pulp. Where were the poems of yesteryear? The Villonesque Ballades of Dreadful Night set in The Waste Land. Peddling fake prose memoirs and not yet twenty six. I ripped out the page from my rattled Erica, crushed it into a ball to throw in the bin. Then thought better. The last sentence had something. Maybe.

I worked on redeeming myself. A prose poem. Shaped cunningly to end where I was at. Falling on the bed, I clutched the half page and recited to the ceiling.

Night. A back room with no windows. A naked light bulb. Someone sitting on a footstool. Bent over a folding table. On the floor beside him a stockpile of old newspapers and a tattered dictionary. Smell of dead laurels.

The poet is free to ignore the rotting insects stamped into the carpet burns.

He pounds a portable typewriter. UPPER CASE LETTERING ONLY. The keys are stuck. The pounding echoes. Silence.

Someone gets up and wanders around the room. Soot falls down the chimney into an empty grate. The stool is kicked over and the folding table collapses. Next door a burglar alarm rings incessantly.

The light bulb blows. A man is heard cursing the dark. Blindly fumbling amongst old papers, tearing out pages from a crumbling dictionary. Only one word is wanted. Only one word. But the letters are missing.

The door opens. Someone falls down the stairs. Picks himself up. He has paper in his hair. A voice utters the word 'defunct'. It is not the word. Out in the street he is heard to mutter. I counted the steps on the stairs. There were only five. Exactly the same number of letters as the word I want. I must find the letters. I must find the word.

Next morning I threw it in the wastepaper basket. It was nothing like that.

'There comes a time in every literary youth's life when he must give up all for his art.' Mr McFee, my landlord, resembled George Orwell in his consumptive phase, a gaunt disjointed beanpole which folded up in slats. He sits with his back to me at his desk, buried in books. 'Only for four months. I have a job waiting

in Scotland in November.' 'The time is immaterial. It may last
a fraction of a moment or a lifetime. It doesn't matter. Poetry
measures itself against immortality, not a way of life.'

McFee had made it clear when I first moved in that he wasn't
really a landlord. A student of philosophy. His thesis ('Aspects of
Eternity. The Irrelevance of Time') was ten years overdue at
London University. 'I can't fix or clean anything. I am utterly useless. The rent does not include a handy man.' And explained how
every day he made a new discovery. To hand in his great work
while it was still growing would be the intellectual equivalent of
abortion.

As I paid my first month's rent in advance, he informed me that
he was against abortions, not on principle, but because his wife
wished he wasn't. Did this contorted confidence mean the house
was full of little McFees? 'Not that we have any children. Perish
the thought.' Abruptly adding, 'I trust you won't be bringing any
children on to the premises, particularly after dark.' He handed me
a key. 'Your room is the one that fits this. On the top floor.'

Next day McFee is more expansive, even paternal. 'Giving up
all for art is not the answer. Neither is getting a job. Penury and
wage slavery are equal and opposite. Each would be the other.
Sacrificing worldly comforts holds the higher moral ground. But
immortality is not morally determined.' He conjures a cigarette
out of the air and sighs. The audience is over. As I leave the office
('my study') he balefully waves his arm like a drowning man. I
rush to give him my last box of matches.

The dilapidation of this Georgian house increased with each
floor. Distressed gentlefolk occupied the heavily furnished lower
reaches. The McFees held court above them in frivolous squalor,
distempered walls draped in carpets. Backpackers and recluses on
the top story took their chances with cracked plaster and rickety
rafters. My room had an ill-fitting skylight. Sun flooded through.

I climb on to the roof. The garden is a rubbish tip. Strains of

Chopin come from below. There is a piano on the veranda. Mrs McFee, redolent of heaving bosoms and another age, a slight woman with spidery arms in a white flouncy dress, fingers trembling with a passion that defied accuracy, an artist to her fingertips, piano her forte, a grand one.

She was Russian, a very White one. On Sundays Orthodox church services took place in her drawing room. Deporting herself like a former beauty (a sure sign of never having been one), Mrs McFee greeted the taxis bearing the patriarch and her compatriots. The sacerdotal chanting commenced, deteriorating into prolonged, monotonous wailing emanating from the belly of the house. I never saw the congregation leave. Permeating incense drove me to Hyde Park. One Sunday I met McFee by the Serpentine. 'Escaping the Black Mass?' he cried. 'Very wise.'

McFee's homily is on my mind. My moral masters had taught me about the demons. Saints and artists wrestled with them. The Rose of Lima and Keats, for example. These were the chosen, chosen to live difficult lives, defeat the demons and create good and immortal works, respectively, for us to imitate.

Many are called but few are chosen to take on the burden on behalf of others, we were told. My life hitherto put me four square amongst the many, just about managing for myself, save for my secret struggle with the demons that possessed me. No saint (I spat on the sweet cake that I wanted to short circuit rivals), I shyly coveted the notion of being an artist, but in a small way.

I was humble enough, knowing that where pride comes before a fall for others, for me the falls preceded the pride. I kept my modest ambitions to myself, advisedly. When J. F. K. was assassinated I composed a commemorative epic. My brother, who shared a bedroom, discovered it and made the line 'He got shot' a family catchphrase.

Outwardly, I was a paragon – also in a small way – of bourgeois industry, caution and modest worldly ambitions. A steady job beckoned. But I was proud of my arm wrestle with the demons, my secret literary life, because it was secret. And now six years on, I had betrayed that and not by accident. At least to McFee. 'What are you studying?' 'I am not studying. I am writing poems.' Tempted by the vision of myself as the Bohemian saint – freedom, penury and not having to shave – I had fallen. I was still in free fall.

But at least I had a moral parachute to delay the crash to the ground. I had not blabbed about the verse drama with the Abbey (to talk about it would bring bad luck). *A Portrait of the Artist as a Young Lunatic* was my magnum opus, based on the Irish Suibne legend. A seventh-century king, concussed in battle, who became a homeless wanderer, spouting poems concerning watercress from the tops of trees. When his wife took up with his father Congol the Squint, Suibne returns from the wilds to confront the pair.

Robert O'Donoughue, books page editor of the *Cork Examiner*, had acclaimed my sound effects in a student production of Pinter's *The Dumb Waiter*. He was particularly moved by my rendition of a toilet whose flush punctuated the action. Locally dubbed 'the talking barstool', he held court in Kathy Barry's, downing endless cups of coffee and encouraging youth. College poets sat at his feet drinking in his wisdom and pints of stout. R. O'D.'s reputation for compiling patriotic pageants in provincial cities had subsided into annual contributions to the Abbey pantomime. He had friends in high places.

His offer to pass my manuscript to the Abbey made me happy, for a week. My chance to make a dramatic career was at hand. The initial response ('We look to encourage new young playwrights and he is clearly a fine writing talent') is framed in my brain. I did not dare entertain hope beyond a workshop production in the Peacock studio theatre. All the same, I have my doubts about exploiting 'pull' in what for me is the pure sphere of literature, unadulterated by thoughts of fame and money. After all it is my secret, my passport to posterity. The dull thud of the humdrum life negotiates prosperity.

I crave the rudderless existence of pure poet. Swept out, on an oar and a prayer, into the great ocean of random experience. Utterly alone, unburdened by responsibilities other than my art. In time – for it is a dream – I would be washed up on an island (imagined by Andrew Marvell) inhabited by immortals like myself. 'Unto an Isle so long unknown/ And yet far kinder than our own . . . / Safe from the storms, and prelate's rage.' O utopia of the 'way out', unspoiled by conventional package tours and packaging.

On the roof, leaning against a defunct chimney, I have found the perfect place to compose poems. The sky is my limit. I look into it and lose my everyday self. The plane moving noiselessly in its descent to Heathrow is a mythical monster. I am here to catch a phrase to seal a sentiment, to scribble down a mix of words nobody else has ever combined, to feel myself into an idea which will change the world, to find my lost self and give it a name. I am living the life of the chosen. Only inaccurate Chopin and cooking smells from short stay Japanese tourists remind me I am not alone.

What grease for cooking fish creates such foul fumes? My skylight scrouch loses its emollient balm. I stuff notebook in pocket and climb down to my room. Its bare necessities return me to sordid reality, also necessary. I look down on to the streets. People. People with placards. Shouting 'Out, out, out'. I decide to follow.

The green, white and gold banners said 'Troops Out'. An Irish Civil Rights march was holding up Notting Hill. I straggled behind sheepishly, noticing a leavening of navvies and priests in plain clothes amongst the usual students. IRA infiltrators, I thought, and slipped off the tail to watch the rump strut on, a pipe band pipsqueaking through blaring horns.

My notebook jottings are demotic.

Anarchistic youth with global shibboleths is giving way to ancient incantations, sectarian organisation and statements in semtex.

Protest (the first two syllables of the ruling majority) losing its voice to the growing murmur of triobloid, *trouble, the Irish Catholic word for rhubarb. The Troubles bubbling up again.*

Playing with words, I want to shout out, is better than playing with guns. I bite my tongue.

The bottle-necking of the early impulse to bring justice is brewing violence, explosions of glass and body parts.

I want no part in cyclical outbursts of tribal bloodletting. They leave only scars.

A boy regimented into the uniform of the green scouts, the Fianna, hands me a leaflet. I tear it up. The pieces whirl into the gutter.

College friends visited me in my redoubt. At pains to impress them with my eccentric lodgings, I forgot they wanted to talk about themselves. I showed them the wrought iron railings on the landing stairs, spiralling down three flights to the basement. It must have been used to winch laundry baskets from the maid's room (mine) to the washroom (now occupied by distressed gentle-folk). One evening McFee knocked at my door. Fuji, a Japanese music student, was hanging from the rails, a hand's grip from a dry dive. Together we coaxed him on to terra firma ('Your shoelaces are undone. Let me knot them.' I grabbed his legs). The student thanked us politely and went back to his room. He played Beatle songs as Bach toccatas on the guitar.

Guests never came back, which suited me. I was a full-time poet, hard on myself and hard on others. Their familiarity cramped my voluptuous isolation, interloping on random experience with homely heart-to-hearts. The point of my pencil was granite (it had to be, to make your mark). People were ghosts on my horizon. In the streets, cafés, pubs and parks. When the lights came up at the cinema, I saw them in a strange glow and myself in their reflection.

The East European poets – Popa, Holub, Herbert – made me wry and cynical towards humanity's slavish submission to authority and fate. My notebooks were hieroglyphed with desperately dry poemlets, divertimentos on dust and the vanities. It pleased me to think I might make my moral masters sleep less easily in their beds, but I rather doubted they read the *Kilkenny Magazine*. But one day – if friends did not come between me and my muse – I would cause mass insomnia.

Women, of course, could not be friends. I knew that from experience and the movies of Antonioni. Love poetry was for fortune cookies. But still I was curious. A pretty girl getting into a car suggested adventure. For someone else. I was not envious. Only sad that I could not drive. Not forlorn, of course. I mocked the word. 'Forlorn, forlorn.' (Something to do with Lorna Doone.) It was not just the driving. I had no car.

I would satirise couples and self-absorption in verse, imagining scenarios that rent them asunder. If it was revenge for my failure to engage, or lack of interest or what people called success, it never occurred to me. Observing lovers in streets, cafés, pubs and parks, I turned them into cruel copy. The Jack the Ripper of poetry. This completely took over. I could not write anything else.

Literary editors in little magazines back in Ireland were impressed. 'New poetry from Swinging London', one wrote approvingly. 'The reality you catch is as sordid as Baudelaire, but more convincing, up-to-date. Slightly shop-soiled songs of experience.' Later, a maiden aunt sighed over a published sequence. 'Poor James, what a sad life he is living.'

Editors (and maiden aunts) were deceived into believing I was living the life I imagined. How could they know that my poems were just intimations of the life I might have led, had I not poetry to write?

Pound's *Lustra* and *Hugh Selwyn Mauberley* were my lookout

posts. I saw London through Ezra's provincial gauze, tracing the
fading tapestries of an effete elite. My sophistication was studied
rather than experienced.

> In South Kensington, I observe the quality
> of women with an ostrich eye for detail.
>
> 'Is it Art?' I mused, as she dissembled
> herself from a motorcar. I noted
>
> the inscape of her knees,
> the well-formulated phrase of her hair
>
> over her shoulders; a silhouette
> of bosom turned round, thighs by Henry Moore.
>
> The look she gave me? A slap in the intellect.
> I went into the Victoria and Albert for a perfect
> relationship with one of Raphael's angels.

Prufrock rising from the ashes. A young fogey before his time.
Published under a *nom de plume* (I was not without shame). Drawn
from Dryden's 'MacFlecknoe, King of Fools' who 'like Augustus/
Young was brought to rule and had governed long'.
    The verse play was in my family name, serious stuff.

[2]

HOW TO WRITE A POEM

My method of composition derived from James Stephens. Recite over and over a poem your peers admire. Listen to the words and answer them with your own. It is the perfect conversation. Allowing you to make the response you only thought of afterwards. Pound advised Stephens to read Browning. 'Bang-whang-whang goes the drum, tootle-te-tootle the fife;/ No keeping one's haunches still: it's the greatest pleasure in life.' His first book of poems began 'I will not dance. I say I will not dance'. Refuting Browning sent him on his way.

East European poetry was fashionable with my peers. I would drink deep of poems by Vasco Popa and regurgitate my own. It was a form of translation without responsibility to the original. The Penguin Modern European Poets series – in English – gave me dispensation. For example:

The Seducer

Popa	*Me*
One caresses the leg of a chair	He pulled on her lips so hard
Until the chair turns	she was sucked into her stomach
and gives him	And there she lies inside out
a welcoming sign	Lining his inside

with its leg

Another kisses
a keyhole
Kisses it Doesn't he kiss it
until the keyhole
returns his kiss

A third stands by
Gapes at the other two
and twists
his
head Twists it

until
his
head
falls
off

Her disorganised
Organs beating
and breathing hope-
less-
ly

'Let me out' she pleads
with acid in her eyes
'Let me out please'
He blocks his ears
until her voice becomes
a gastric rumb-
le

'Rape Rape' she shouts
And a policeman stops him
'Repeat yourself young man'
He keeps his mouth
shut

Miroslav Holub's poems were more than a starting point for me. I had come across his work in biochemistry in my studies and, learning he was a poet, wangled a Holub reference into my thesis. (My complicity with a fellow-scientist with literary leanings escaped the external examiners' rigorous scrutiny.) Holub's poems were those of a man of science rather than literature. He made himself an instrument to register life with accurate readings. Understated, avoiding exaggerated claims, he made a mockery of neo-romanticism, confessionalism and other subjective literary modes.

I could not hope to compete with Holub the scientist, let alone the poet. His poems were main features in a picture palace. I entered the darkness and lived through them. My own were the B movies I stayed on to watch because they were part of the same programme. The movie analogy is not casual. I saw in art-house cinemas (like the Academy on Oxford Street) a life more real than that around me. And the sub-titles were as poetry, giving snatches of meaning to the narrative of existence.

I did not need to read his poem 'Love', knowing it by heart. My answer to it was a modest mood echo. I did not dare to upstage the main man generous enough to allow me a little solo.

Love

Holub	Me
Two thousand cigarettes.	I have been sad.
A hundred miles	How easy to be sad.
from wall to wall.	November giving up the ghost
An eternity and a half of vigils	on the reality of a clear pane.
blanker than snow.	
Tons of words	The missed train – the tale of
	a track
old as the tracks	that makes you think
of a platypus in the sand.	its coming back
A hundred books we didn't	
write.	with its tongue out.
A hundred pyramids we	
didn't build.	I have been sad.
Sweepings.	How easy to be sad.
Dust.	The first step, the last.
Bitter	The first word,
as the beginning of the world.	the last. Have you noticed
Believe me when I say	how sad they are?
it was beautiful.	How easy and how sad.

What London editors returned without comment, their Irish counterparts snapped up. There at that time the cult of the showband raged. Glitter-suited combos performing covers of American hits –

from Jim Reeves to Little Richard – in provincial halls. They supplanted the originals in popular affection. I should have realised that my little vogue was somehow analogous to this phenomenon, the wren riding the eagle to rise above it. I was local-boy-made-good, Hank O'Loughlin imitating the Yankee yodeller, Hank Williams, topping him in Ballyvoehane.

Next I eliminated the inspirational kick-start, reading my own published poems before striking out on new ones. I began to repeat myself, writing the same poem over and over. This was what my public wanted. I gave it to them. Beethoven's 'Variations on a Theme by Diabelli' became Beethoven's 'Variations on a Theme by Beethoven'. I lost the point of departure and stayed put.

A poem called 'Euclid' was my QED. It stated definitively the proposition of my afflatus:

> Two legs start at the bottom
> of the stairs: one of them a club foot.
> The club foot takes steps
> separately while
> the healthy hoof gallops up
> three at a time. And yet,
> having a body in common,
> they come together at the top.

No corollary necessary. I had reached the limit.

Recognising my limitations took more than four months. But the seeds of self-knowledge were planted during this time. The not-so-slim volume appeared a year later with harmonious reviews. 'A new voice', 'Young poet finds his voice', 'A still small voice', 'A monstrous little voice'. The 'voice' accolades sounded hollow. I knew that mine was somewhere between a ventriloquist's dummy and a promiscuous parrot.

Still, flattery sustains vanity in a literary youth. He doggedly learns to chase his own tail to fulfill expectations. Poetry press editors and contributors (the main readers) are hypnotised by pirouettes spun on a fulcrum of preconceptions. Repetition – the same names, the same poems – reassures the uncertain in this dizzy world. Averse to the prevailing vertigo, I began to see some merit in keeping the head down and achieving a modicum of self-respect in obscure stability. The romance of the posthumously discovered body of work dies hard in the attic of the healthy young.

Meanwhile, I began to have a literary life.

[3]

THE BLOCK

R. O'D. reported the Abbey were 'taken' by my Suibne play. Deila Dunne, the artistic director, told him the form was so new that she was not sure 'if it is very good or just somebody indulging in an exercise'. The play was now in the hands of their 'best readers'. A nervous tic in my eye calculates my fear and trembling. When hyperbole is tempered with doubt it is time to watch out.

I found myself at a loose end. Poems no longer tumbled out at every impulse. In Notting Hill I walked streets which had seen better days, distraught. The smug nineteenth-century family houses, reduced to flats and bedsits and owned by latter day Rachmans and Church Commissioners, accommodated my anguish. Drug abusers, decayed gentry, blacks and tourists passed by. How could they know? I was experiencing writer's block, which meant I had a serious literary career behind me. I cultivated a blank, baleful expression, the true reflection, I imagined, of writer despair.

Mrs McFee recognised a kindred spirit. She smiled wanly, ascending the stairs for her evening recital. Colette appraising her callow youth. That evening, I fancied, she played for me from the veranda. I opened my windows and allowed Scriabin and Godowsky to fill my room. I imagined her fluttering party dress and lilting shoulders. The lace curtains, drawn back to embrace the evening, stirred with the ectoplasm of the female soul. The temptress of the ivories abandoned the pedal of unrelenting passion and ambushed my self-pity with a Schumann humoresque, a faltering *Papillon*.

I looked in the mirror and saw an emaciated stubbled face peering out through a tufted bush of hair, a hanging basket upside down. It itched in the damp evening air.

Next day I submitted myself to a two-bob barber, emerging, ears intact, with a convict cut. Disciplining the hirsute was my first step towards rehabilitation (though I let my incipient beard be – it deserved a chance). Bristling with renewed vigour, I phoned a college friend. My return to life began with an invitation to a party in Putney.

I wore a French beret on my bald pate and walked from Kensington to Fulham in a thought capsule. My need for external inspiration perplexed me. Time, and the will to imagine things, should have been sufficient. I believed experience was necessary for a writer, but second-hand so as not to distract. Writing was life enough. Not writing wasn't. Should I allow myself a diversion? Pascal was all against diversion. The fool's way of not thinking of death. Get myself a girl. Give my mind a rest. I thought of death a lot in my writing, rarely in my everyday life. I should be true to my everyday inclinations. Maybe my writing was merely a distraction from not following my inclinations – a girl, a thoughtless existence, being one of the boys? I shuddered, but persisted. Real life experience could create a muse. After all Beatrice existed, flesh and blood. Dante was inspired by her. Though clearly more by her existence rather than palpable flesh and blood. *La Vita Nuova* is not about desire or even love. It is a quest for the abstract ideal. On balance, Pascal was right. At least for me.

Crossing the river, I woke to the world around. The Thames is less a waterway than a great divide, separating an international city with its grandeurs and gangrenes from massive sprawl. Wharfs and power stations giving way to soul-destroying outskirts. Battersea, Wandsworth, Clapham and Streatham. Chaotic conurbations gradually leveling out into suburban settlements, the Green Belt beyond.

Putney is an oasis of polite living by the river, though squashed by the ugly intrusiveness of its surrounds. On a sultry evening in early July a sluggish weariness lingers. Walled gardens and fine houses cannot disguise the tainted ordure of proximate squalor. The pavements are littered with transient interlopers from another world. Nothing is indigenous here except the dull thud of normalcy in an invading wilderness, cluttered with anarchy and poisonous with pollutants.

I despised Putney with its fake exclusiveness. If suburbia is where lesser mortals are made to feel comfortable by what is predictable, it presupposes orderly lives. Births, marriages, mortgages and death. It requires clerks, insurance men, teachers, policemen and shopkeepers to home here with their families in neat denatured gardens. Greener than north of the river, the bosky verdure had a reptilian sheen as though lacquered in noxious trace elements. Smell also seemed suppressed by unsatisfactory deodorants, seasonal changes more like scene changes – trees, lawns and flower beds as props.

It was Henry Green territory, a hotbed of undivulged crime and passion. Putney's shady terraces, I decided, harboured embezzlers, wife-beaters, child-molesters, bigamists, poisoners, respectable madames specialising in whippings and nannying nasty clergymen guised in rubber knickers and frilly bonnets, and ordinary people taking murderous fantasies out on hedge clipping. A lifetime of painstaking sleuthing would be ill-rewarded with a sad accumulation of sordid little items in the back pages of the local press. I wallowed in my opprobrium like a piglet in an alien trough, liking Putney more and more as it gratifies my lust for a T. S. Eliot quagmire.

I arrived at Adrian Naughton's bedsit at the appointed hour, to the minute. A string hung out the letter box. I pulled the message. 'Gone to The Kings Arm's. Gatecrashers welcome.' My heart sank, a pub crawl party. Tired and thirsty, I submitted to student convention. 'Augustus, the poet', a florid face yelped from the bar. 'What's that under the beret?' My symbol of bohemian distinction sat like a ballcock on my head. Adrian tore it off. 'My God, he's been in the nick.' Vaguely familiar college cronies on adjacent stools hooted appreciation. A pint was handed to me. 'Drink that down, Augustus, we're moving on. From the King's to the Queen's Arms. An heir will be born.'

His ceili yelps amazed and appalled me. Naughton, the only son of a perfectly respectable suburban family – his father worked in the bank – was no roaring boy. Exemplary student, never one of the lads. Dutiful Adrian, many a time I saw him walk to Mass with his father and sister, now a nun. I watched him grow (not very much) from schoolboy swat to good student, a weedy tweedy fellow beneath bullying or contempt.

I had befriended him briefly in our last year. Serious, studious, he talked of Teilhard de Chardin, attended the Thomas Aquinas Society. Once we went together (I disgraced myself by mentioning Piltdown Man, the hoax that de Chardin fell for), and met occasionally on the fringes of the One Ball Gang, an intellectual coterie that I abhorred but could not ignore.

How could this wimpish mannikin have evolved in a couple of years into a gallog, out-navvying the navvies in Irishry? I understood him to be a financial journalist with an evening paper. Grub Street, I thought, there is no accounting. He'll be back in Cork working with his father and married to a mouse once his apprenticeship is complete. Just a bourgeois youth making whoopee abroad, before settling down.

'I'm staying here', I muttered into my glass. 'I've only just arrived.' 'Young Augustus, always trying to be different.' Adrian jumped up. 'We're off, if you don't want to come.'

Some androgynously dressed-down girls rose from tables in the saloon and followed his entourage. I sat sulking with rage and shame, rage at being outnumbered by the clods, shame at being Irish or ashamed at being ashamed.

I noticed not all of his gang had left. A pale willowy girl remained on her stool. She gave me a ghostly little smile. And face down on the counter began to bang her head. 'Are you all right?' I asked, concerned. 'It depends on what you mean by all right.' Sweeping her golden shoulder-length hair up from the bar, her wistful reply and proud forehead intimated bitter experience. That is how I met Alma.

[4]

MADE IN HEAVEN

I was ill-prepared, like most of my coevals, for Alma, an English girl.

Back home, our acquaintance with the opposite sex was not encouraging (or encouraged). Stereotyping girls kept them at one remove. Clinging vines, high-minded harridans, hopeless flirts, tomboys, friends' sisters, sisters. Ignorance of intimacy preserved their mystery and our worst fears.

What were women for? The received answer was marriage and children. How did they achieve these – to us – undesirable goals? Sirens and female spiders exploit male confusion and weakness. They lure victims with fatal charms into perplexed impotence. Compromised male cripples are courted, flattered to deceive. Once trapped, males are released into domestic captivity and fattened to become sperm donors and breadwinners. Marriage and children accomplished, virility is gelded. The cycle of the sexes, and affairs of the heart, close in coronary thrombosis. The females of the species collect the life insurance.

Alma was different. Though not much older than me, she intimated many lives, false starts on a treadmill that lead to ... I couldn't even guess. Her vampish egotism enthralled, appalled me. Like Walter Pater's Mona Lisa she had been 'a diver in deep seas and keeps her fallen days about her'. I felt sure she only thought of marriage to regret its existence, and of children to revoke their potential.

Alma's dream of becoming an actress realised itself that evening in a solo show for an audience of one, me. The King's Arms and clientèle evaporated in smoke. Our theatre in the round excluded the world. I was the fall guy coaxed on stage for the main protagonist to demonstrate her arts.

The performance gave me an opportunity to examine her person. Everything about her was regular – cut of hair, line of features, fall of clothes (upmarket boutique), shape of figure, clip of speech, mien of mime, change of mood and the measured sipping of three gins and tonics to last the evening.

Slapstick gave way to Greek tragedy (in estuary English). I became its prop, an anachronism (Greek drama does not have scenery). But still I played my passive part to the hilt, patiently waiting. When the heroine dried up the chorus would jump in.

Fate had been unkind to Alma. Antigone, Electra, Eurydice came to mind. Arachne too as she began to lose the thread. Her tale of woe knotted. The flow faltered – tears that would not come, sighs between urgent sips of gin, dying swan contortions. My time had come.

As I cleared my throat a yelp shattered my cue. 'Augustus, you're a sly one.' The King's Arms materialised again out of the mist, Blake-like at first, then sharpening into a Hopper painting, 'The Long Bar'.

Adrian and his bacchantes shimmer at the door, a mirage finding its oasis. He staggers over, embracing our shoulders for support. 'Augustus and Alma, a marriage made in heaven. Him a promising poet. Her an employee of a grand publishing house. Now isn't that nice?'

Steering a furious Alma out through the drunken hordes, I escorted her home to Kew.

Walking off the gin reduced her from a stumbling Sarah Bernhardt to a brisk Wren off-duty. I was on sufferance. Matched her stride for stride, too breathless to talk. She admitted to being 'nothing much at Hutchinson's'. Her theatrical tale of woe did not resume. We arrived at a four-square terraced house with an immaculate garden. I am dismissed, but not before giving her an envelope of recent poems and my phone number.

Alma did not write it down. When I offered pencil and paper, she curtly remarked, 'I always remember phone numbers. It's my bloody job.'

The tube back to Notting Hill at midnight is the anteroom to a morgue. Drunks, drug abusers and vagrants. I empathised with the latter. Being the sounding board for three hours of a middle-class English girl who is not happy made me feel marginal. Despite the rocky ride in the half-empty train, I reconstructed the jigsaw of her life as told, scribbling fiercely.

I typed it out in my room, embellishing where there were pieces missing and framing it in a prologue to make it less one-sided. Not only was I living but I was writing it down. I slept without dreaming as an author of honest prose should.

[5]

ALMA'S TALE OF WOE

The English pub is a palace of confidences. Royal loneliness slums with common strangers. Dr Johnson described the tavern stool as 'the throne of human felicity. When I am seated, I find masters courteous and servants obsequious to my call. Wine there exhilarates my spirits, and prompts me to free conversation.' The meeting of parallel lives in a neutral venue releases an existential atmosphere where more rather than less is said. The consequences of this 'interchange of discourse' are absorbed in the moment. Truth is subservient to the immediate effect. It is more likely to be exaggerated than understated. But it is not eluded. In vino veritas cum grano salo *should be framed behind every bar.*

All will be forgotten tomorrow. The princess returns to her unhappy tower, a prisoner of her hair. Commoners rub their eyes, scratch their heads and wonder what to believe.

My local pub is The Battle of Alma. Alma means soul in Spanish and dancing girl in Egyptian. How are these three facts connected? A girl called Alma who trained as a dancer (classical not belly) bared her soul to me in a pub (not The Battle).

Alma was conceived on the night before her father joined up. A trainee accountant, he fought the war behind a desk and, posted to North Africa, discovered his homosexuality. On demobilisation he returned to Surbiton. His wife took to her bed when a minor scandal made the local papers.

Alma was brought up by a succession of indifferent maids. Her mother entered a mental asylum. The family prospered. Alma's daddy always gave her evening baths. The perfect father for ten minutes – splashes and suds, laughter and kisses. The final embrace of the towel was bliss.

Alma noticed daddy began to avert his eyes from her growing body. His touch lost its playfulness. School friends taught her the facts of life. She confided in her father. He left the bathroom abruptly, calling the maid, and didn't return. The maid said he was sick.

Alma then threw her first epileptic fit. She claims to be able to will petit *and even* grand mal, *a psychosomatic gift available to her in times of danger and distress. It is an extreme form of acting, not unknown in stage history. Donald Wolfit, Anew MacMaster and Edmund Keane could make Othello fall into convulsions at the drop of a handkerchief (Act 4, Scene 1, lines 44–60).*

Alma's father avoided touching her, absenting himself henceforth from evening baths. She took up ballet lessons and became untouchable. A whirl on embonpoint. *Her ambitions to train as an actress were ironically thwarted when she failed the medical for drama school. Instead she went to Hull University to study theatre history. Distracted by love affairs with older men (for instance her professor and his assistant: 'Life in Hull was like a rugby scrum'), she only achieved a second class B Phil. Her frustrated acting skills were put to good use – not blushing before wives and the occasional bedroom fit.*

Alma said older men subject their lovers to 'artificial complications'. She regretted missing out on carefree flings with students more her age.

Alma is secretary to an assistant director with whom she is having an affair. It is more serious and hopeless than any previous entanglements. Recognising her acting skills, he covers his tracks by bringing her home to take dictation. She plays the role of the working secretary to perfection. His family has become fond of her.

Alma relates the details of their covert relationship. Furtive trysts after hours in the office. Home is too sacred to defile. She knows he is unworthy of her ('a real bastard'), but likes being part of the family ('one up on the furniture, but that's something'). She would like to break it up, but fears for her job, and worse, she has a crush on her boss's wife and, she thinks, on his eldest son ('scarcely out of short pants'). The ramifications and complications are endless, unresolved, a story doomed to an unhappy ending.

[6]

PETALS IN THE MUD

The Putney adventure revived my poetic powers – six or seven poems a day, typed on grainy yellow sheets that carbon copied nicely. Alma had my number off by heart. That was enough for me. I had listened, made no demands. She would ring me in a week or two. A long poem about Fluff, a lady of the night I admired from afar in my college days (she worked the port and mocked students – 'all balls and no money'), ended:

> But when the Harbour Board turned in
> for Custom & Exercise dreams,
> halfway to Dunlops on bad nights,
> Fluff tendered the trawlers upstream,
> harbouring them from their stormy plight,
> docked them down in the arms of sin.

Alma was far from my mind. I attended the Poetry Society and saw Marianne Faithful, a fallen petal stuck in the mud of Pop, drinking in the bar with a bearded guitar. This was living and writing. A tentatively handsome fellow in a suit with a BBC accent asked me who I was, did he know me? I played mysterious. He recited a litany of current Irish poets. I laughed to hear familiar names. 'You know them?' 'Yes.' I didn't say on the page only.

My new friend, Tony, introduced me to a French poet, Michel Something, whose disinterestedness impressed me. Dissipation personified – carrot head, hair like straw that stuck on any way from a night in a haystack, dirty hanky sticking out of his breast pocket. 'Michel is writing an epic poem about the Ablative Absolute.' We talk about the French grammarian as though he is not there.

'Popa is reading with Robert Bly next evening. I think I can wangle an introduction.' Tony must know my work, I think, and disappear off on a cloud. 'See you tomorrow.'

McFee calls to me from his study. 'Out on the town! What has happened to your Art?' 'I'm making friends in the poetry world.' 'Ha! friends.' He wiggles his cigarette. I match it. The evening and its consequences bemuse. Telepathy, I decide on second thoughts. Tony could not know my poems but he can read me like a book. I jump up the stairs, two at a time.

I felt strong enough to compose an Alma poem. It came in one breath.

> Her body was found stripped
> of flesh and even the memory of flesh in the drained
> bed of a river. She had said:
> 'I must leave the river.' But how could she
> part with a part of her, more than a part, more
> than her bloodstream and brain put together: they couldn't
> carry on without it. It was within her. She said:
> 'I must leave the river.' But the river left her.
>
> It was within her. Nevertheless, she hardly felt it.
> If she did she would have made a boathouse of herself

with herself. Once she saw it, posing on a wound,
and was so frightened she called for a hospital.

As to its history, just accept it has one.
The river if it's checked is unsafe,
builds up the dam until it breaks
in a flood that strains to mud flats.
As to its history, just accept it.

She thought she was free. She said:
'It is easy. I must leave the river.'
And her body was found stripped
of flesh. She thought she could leave it,
but it left her. Yet, not without
running through her with its only finger,
leaving its fingerprint. The river left her
in its empty bed. Her body was found.

I knew Alma would ring. People who divulge intimacies cannot
wait to find out how the confidant is taking them. 'How are
things?' 'The same.' I took the call in McFee's study. He was
enjoying breakfast. I felt constrained, but recovered well enough to
ignore his chortling asides. 'Let's meet and you can tell me about
it.' Her silence was not encouraging. 'We could go to a show.' A
show sounded neutral to me, unlike a film or a meal. 'Making a
show of yourself.' McFee tee-hee-ed. '*The War of the Roses.*' 'I hate
blank verse.' '*Danton's Death?*' 'A bit too moral.' 'What would you
like?' 'Just get tickets, I don't mind.'

She left a number. No mention of my poems, I thought. Perhaps just as well. McFee threw a parting sally. 'Take her to *Hair*.'

My attention at the reading was distracted by Vasco Popa's presence. A neat little man like his poems whose gloom discouraged

laughter. Tony surpassed himself. He became Vasco's da Gama, navigating him to a Chinese restaurant for a meal. Bly joined the party. I sat next to Popa, whose Slav blinds were down. I despaired of communicating. Tony addressed him in fluent French.

Robert Bly disappointed me by being friendly and unchallenging in his converse. I thought a minimalist American poet should at least be rude. Instead he was brotherly and a bit boring. Not that his poetry meant a lot to me. Still, I felt his off-duty mannerliness was a sell-out.

Popa ate as sparingly as he spoke and picked his teeth. My attempts to be reverential ('I have read all your books in English translation and you are my inspiration as a poet') fell flat. Tony came to my rescue, lauding me in French as an adapter of Popa's work. 'Recite.' Popa turned to me. 'Recite an example.' I explained through Tony I did not exactly translate, but I could mime a poem. The glum Slav's tablecloth-transfixed eyes lifted to mine, a brief glint, as he recognised his 'After Play'. Tony made me repeat the performance for Bly's benefit. Everybody laughed except Popa.

The poem roughly goes:

> The hands clutch the stomach
> lest the stomach bursts with laughter.
> But there is no stomach.
>
> One hand just manages to lift itself
> to wipe the cold sweat from the forehead.
> There is no forehead either.
>
> The other hand reaches to the heart
> lest the heart leaps out of the chest.
> Of course there is no heart.

Both hands drop
into the lap.
Where is the lap.

On one hand rain is falling.
From the other grass is growing.
What more should I say.

[7]

THE GARDEN PARTY

Tickets for *Hair*, hip musical of the moment, were unobtainable except for returns. I queued with hordes of hippies in the rain. The coming of the Age of Aquarius, I gathered, was the message of the show. I knew Aquarius figured in the Greek sky as the Water Carrier, a constellation the sun entered in early spring to refresh the heavens. What could it be about? A dissolved version of *The Iceman Cometh*, perhaps. Amongst hairy pilgrims counting their beads and chanting the hit song 'Good Morning Sunshine', flippancy seemed out of place. All I really knew was that at the climax the full cast stepped out of their loose-flowing flower child cheesecloth and tossed back their long hair in a moment of collective nakedness. Every night was packed.

I paid for my shame at queueing for an entertainment I despised by shelling out for two outrageously expensive seats. The thought I might consider it an 'investment' made me wince.

McFee had taken to sorting my mail, weighing and considering the envelopes to speculate on contents. A fat one elicited 'rejection', a thin one 'acceptance'. Inscribed 'Mr' with a degree in the tail, 'your family'. He flipped through them consolingly. 'At least you get letters.' Deila's assistant wrote me a holding letter from the

Abbey. 'We are waiting for the third reader. So far the majority opinion is that you are a writer to be reckoned with. However, the final decision is not in our gift. It rests with the directors.' Both my eyes twitch.

Today McFee handed me a floridly addressed lavender envelope braided with serpents. 'I fear the tax man has caught up with you.'

I took it to my room. 'Tambuki and Ursula are back from their sojourn in Bangalore and cordially invite you to a soirée. Guest of honour, George Barker. Bring a bottle and friend.' The address was Chelsea with the magical word Mews in it. How did I get on this famous editor's invitation list? My trips to the Poetry Society were largely incognito. Supping with Bly and Popa would not have helped. This was mainstream *belles lettres* territory.

I certainly was making my way. Courtesy of whom? Gobsmacked, humbled, suspicious, I racked my brain and came up blank. I rang Tony. 'Not me.' My mystery benefactor remained a mystery. I checked the date. The party was tonight. I went out to buy a cravat.

Chelsea Bridge Mews is a genteel jumble of yeomen's houses. Roses and virginia creeper ramble all over the place. Garden flats are the prized residences. Tambuki's wins the gold ribbon. The front door is open. I see through to flowerbeds where people stand, fingering glasses. I enter unannounced, passing through the french window into a bowered grove perfumed with orchids. The chatter is muted but punctuates the warm evening air with multifarious murmurs. In the ornate garden guests are thick on the ground, exotically plumed statues paling into the dusk. I have entered the world of a Marvell poem.

A poet I know by his book jacket comes into focus. He was once a boxer. I grab a glass of bubbly from a tray (the bearer a white suited Indian boy) and attach myself to his circle. He is expatiating on publishers' advances. 'I live on commissions. It's a form of literary alimony. Having put your best years into the marriage of words and music, all you get is housekeeping money. The divorce settlement is pot-boilers. Anthologies pay the rent. A book on jazz for Phoenix allows me three months respite in Ischia. *Bomber Poets of the Second World War* puts the clothes on my back. School texts subsidise booze. I don't know how I eat. Of course you don't have to honour commissions. The good thing about editors is they move on.'

A toady simpers, 'But Vernon, your poems must bring in something. They are everywhere.' 'Next to nothing, loose change. The answer is to marry a rich widow. But you have to live with them, pander to their ways. I can't do that.'

A lanky hawk of a man with swarthy complexion nearby raises his glass. 'Vernon, old pal, you've married more rich widows than I have had hot dinners. And, if I'm not mistaken, you're married to one still.'

The circle breaks up and reforms around George Barker. Only Vernon and I remain. Endeavouring to cheer him up, I say, 'Cassius Clay could do with someone to tart up his poems. I'm sure there's money in that.' The boxer poet is not amused. 'Who in God's name are you?' And walks off. I join the Barker circle.

I have this man's poems off by heart, I think. I am in the presence of an immortal. 'And in the cold sheet of the sky/ Lifelong the fishlipped lovers lie/ Kissing catastrophes.' Lines to make me smile. Inexperienced adolescents associate serious kissing with suction. Fishlipped suggests the palpating *moue* of incompetent lips. Catastrophies are slack-lipped. Fats Waller had a song about a cuckold called 'Liver-lipped Jones'. I had written several poems playing with the conceit of osculation and leakage.

George's tongue spits insults like lizards' saliva. His circle implodes as women flee for shelter. Men stand their ground. This is war. But his rules of engagement are unruly. 'Laurie Lee is a sissy, a little missy. Mixes rosé wine with his cider. Spain ruined him. Who has ever seen a "pink moon"?' 'Ha! George, you should know. The moon seen through bloodshot eyes.' George shrivels the clever literary critic with a poisonous dart. 'How much do they pay you for your reviews? I mean the authors. Laurie Lee writes through his arse. "And as they go their wandering tongues embrace." His lovers are contortionists.'

I am alone with George.

If drunk, it does not show – except for snail-tracks of froth at the angles of his mouth. 'Ursula, come over here and I'll behave myself.' A plump diva in a flowering gown turns her back. 'Ungrateful creatures, women. "Let her lie naked here, my hand resting/ Light on her broken breast, O sleeping world./ And her hand of a country trembles against me." I wrote that for her.'

'Why broken?' I ask. 'What?' George snaps at a gnat. 'The breast.' 'What breast? What are you talking about?' and spins away, waving furiously to someone in the shrubberies. 'I'm a fan of your poetry. I know two of your poems off by heart.'

'Two?' George rounds on me. '*Who are you* to reduce my work to two poems?' He looks at my cravat and beret, laughs bitterly. 'What two, sonny boy? You might as well spill the beans.' '"Summer Song" and "To My Mother".' 'Christ!' 'I am Irish like your mother and . . .' 'Leave my mother out of this.' '"Most near, most dear, most loved and most far"', I stutter, hoping his own words would calm the waters. '"She is a procession no one can follow after".' 'Cut it! You read too many anthologies, young man. Early work is the death of reputation.' George throws his hand in the air to relieve chagrin. 'Malcolm, I'm coming.'

Already two well-known poets had abandoned me in despair, their despair. I feel justified. 'How vainly men themselves amaze/ To win the palm, the oak, or bays.'

Suddenly electric lanterns planted behind bushes light up. The garden becomes an artificial paradise. Guests shadow into insignificance, dull crouching shapes. 'When we have run our passion's heat/ Love hither makes his best retreat.' Time to go.

Ursula catches me sneaking past the crowded buffet in the drawing room. 'Thanks for saving me from *that* rude man. I will be *ever* grateful. I must introduce you to Tambuki. But *what* is your name? I don't believe we have been introduced.'

If Ursula did not know who I was, her pasha of a spouse knew who I wasn't. His guru eyes glide over me and settle elsewhere. 'I'm sorry, he is *preoccupied*. Jet lag.' I am more impressed by her apologetic tones than Tambuki's trendy (I feel) rudeness. '*Who* did you come with?' Her curiosity flattered me, made me someone, but it wasn't me. 'I think probably I came to the wrong party. Is this Harry and Doris Hopkins's Silver Jubilee?' 'Good heavens, a *gate-crasher*. I suppose I should *throw you out*. How exciting.' 'Would it disappoint you if I just go?' 'No, stay and *talk to me*. I'm bored horribly.' 'I'm sorry but Harry and Doris will be waiting for me. I am part of the band.'

By the time I reached Sloane Square, regret at rushing off had receded. I recited Marvell to myself. 'Meanwhile the mind, from pleasure less/ Withdraws into its happiness:/ The mind, that ocean where each kind/ Does straight its own resemblance find.' Why was I invited? And by whom? Had I acquired a mystery patron? The thought thrilled.

[8]

A SHOW TO REMEMBER

Alma was almost radiant. Hair washed into a Twiggy trawl, leather mini-skirt, hands up to her thumbs in a silky short jacket, hazardous high heels, she was well pleased with her appearance. I was taken aback. Last time I saw her she was a quietly dressed dying swan. Now rigged up like a dizzy secretary, she looked older but not wiser.

'How did you get tickets? No-one I know could get them.' 'A friend of a friend', I lied. Queueing could not be admitted. She looked at herself in the foyer mirror. 'My God, I'm a mess.' 'No, just a teen dream', I wanted to quip, but I had seen myself. (Deciding a beret would be uncouth in a theatre, I had waxed my head stubble to make it bristle. Jeans and turtleneck sweater completed what I fancied was a Steve McQueen look. Now I saw baggy slacks, constricted sweater and hair that stood on end. I was the Good Soldier Schweik.) Instead I resorted to the interesting. 'Looking good when feeling bad is very hard to do.'

A mistake. I had to explain. 'Jack Teagarden.' 'Oh, yeah, Teagarden? Angus has lots of 78s.' Her 'Oh' was a sigh.

Before reaching our seats I had conjured up the cause of her woe.

The theatre, a converted cinema, was designed for darkness, to be felt rather than seen. Lights up, the space was infinitely boring and terrifying. The audience in its basin resembled a field of corn stubble cowering under a threatening sky. Our seats were a spitting distance from the stage, semi-detached (ample elbow and leg room) and anything but intimate.

When the house lights dimmed, an explosion of sound and psychedelic strobes isolated and trapped me. Once I became reconciled to my fate – two hours without interval in a hippie hell – a simple enough story emerged through the musical equivalent of Pop Art. Amplified and enlarged, the comic-cut plot blew the mind into neutral. Any temptation to think critically was hopelessly zapped.

A boy from Oklahoma on his way to enlist in the Marines for the Vietnam War stops off in New York and falls into a flock of flower people in Central Park. These children of nature lure him into dance and song to make him politically aware. Earth mothers and flower daughters touch his feelings. It is a time for tumescent growth. He becomes aware of his body. Gradually the risk to his person in Vietnam dawns. He won't be able to dance around the maypole in the Killing Fields (the hit song '3-5-0-0' numbers the monthly casualty figures, Americans only).

Wimpy draft dodgers bond with him in a ballet of peace and love. The farm boy gets natural, grows his hair, learns to let it all hang out. Hair is everywhere, symbol of freedom, fun, health and not doing what you are told. What is lost in jail, enclosed orders, cancer and war flourishes here. Absalom's two hundred shekels of tresses – weighed after his annual polling – is not in it. The Oklahoman's shock sprouts and thickens, gollywog-like, shrinking his face until it disappears. The spoilt marine's hair becomes a sea urchin which grows into the original Hairy Mammal, around which massed ranks of especially grown supporting locks prance the hippie hippie shake with Blakean abandon.

The audience is wowed. Farm boy sings the song of flower power ('I got life, mother./ I got laughs, sister./ I got freedom, brother./ I got good times, ma'am') and goes 'Underground', which paradoxically means finding himself a place in the sun, a rather cartoon celestial body rayed by apple pie-in-the-sky and choired with clap-happy come-all-ye. Beach heaven meets musak.

The collective flash, which harbingers the Age of Aquarius, lasted a few seconds. Chorus line bows and hair covers their all. Its brevity surprised the audience. There was a pause ('Is that all?') before applause drowned out the squealing sound system. But still the famous finale gave me time to be touched by the jug-like breasts of the earth mothers and the egg cups of their daughters, and to be shocked by the pudenda on display – as far as I could see all were shaved.

Afterwards in the Unicorn Theatre café – a haunt with cachet – Alma raved about the show. Though the only hair I could think about was my own, or the lack of it, I was pleased and nodded along with her enthusiastic explanation of the Coming of the Age of Aquarius.

Apparently it meant that once everybody learned to stand naked holding hands (for an unspecified length of time) all the problems in the world would go away – war, pollution, personal difficulties, pimples and so on. It sounded all right to me. (All it needed was cool water and an aspirin. I would be happy to carry the glass to casts of thousands, audiences in millions.)

She touched the hand of the good listener as she warmed to peace and love and a better world, and that included me. My hand was almost in hers. Should I kiss it? I felt that once she dried up I could ask her about my poems. But it would need patience. My second cup of coffee turned a headache (loud music, neurotic lighting) into brain meltdown. It helped.

The Unicorn was a favourite haunt for resting actors. Easy to spot, off-duty they personify heightened ordinariness. Out of the side of my eye, I observed them perform an impromptu crowd scene. Everyone was auditioning to be discovered by Miss Wendy Toye, the resident impresario. Exits and entrances to the toilet increased their chances. The same people kept coming in and out. Flux – the dish of the day – gives phantom indigestion.

Children's plays were the theatre's speciality. A policy of not condescending to the latent adult in them prevailed. Post-Spock *mores* promoted a respectful seriousness, encouraged infant sexuality. While adult theatre became more infantile, its kids' equivalent grew didactic. Educational and Brechtian dramatic values found their true home.

An apocalyptic version of C. S. Lewis's *Screwtape Letters* was on tonight. A safe enough subject, though a bit Christian. His *The Lion, the Witch and the Wardrobe*, a recent hit, had invoked Christ, Joan of Arc and Art Nouveau. I considered more liberated possibilities. *Young Schopenhauer and His Magic Flute* (the 'young' would present a problem). Or *What's Wrong with You, John Ruskin?* (perhaps not). Or *The Little Prince and Einstein: A Time and Space Odyssey.*

'You're not listening to me.' Alma drops my hand. 'Sorry, but I couldn't help noticing the toilet performance of thespians. They suffer for their Art with frequency.' Fingers digging into her palm, she flexed them like a crab in peril – nails bitten to the root. Suddenly business-like. 'Augustus, I looked over your poems. Not bad, no worse than others published by Hutchinson's. Certainly as good as Adrian Mitchell. I have passed them on to Angus.'

I managed to hail a taxi by risking my life. Pressing pound notes into the driver's hand, I waved Alma off. She looked startled. What did she expect? All men are the same and want the same thing? I felt happy at scotching that slander. But the cathartic energy required to dispatch Alma froze into misgivings. I began to have doubts about my acting ability. Did my anger show? Had I in my haste lost the part forever?

The Saturday night tube is a leveler. Anticlimax makes everybody ordinary. Returning entertainment seekers are already home in their minds. The beckoning consolation of the familiar glazes the eyes. Excitement is reduced to nodding. Revels ended, return to the humdrum.

I knew the abruptly truncated evening was a surgical failure. Rage at not being proclaimed exceptional was cured, but the patient of hope (why did she have to mention her lover?) had died. I was not surprised – I surprised her, after all. But I mourned the loss.

Climbing the stairs, lonely with my success and failure, failure and success, vaguely dissatisfied with my own company, even a little confused, I passed Mrs McFee's door. It was open. She stood in a silken dressing gown facing me, robe not fastened and eyes elsewhere. I was not there.

I had time to regard the aging body, not beautiful, but human. She did not move, a *tableau vivant* of frailties. In that glimpse of humanity in the abstract I could believe the Age of Aquarius had arrived.

I did not write a poem. After drinking tepid water from the tap, I fell asleep, fully dressed.

[9]

THE SERPENTINE IN
THE GARDEN

A heatwave hits London. I basked in my rooftop perch, reading
Nabokov and changing colour. R.O'D. had written again. 'Barging
the Keepers of Parnassus is a slow grind. Deila means well, if given
a chance. But trouble in the Abbey is deep-seated, of dishonour-
able duration. The basic problem is civil-servicery. Zeus Blythe
is in cahoots with Bord Failte. I gather one scene of male nudity is
causing concern. National identity and genitalia don't go together.'
My nervous tic accelerates. What nude scene? Could they be
reading someone else's play?

Mrs McFee fled town, her flutter fanning the way to cooler
climes (Polish friends in the Cotswolds). My idleness was enriched
by chats with her husband. Always happy to pass the time dis-
coursing on its irrelevance, he took to sitting in the only chair in
my room, smoking, talking to me through the skylight.

'Time is not the essence. It is an imposition of the Industrial
Revolution. Take clocks. Until the eighteenth century they were
just toys – to measure the confluence of constellations in order to
read horoscopes. Sundials, clepsydrae, sand-glasses were just play-
things for myopic people. Though looking at the sky was infinitely
better for astrology, these timepieces compensated the visually
impaired.

'Age diminishes the eyesight. So these aids were widely used. Old men needed to know what was going to happen (is it hell or heaven for me, and such). Believing fate is written in the stars (which included our sun and for the more romantic or ignorant our moon), these early versions of the clock passed the time between life and death.

'Cabalists invented the pendulum in the seventeenth century to mesmerise time-watchers. This early form of hypnosis put them to sleep in order to control their destiny. It was a game, a sinister one, like most games.

'Precision became an imperative when the Enlightenment sought to moderate the worst excesses of the Industrial Revolution. Day was divided into smaller and smaller units so that factory slaves could be allocated an acceptable workload, one that did not kill them and make them prematurely redundant. Stellar epochs, rotating seasons, night and day, morning and afternoon were reduced to hours, minutes, seconds, micro-seconds and so on. This served to determine recovery time – sleep and leisure, meal times, tea breaks – and opportunities to procreate (the next generation of labour assured). Exact time measurement was necessary to sustain the means of production.

'We have moved on. Clocks once were adjusted to keep in step with the rotation of the earth on its axis. That kept them in touch with their origins in reading the stars. Now an atomic standard of time has been developed. Time is no longer drawn from heavenly bodies but from molecules, the primary unit of human bodies. The reduction of time to absurdity is complete.'

McFee was reading from his thesis. The sun on my back, I found it soothing.

We had discussed the future direction of my work. He proposed a poem on women for three-part male voice choir. 'It will be performed in the Royal Albert Hall, last night of the Proms.' Without commenting on his peroration, I called down, 'Want to hear my latest version?' 'Have you any matches?' I threw a box down and recited in orotund tones an old student poem:

> Women are so seasonable.
> We don't know where their spring is.
> We don't know where their winter is.
> Where is your autumn, dear?
> Where is your summer?
> Tell me, what year are you?

'Is that all?' The chair scrapes the floor. 'I'm sure I can get Mrs McFee to arrange it.' I hear him leave the room, humming speculatively. He is composing my chorale.

I was drowning in my own sweat. My torso shimmered like a bodybuilder's, but without the muscles. I needed a swim. The Serpentine in Hyde Park was the only open-air bathing in Central London. A man in a row boat continuously raked litter out of the ring that cordoned the swimming club from the fetid lake – entrance fee, five shillings. It was said to be clean. I took to having a daily dip to refresh the pores and ward off sunstroke. But it was like swimming in bodily fluids, other people's. The backdrop was Rotten Row.

My custom was to loll on the scorched knoll in front of the boathouse, dousing myself in the torpid waters from time to time. I read the newspapers. The monarchy restored in Spain. A Civil Rights movement in Northern Ireland halted in its tracks and taken over by gunmen. What were these events to me? I was no longer an intellectual: ideas were distractions. I was an artist, a poet. Leave propaganda to the Adrian Mitchells, the chanters of shibboleths (I had not forgiven Alma). Art is forever, not for now. Now was other people's business.

Nabokov justified my indolence. 'After all, for a man to be happy he must feel ever so often a few moments of perfect blankness.' The 'few moments' bothered me. But McFee opined, 'Your writer friend is generously vague. A moment in time is what you make it. The world is billions of years old. A few moments could amount to an epoch. Or a hiccup. Take your pick. It is all relative. Time is just a convenience.'

I did not need his encouragement. Time for me had stopped. Nothing could happen. Politics in the Abbey would kill my play, and Alma was history (needless to say she had not contacted me). Only a note from Tony disturbed my peace. He alerted me to various diversions. A reading by Heath-Stubbs at the Irish Club, possible inclusion in Dial-A-Poem, an evening with André Frenaud (he entertained the great in his modest flat). My evenings began to fill up, despite myself.

McFee was in an approving mood. 'A young man should waste time on frivolities. Particularly of an evening. Stops him brooding in the dark.' Ensconced in his study, he point-policed my comings and goings, throwing felicities like horseshoes over his shoulder. His cautionary remarks on the Serpentine ('the Black Hole of South Kensington, crawling with sodomites and infectious diseases') I enjoyed, more for their bile than instruction. But I could not ignore his solicitude for my artistic nights on the tiles.

Heath-Stubbs and his admirers reduce the Georgian splendours of the Irish Club to a fit setting for a conference of back-street abortionists. In a gallery crammed with ill-matched paintings of no great artistic or educational value, the reading is a sideshow to an impromptu bar, hosting a firkin of Guinness, a free gift from its sponsor. H-S, distinguished classicist and poet, a tower of a man tottering on scholar's pins and half-blind to boot, much given to arcane metrical elaborations concerning Naiads and Poseidon, might be expected to draw a polite coterie. But the crowd – one ear cocked to his sonorities and the other to the gurgle of the firkin – represent the lower reaches of the Celtic literary fringe.

This latter-day Dr Johnson is at home in his makeshift tavern.

Hoisted on a blackthorn stick, the windmilling beat of his verse harnesses sun-driven phaetons, white winged horses in their wake. He almost levitates – fingertips feathering the air – at one with his musings.

But a thoughtful rallentando – the drag of scholarship – strings the kite of his imagination, keeping feet on the ground. Common sense observations pop up. Their shock earths the high flown embellishments of learning into fragments to be displayed under glass in his poetical museum. For H-S is more a commentator than a maker of Pindaric odes.

If a painter, he would have been an eighteenth-century Mannerist, drawing into his vast canvasses tributes to past glories, trenchant in self-effacement. Tonight his wall eye scans the ceiling, finding perhaps imaginary Tiepolos above the pall of cigarette smoke.

The audience slurp in the atmosphere of gods and Guinness.

I see Sean Tracter, an ambitious clown I'd jaywalk to avoid. His country boy physique and sentimental ditties ('Donna's Cat') wrestled with each other in a visage born to lick the head off a pint of the black stuff – jowls wobbling before the sacrament, gleeman eyes half closed in ecstasy. A gallimaufry of begorrah sounds froth as he celebrates oxymorons and pulled pints in equal measure.

I see Neddy Willow, shrunken wide boy, promoter of himself and a thousand subsistence ventures in the underworld of poetry. A product of Glasgow tenements and boys' homes, his rhyming prayers for Church functions commissioned by kindly Reverend Mothers kept him in drinking money. He once showed me a small batch of weird hymns to choir boys. Innocence debauched by cloying sentiments. A cult of charity developed around him. Helping Neddy became the one good deed of many middle-class poets, made more conscious of their advantages from birth by this ageing orphan and holy fool on the rump of the body poetry. What wits Neddy had he lived on, in literary poverty.

I see Northern Ireland poets aplenty, mostly schoolteachers on their summer break. Tweed jackets and ties, thick spectacles, briefcases. Ambitious in a small way. Whatever you say, say nothing you will be ashamed of later. Good at exams – set questions answered as expected. No need to check the back of the book. Anecdotal poems about putting out the milk bottles ('Closing the main door at night is the day's/ Last act of/ Isolation./ Doorstep and what's floating there,/ A message in a bottle, reading "Three pints"'). Instead of the Three Graces you have the three empties (does that mean a family of three?).

Fear of getting things wrong is a terrible thing in a poet, I think. Correct sentiments (the precise number of milk bottles) are useful but not for poetry. Spiritual policemen and their dogs cannot sniff out a Mayakovsky. Mallarmé is 'a terrorist of the polite' (Sartre's phrase thrilled me). And Paul Celan? Who would say he thinks right or is right thinking? His poems are something else, oblivious of the obvious. I make a mental note to ask Tony to elucidate Celan's and Brecht's use of German. It's hard to reconcile – in translations – that they speak the same language.

'Seamus Heaney's spawn have hatched into tadpoles' began my first (and last) review in a Dublin little magazine. It concluded, 'Poetry not only dead but stuffed.' Would this huddle of aspirants recognise me? The strutting dismissal was signed. My incipient beard bristles at the prospect of an affray. But the Northern Ireland poets stick together, taking notes, offending nobody. I lament the death of manly passion in the world of poetry.

I see the young English hopefuls trying to catch the eye of H-S, a prolific mainstream anthologist when off duty. His weak spot for Celtic readings means they have to learn to put up with uncouth stompers in ignorant brogues and Aran sweaters, not to mention the costive Ulster brigade. Their etiolated free verse is unaffected by exposure to folksy orisons and wild words, or minimalist Mass Observation, or by anything much beyond their sensitive upbringings in cotton wool. Nevertheless they turn up, down pints and participate in the *craic*. Honorary Irishmen for the evening, tutored in the *blas* and blarney. But while they suffer for their Art, who is watching? Certainly not H-S. He feels their faces and only recognises their youth. 'Wonderful boys.'

The stifling gallery is a thicket of smells. Rank sweat and stale sick predominate. Brut isolates the Ulster contingent, rose water and eau de cologne the English hopefuls (only the blind can appreciate their subtle penetrations).

Musky privet draws me to the sole female – a full-blown English rose in a maxi-skirt and voluminous blouse. 'Do I know you?' Her sad, sweet face reminds me of something. Raphael's 'Poetry' in the Victoria and Albert Museum. The same agonised look and fulsome body, though not clutching a harp and book. 'I'm Sabine, from Montreal originally.'

The intonation of her voice is that of a cello. Colourful long bows interrupted by painful plucking. Expansive and contained at the same time. 'I don't get poetry readings. H-S strikes me as old-fashioned, but why are the young poets showing him such respect? They should be heckling.' I want to agree with her ('Crabbed Age and Youth cannot live together'). But, realising on closer inspection that she is not much older than me, I become shy and can only shake my head.

Throughout the reading I had been putting smart phrases together on the off-chance of impressing somebody. Now Raphael's Poetry is standing before me, I am dumb-struck. I could have wowed her (some weeks later in a review published in a little magazine nobody read I wrote, *Heath-Stubbs is not your usual Living English Poet. The type 'who writes self-effacingly on how much he hates his record collection' (James Dickey). He is eloquent, a painter of words, though with a highly selective palate – greys and whites with the odd thread of silver – for he is painting pearls. But the Gadarene swine of literary fashion can only see the oyster shell.*

149

Sabine loses patience. 'God, where's my husband? Have you seen Christopher?' She dervishes off through the crowd at the bar. Flounces and folds whirling into a lost cartoon by Hogarth ('Poets in a Cabal').

In the gents an elegantly effete gentleman is buttoning his fly. Drooping deportment, blazer, pomade held together by an invisible hairnet. He is the retired major in a Terence Rattigan play. McFee had warned me against homosexuals on the poetry scene ('they prey on the young who fancy they are different'). I exit without urinating.

Back among drinkers I feel safe. But the major pursues me holding my beret. 'You left this behind.' Tolerance being the hallmark of the Bohemian life, I engage this predatory Bulwer Lytton in polite conversation. I learn Mr Delahaye is a novelist who occasionally writes poems. Anglo-Irish. Once a correspondent for *The Times*.

He honours me with attentiveness. 'You must be one of the new breed of Irish poets. I am secretary of Yeats's London-Irish Literary Society. Could you possibly round up a few poet peers with a modernist bent? I have promised the ladies young blood.'

The only name I can think of is Tony. Mr Delahaye knows him. 'They must be Irish. The ladies are insistent.' I mention my friend Jeff and some young poets that I've come across in little magazines. He writes the names down in a patent leather notebook. Suddenly Sabine appears. 'Christopher! Where have you been? I have ordered tea. You know one another! Well, goodbye, we must fly.' She dervishes off. Christopher Delahaye grips my hand briefly. 'We'll talk. I have Tony's number.'

The Serpentine at night is Lake Pergusa, entrance to the Underworld. I have drunk too deeply of the Black Stuff and sit down to settle a spinning head. If I can get my body upright, steady my legs and propel them forward towards Notting Hill, a downy couch awaits. But it is hopeless. Happy in my helplessness, I lie under the stars. I can't make out any constellations. The Milky Way is all I see. The light from it is ancient history. And by the time mine reaches the stars I will be amongst the immortals. Time is not as irrelevant as McFee posits. Now perhaps it is, but not always. I survey this Garden of Eden in negative above me. I would like to develop it.

When I wake up, it is lighter. The grey snail-track of dawn is crossing the sky. A mound of sacks clumps on the grass bank beside me. It is inhabited. I jump up. The mist of day is rising, a prehistoric monster evaporating out of the swamp.

I walk thought the park. The city is waking. People walking purposefully in every direction (more L. S. Lowry than Hieronymous Bosch, I think). Trucks and buses lumber along Bayswater Road, cars scream between them. A pale moon fades into its own milky wonder. Kensington Palace Gardens is smelling of roses. All is right with the world.

As I creep past McFee's study, he calls, 'What a time to come in.' 'I thought time was irrelevant?' My night out ends in triumph.

[10]

ALMA'S MATER

What I want and don't expect to get inspires second-hand satire. I am trawling my notebooks for iconoclastic poems in anticipation of the reading at the London-Irish Literary Society. Fame, money, affairs of the heart, being liked by everyone. Others' imagined lives.

> Knowing no peace but war
> at breakfast, he fell over
> the milk bottles for the third time.
> The women wept as they stripped him and he
> was grateful for their tears.
> Rub me there, he said woundedly.

Superimposing a self-portrait by Rembrandt on mine makes for another poem.

> A turban on my head,
> the pipe I smoke is not
> for other men to puff –
> unless they serve to swat
> the flies, and breathe my breath
> and give me right of love.

I stand for my portrait
beside myself with pride
against a canvas of blue;
the artists I've tried
sketch my image with hate
and with wonder too.

I stamp into the mud
the shadows that have grown
behind me. It is clear
sand is the grain I've sown.
Only anonymous scrub
can take root here.

I confide in McFee. 'I can't put two words together on my life.' He
congratulates me. 'You are progressing. Juvenilia insists on making
every moment significant, every movement a symbolic gesture.
The very socks you wear are offered to the world to smell. Better
to wash them in the privacy of your bathroom.' I light his cigarette.
We watch the smoke rise. 'Writing the life of your time is to waste
the moment. Self-consciousness takes over, ruining both the experience and its expression. Other people's dreams and disasters
should suffice until you have exhausted living and retire to reflect.
You are on the right track.'

Nevertheless, I returned to my room and composed a poem
about Alma.

I want this
to last, he said,
breaking it up
into little bits
to put in the pocket

of his sieve-suit:
the pocket with the hole.
O love too small
to stay.

I felt better.

Jeff Squires comes with a rucksack to sleep on the floor. Mr Delahaye wants us for his ladies. (Gary Snyder and California mediated through a Protestant aesthetic would chord nicely with edgy Irishry cut loose.) *The Honest Ulsterman* had just published Jeff's pamphlet *Sixteen Poems*, a Taoist triumph of shards from the pot of profundity, I thought.

His lucid fragments – so different from the rounded linearity of his Ulster contemporaries. They spin vessels that are functional (to contain milk). Jeff returns utensils to their original form, restoring their non-utilitarian essence. The poems have an archaeological calm about them.

Now meeting him for the first time, I realise that the shards and the man are one. He speaks in bits and pieces. The unsaid is what is important. Nothing is obvious to me. But Jeff assumes it is. My disadvantage is compounded – he has a marriage behind him and met Samuel Beckett once.

My affable attempts to impress with wit and wisdom are ignored. I presume loquaciousness irritates. It did not show. But one of his asides ('cleverness is overrated') made me blanch. Here was a man who lived the Confucian belief that 'it is wealth to be content; it is willful to force one's ways on others'.

Later, over a pint, I asked him what his poems were about. He laughed – not at me, but at the banality of the universe. 'Poems are not about anything. They just are.' 'But they must mean something other than that they are poems?' 'Isn't that enough?' Pressed, he admits, 'My poems are surfaces, that's all.' 'Highly polished ones, if I may say.' Jeff bypasses my cheeky conceit. Patiently, calmly, he resumes his shuffling of shards, an object lesson to prickly me. 'In the final analysis one does not write to say something. You write not to say something. Guilloux. Have you read him?'

While he snores on the floor, I lie in the bed, restless with self-dissatisfaction. A line by Squires – 'The noise of them as she put them on' – reoccurs in my mind, endlessly repeating itself like a mantra. It lulls me to sleep.

Yeats's London-Irish Literary Society has seen better days, but the hats are still wonderful. The library in the Irish Club is a feast of fruit and feathers with lashings of lace. Row and rows of ladies of a certain age, in time-honoured apparel, thrill to the Honourable Mrs Elodie Burke-Daley's rhapsody on last week's cultural evening. Evidently Mr Sheridan Trench's lecture on Maeterlink's *Life of the Bee* went down well, particularly the slide show. Next week the Very Reverend Malachy Stoker promises an enlightening talk on Emanuel Swedenborg, the Swedish mystic. Afternoon tea will be in an hour. No mention is made of a collection plate. I think it is understood.

Christopher's introductions are brief and to the point. Lineage mainly. He accredits us with keeping the torch of Irish poetry alight. 'Twenty minutes each. Ten for questions.' Jeff's brown corduroys and loose white shirt go well with his rust red hair and pale complexion. His brow is suitably noble – a distant relative of Cecil Day Lewis, the Poet Laureate – and voice pleasantly audible (West Coast undertones smoothing out a faint Ulster brogue). His brief, immaculately shaped poems are delivered like rare coins for inspection. The ladies test them with their teeth.

> What is here is
> not time passing
> but time changing

My mother growing
old does not understand
me growing old

What is here is
not time passing.

The Honourable Mrs Burke-Daley asks him to repeat a mysterious haiku.

Flower
that opens to me
in the dark
when flowers do not open.

Second time round the ladies sigh and primp their hats.

The reading is going too well to please Jeff. It shows in his choice of poems. More abstract, less obviously pleasing. At breakfast I had elicited a slight elaboration on his aesthetic. I provoked him by suggesting he was an imagist. His vessel of composure disintegrated in slow motion. One shard caught the light and illuminated his work. His vignettes are images that evoke thoughts rather than pictures. Not ideas, mind you, he emphasised.

Jeff suspects his audience are enthralled by incidental pictorials and miss the underlying thought. The more the ladies murmur appreciation the less he believes in it. I am alarmed by the discrepancy between his delivery and its reception. Hats are metaphorically thrown in the air when he ends, a broken poet protecting his images from metaphorical camera flashes. Jeff knows he has been misunderstood.

I am not taking any chances and launch into 'Dream of Caged Beasts'.

The beast is uncontrollably gentle:
allowed to take the air,
a circus of acrobatic clouds:
but strokes the wrong way,
smothers himself. Room

remote. The ceiling moves
the silence within a silence.
If the clouds would break
naturally it would be rain.

The windows blind
as he assumes the walls.

Touch and he comes away in your hands.
Coax and he disappears into your eyes.
Soothe and he bleeds into your mouse holes.

Tonight the beast will come
to drench your bed.
And there is no room.

Without pause for breath, I announce my next poem. 'Tabes
Dorsalis or Syphilis of the Backbone', transfixing frissons of incipient revolt with a gimlet eye. Edgy Irishry cut loose is dangerous. I
wear a woolly Texaco blue sweater my mother knitted – the wrong
clothes for a close afternoon. My low Bogman brow beads sweat.

> Do not let me judge
>   the whites of eyes,
>   the whites of eggs,
>   the knots of nails,
>   the loose hair.

I have (been) ((blind)),
too blind to know
where my arms are
– where are my arms?
I know my legs are leaps
– into the darkness?
I cannot find
myself.

My catalogue of clap symptoms from Graves's *Pathology* coincides with a break in the weather. A thunderstorm rages outside. The audience huddles to witness General Paralysis of the Insane enacted. Infarctions breach the heart in a downpour.

The rest of my reading is scarcely heard. But wild gestures, personal disintegration and the imagination of the ladies compensate. My concluding doxology ('And I must insist/ in making every/ moment important,/ every movement/ a cause') is interrupted by Christopher. 'Thank you, Augustus. Five minutes for questions.'

I can hear the after-drip from the chute outside the library. The silence heightens the return of the birds. The Honourable Mrs Burke-Daley stands up and eyeballs the frozen throng, coaxing with contempt a query, even a misgiving. Her imperial eye finally settles on a squirming victim. 'Miss Hackett, surely you who teach English at Cardinal Vaughan School have something to ask? You had plenty to say for yourself in your talk last year on "Among Schoolchildren".' A tiny woman in a cardigan, with a perm rather than a hat, rises. She is no taller than the back of her chair. In a surprisingly sonorous tremolo she addresses Christopher. 'What is poetry, the eternal question? Laura Riding, whom you once knew, told a child "Making a poem is being alive for ever". I hope and pray the young poets we heard tonight make poems and live forever. That said, I must admit to being old-fashioned. If I don't understand the young it is my failing, I'm sure. The question

I ask is what distinguishes their work from predecessors. Lionel Johnson comes to mind, and of course yourself?'

I have a card index of anarchistic quotations on Art and poets up my sleeve. 'The poet is a nasty cur even when he isn't having a fit' (Ford Madox Ford) and 'Art is a chamber pot ready to receive the crap of the earth' (Flaubert). I start a reply to Miss Hackett, but Christopher's world-weary hand stops me. 'The new poets do not finish their poems. That is the sum of it.' Jeff brightens up. I make a mental note to ask Delahaye why Sabine didn't come to the reading. Is she by any chance the Madame Bovary of Montreal, I muse? And dismiss the thought reluctantly.

The ladies flock around, questioning Jeff and me about our families. One comes from Sligo and tells Jeff he is probably descended from Oliver Goldsmith ('the Squires all are'). Another knew my Aunt Mary from dancing days in Ballinasloe. I am aware that caked sweat under a heavy pullover would probably smell only for the parade of perfume that engulfs me. My Bohemian bouquet is masked by womanly considerations. I don't wait for tea.

McFee meets me at the door. 'Your floozy is on the phone.' It is Alma. 'I am worried about my mother. She threatens to throw herself under a train.' I am back in the real world.

[11]

A FINE ROMANCE

Restoration to Alma's favours confuses my plans.

Deila had written a perplexing letter, praising my generous, nimble imagination, but questioning my ability to control and humanise a new theatrical form. Virtuoso displays of language master rather than serve the protagonists. She complains about lack of resources to nurture young writers. But wants to keep in touch. Come over after Christmas. Tom Kilroy has offered his house for dramatists to read their work. Let me know if you are interested. My twitch tells me I am not. I reply, asking for the return of the manuscript.

The new job started in six weeks. I needed an idea from my Bohemian days to carry into drudgery which would sustain my true vocation – poet of life and love – throughout the adversity of necessity. McFee had introduced me to Soren Kierkegaard. The Danish philosopher – half-Virgil, half-Mephistopheles – would be my guide.

'Life must be lived forward, but understood backwards. No time in your life is complete. You cannot stand outside and understand the present until it is past. You cannot do that unless you go through the mindless motions of living. Progressive daily decisions and actions eventually achieve the absurd moment when you can reflect and look back. Life and its understanding are the two sides of a seesaw. Life up, understanding down. Understanding up, life down. They cannot be up and down at the same time.'

This epigraph to McFee's thesis changed my life. Kierkegaard's Principle of Teleological Suspension in Relation to Communicating Truth suppresses reflection for the time being in order that the truth may become truer. I would submit to it.

I was not destined to a life of thought. I must live now and think later, dog through the humdrum – job, courtship, marriage, fatherhood, the escalating scale of adult responsibility. Their weight in time tilts the balance back, reversing the seesaw. Then the plank of life will rise up, a totem revealing its meaning. Out of the bathos of my choice, the truth will emerge. I will find words for it.

'Engaging the ordinary is not absurd.' McFee finds the passage in his tattered *Either/Or*.

'There seems to be something wrong with cause and effect. They do not rightly hang together. Tremendous and powerful causes sometimes produce puny, pathetic effects – sometimes none at all. Then it happens a slight little common or garden cause produces a colossal effect.'

What about happiness, I ask? He laughs bitterly. 'Happiness is a sentimental notion, only entertained by fools and ladies of leisure. It does not have a definition. Except in memory. We feel we were happy once. Delusion is a great consolation.'

And love? I hesitate to utter the sweet, forbidden word. 'It is an idea, not a reality.' He finds the quote in *Repetitions*.

'The idea is the vital principle in love. If you embrace it you must be prepared to sacrifice life itself, yes, and its practical application even when its object is favourably disposed. You ban yourself from poetry and pleasure. But still being in the service of love heightens your everyday life. Every fleeting emotion is not without significance. Your life is relentlessly moving toward poetic collision. Something terrible like death. The idea of love is exacting. It cannot serve two masters or, to be more precise, a master and mistress. The woman's beauty – or disapproval of the idea – cannot be allowed to distract you. In love the word distraction has two meanings. Driven to distraction, distracted from its course. This is not an accident of language. It represents the poetic collision.'

McFee digresses. 'Soren spent his youth diverting his fiancée Régine from the path of true love and the rest of his life writing about it. The next bit is the best summary of the poetic collision in his work.'

'The story of the young man living the idea of love can be told in the poetical manner through a multitude of irrelevant matters – salons, clothes, scenery, families and friends. Forget it. I eat lettuce, it is true, but only the heart. The leaves in my opinion are only fit for swine. I prefer the rapture of conception to the labour of childbirth. If there is anybody who has anything to say against this, let him say on. It makes no difference to me.'

'The rapture of conception. I thought Kierkegaard was a virgin?' 'Don't be so literal.' McFee was displeased. Nevertheless, he presented me with the relevant passages next day in immaculate copperplate. I carried them in my pocket and read them like a priest would his office, while on my walk past the Serpentine. The direction of my life was clear. I would take up the job in Scotland, eschew happiness, embrace Kierkegaard's tragic vision and live an idea. Poetry would be a bonus.

Alma's return upsets my resolve. I thumb through McFee's *Either/Or* for redemption. One entry meets my mood. 'Time flows, life is a stream, people say, and so on. I do not notice it. Time stands still, and I with it. All the plans I make fly right back upon myself. When I spit, I spit into my own face.' I am in poetic collision and weakening.

We meet at the Poetry Society ('your patch'). I was against it ('I'm interested in poetry, not poets'). But she had heard Marianne

Faithful was seen with a Rolling Stone in the bar. Her mother is a pretext to talk about herself. She had moved from Kew to South Kensington and feels good about herself.

Her well-dressed look has been abandoned. She is now the waif. Straggling hair with little butterfly bows, loose pre-Raphaelite nightie-frock, oriental trousers underneath, no make-up. Alma looks to me as though she just slipped out to put something in the garbage and lost her key. Certainly not dressed for a date. This does not displease me. I am the trusted friend and ear apparent.

I know she feels safe with me. She touches my hand, occasionally squeezing it to make a point. Almost girls together. Her amiability expresses itself through ripples of carefree laughter, a new-found feature which she displays without regard to conversational con-text. Alma, the babbling brook of good humour, is performing and not only for me. A trendy couple in matching lilac Beatle suits and hair turn around. She gives them a little love-in wave. They reciprocate peace and love.

All the seats in the bar are taken, but nobody is buying. The occupants are all female and alike. Poetesses garbed in the style of highly respectable bag ladies, each in her own world, scribbling on letter pads or cloistered with their thoughts. Names like Netta, Greta or Peta would become them, I think – witch and nature poems stuffed in their corsets; friends of Emily Dickinson, Stevie Smith; commodious shawls. The Life Closed Twice Club, Tony calls them. Their presence is reassuring, great self-contained couchant cats.

Alma is high with uplift. I miss the drama queen. Onslow Square is heaven, Hutchinson's a happy haven. I ask about her mother. A moment of petulance threatens to break the tedium. 'That has been dealt with. We talk on the phone.' And Angus? 'He's a dear.'

I begin to wonder what change has brought such calm. She even asks about my life. I tell her of days by the Serpentine and nights on the poetry scene. The Serpentine interests her. She titters. 'Have you made friends there?' I recall McFee's remark ('The Serpentine is a hotbed' etc). Alma thinks I am homosexual and she is my fag hag.

I am appalled, and thrilled. Have I become a surrogate father figure to Alma, stepping into his dark side? Not importuning her after three outings has been misunderstood. I scrutinise her fine equine features and coiled-spring physique. I don't fancy her. The age difference – three years. She is too old for me.

But I am not sure of myself. Does my reluctant libido mean I'm a latent homosexual? Is my rugged exterior just camouflage? Even more incriminating, I like women and normal men – I know this from locker room banter – do not.

'Friends?' I force a laugh. 'I haven't even been approached.' 'I know what's its like', Alma murmurs. My confusion is serious. Obviously I'm not a homosexual. I smoke a pipe. I see myself stepping into the waters, like Monsieur Hulot, pipe first. Satyrs snigger in the bushes.

I am saved by a Happening. Three young men in velveteen leap on to the bar and stage an impromptu reading. The Lilacs sit holding hands, delighted. So is Alma ('This is more like it'). The Life Closed Twice Club ignore the action. The trio mime The Crucifixion with slapstick emphasis. The words sound vaguely familiar. 'Ersatz Vasco Popa', I whisper to Alma. 'All poems sound the same to me', she replies. I am in despair. These impostures have stolen the secret source of my new mode. Was one of the velveteens under the table at that supper with Popa?

The young men climb down from their imaginary crosses and trot over to our table. They conjure up a wine glass and a roll. 'May I?' Jesus tips a splash of Alma's martini into the glass. 'This is my body.' He drinks and divides the bun between the Two Thieves. They scoff the bread, mouthing 'This is my blood'. And run off.

'Queers are so amusing.' Alma is ecstatic. 'Are they homosexuals?' 'You should know.'

I feel kindly towards Alma. Attributing me with her beloved father's weakness is, after all, some sort of a compliment. My offer to walk her home is refused ('It's only round the corner'). The spring in her step is unnerving. She knows what she wants and is bridling for home. It hits me like a slate falling from a roof. The change in her life that brought her calm is obvious. She has moved in with Angus and it is working out.

At Earl's Court tube station a poster diaries the South Bank. Popa and Holub appeared at the Poetry International Festival on the night Alma and I went to *Hair*.

Back in my room I flip through my notebooks. Surprisingly few recent poems are Popa-esque. One or two closet Holubs. None resemble O'Brudair, Yeats, Eliot, Pound or the Imagists. Most read like translations from a language I do not know. I fall asleep, knowing my secret is safe.

A CRISIS IN POETRY, A
CRISIS IN PHILOSOPHY

I compose a poem in my sleep, tortuously putting together a house
of cards. I rush to write the words down. Sleep's scaffolding
removed, the Babel collapses. Only one line survives. 'Can death
be sleep when life is but a dream?'

I show it to McFee. 'You have been visited by a Shakespearean
succubus who moonlights in music hall', he chortles merrily.
'Surrealism is an uneasy bedfellow. Tell me why so many of them
are charismatic Catholics?' I know from Tony four Surrealists –
André Breton, Paul Eluard, David Gascoyne and Brian Coffey.
Three out of four are indeed RC. I speculate recklessly. 'Catholics
are allowed an antinomian dispensation in sleep. A sin-free zone.
You are neither responsible for your dreams nor nocturnal emis-
sions.' 'Jews take their dreams more seriously. Freud?' 'And
Delmore Schwartz. And look what happened to him. Dreamed
responsibilities but could not take them seriously. You'd like
Delmore Schwartz. When he divorced his wife and muse, he sent
her a postcard – take the piano, I need the space for books.'

He lights his cigarette from my pipe. 'Dreams are all right. It's
our response to them that is deficient. I have made a special study
of dreams and time. Most people believe dreams last the night. But
they are a mere flicker of an eyelid. Too fast for the untrained mind.

Breton, for instance – he practised dream retention until the time factor became irrelevant. Boring dreams, but not forced like Jules Superveille and your other Catholics. I except Pascal of course.'

He roots amongst his papers and comes up with a fistful. 'Yes, Blaise Pascal hadn't much time for dreams.'

'If a labourer dreams every night that he is a king and a king dreams every night he is a labourer, neither would wholly wake up. The king would almost escape responsibility, the labourer work. Nevertheless, the king would continue to rule and the labourer to live by the sweat of his brow. If a clerk dreams every night he is in a battle and a soldier dreams every night he is counting up columns, both would be afraid to go asleep. The clerk would almost live in fear of being a hero, the soldier in fear of being a drudge. Nevertheless, the clerk would continue at his desk and the soldier suffering wounds.

'But no two dreams are the same, every night a different one. So kings, labourers, clerks and soldiers scarcely notice them. Once awake they are forgotten. There is continuity in the waking life. Kings, labourers, clerks and soldiers see that and know their place. Of course their waking life changes. But this is usually too gradual to notice. And when the change is abrupt – like when we are dislocated by travel – they say, "It seems to me I'm dreaming." For life too is a dream, though not so inconsistent.'

Pascal induces a quiet despair in McFee. He can never hope to finish his thesis. Time is running out. For McFee, and for me too. Its irrelevance is an illusion. I light his cigarette again. The glow revives him. But our mood of shared sadness is broken. He picks up another scrap. His voice is sharp, cutting through the crap.

'We eat the ideas, opinions, expressions and moods of the dead, a form of cannibalism that satisfies us. Everywhere it is the same. The past mashed into ostrich brains nourishes us. It is disgusting. As to our lives and how we live them? No thanks. We will have none of that.'

McFee balls the scrap and throws it towards the wastepaper basket and mutters, 'Kierkegaard mocked men's dreams. He was right.'

'Everyone wants to live at the same time as great men and great events. God knows how many manage to live at the same time as themselves. To do that you would need to understand yourself and be at peace. But that is impossible. At no particular moment can we find the necessary resting place.

'Dreams are what you eat. Happy the diet that made people believe God spoke through them. Simple food and drink brings good news from above. Shepherds lived on olives and bread.

'Now in cities we dine on high game, rotten cheeses and old wines. No wonder we attribute what speaks to us in dreams to devils and demons. We learn, not about God, but about ourselves, and it is a nightmare.'

I return to my room for an early bed. But cannot sleep. I do not want to dream.

> Dreams are the junk of the mind.
> I'm always glad to wake up.
>
> Waste from the lower brain stem
> draws the rats to the rational.
>
> The perfect circle of sleep
> is bombarded by the remnants
>
> shed from the scab of our lives
> to make garbage of the self.
>
> Remember to put out the bin.
> Give me dead sleep and not this.

I tear the page from my notebook, put it under my pillow and phone Tony. He has been finding out why I was invited to the Chelsea party.

'Augustus! I was just going to phone you.' Tony sounds constrained. 'Can I come round? Is it too late?' I do not ask why, respecting his mysteriousness. And time is immaterial in the Bohemian life. But as he enters my room I notice the jacket of his suit and trousers do not match. Something terrible has happened.

Perched uneasily on the only chair, Tony looks like a refugee from a painting by Edward Hopper. The title is 'Bad News'. Young man slumps on a bare bed. His visitor sits at an awkward angle. Scaffolding outside the window aligns with it. The simple lines of the sparse room are intimations of innocence about to be encroached. It is the moment before the chaos of the city enters – cranes, demolition squads, tangled webs of ruin. Things never to be the same.

Tony evokes both the young man and the messenger. Despair makes me his guest. I encourage him to talk, to tell all. He takes out a crumpled sheet of paper. His hair crinkles with perspiration. This is not the suave Tony I know, the Diaghilev of the poetry scene, fixer of egos and events. The young man who knows every-body. The sheet is covered with scribbles, heavily crossed and written over. It looks like the Dead Sea Scrolls, the famous 'War of the Sons of Light with the Sons of Darkness' page. Or could it be a schizophrenic's shopping list?

'Augustus, don't think I'm crazy. It's a poem and I'm several words short. I had it this morning. Now it's zero, a blank. I can't read my own handwriting.'

His laugh is half-hearted. I tell him about my dream poem. Make jokes about telepathy ('If you remember mine, I'll remember yours'). But recovering words from sleep is self-indulgent, I realise. This is serious, a man's conscious memory at stake. Tony is facing real, rather than imagined, loss – memory, poetry and possibly his mind.

We settle down to decipher, crouching on the floor. In my excitement, the page becomes a Blakean blur, a gnostic scrawl. I can read the title, 'Untitled'. The poem is fourteen lines. Under each line there is text in parenthesis. I gradually acclimatise and make out a line. 'This sentence is not the same as the previous one.' Tony informs me that 'all fourteen lines are the same. The missing words are in the round brackets.' The maze of script wanders off the page. I light my pipe. 'Mark what you can't read.' He only underlines four phrases.

Midnight strikes. Breaking for tea, I ask Tony about his sleuthing. 'You were the man from Hutchinson's. A friend of mine is a friend of Ursula. She remembered you because of your cap and unusual manners. She thought, what are publishers coming to?' My mind races. Alma. Angus. Alma. Me. Perplexity clears, clouds again. Jealousy (Angus) commingles with pleasure (Alma) and anger (their complicity). All the same, pleasure prevails (Alma looking out for me).

I want to ask him about the Serpentine and its reputation, but demur. How do I know Tony is not homosexual? He is married, just like Alma's father. I pour the tea, consciously restraining myself from saying 'I'll be mother'. He adds a pill to his cup. 'Valium. I hope you don't mind.'

I hold the page up to the light and declaim, 'This sentence is not the same as the previous one (Because of what follows I have had to write the words this sentence etc, despite the fact that these words are the first words of the text and therefore have no antecedents on the page).' The last clause of the next parenthesis is marked. I scratch it with the sharp point of a paper-clip, the technique to bring up words written in invisible ink. In the bulb's glow I read 'the word rose twice, or what have you'. Gertrude Stein, surely? A rose is a rose. Tony, pleased with my reference to an author who is well thought of, concedes. 'Subconsciously. She is one of my favourites. I thought the phrase meaningless.'

Taking that lead, we redeem the incomprehensible from the tautological in the other three marked passages by constructing a nexus of references. Tony could read his own handwriting after all (only one correction necessary – 'Lacan' for 'Lucan'). His memory – or his confidence in it – was the problem.

Together we recreate the cultural context that clarifies the obscure or eccentric. 'Should I include footnotes?' I advise against. 'The reader will give you the benefit of the doubt.'

Topping up the tea with brandy from my medicinal flask, I think I understand what the text is about. But, wary of Jeff's caveat, I couch my understanding in roundaboutness. 'The subtext is the conflict between repetition and recollection. The real poet cannot repeat himself unless he fails to recollect what he has already written and quotes himself.' I find myself in the same relation to Tony as McFee to me. He, to my surprise, is all ears.

The night is young and I am Augustus. 'Repetition is the opposite to the exceptional. It comes from the assembly line which determines most people's lives. Call it mass-production.' Tony murmurs 'Walter Benjamin'. I nod agreement. Admitting I had not heard of Walter Benjamin would divert my flow. 'If you repeat something often enough everybody believes it. And you make a profit. Repetition is to the modern world what recollection was to the Greeks. Kierkegaard . . .'

I notice Tony sags in his chair. I hope it doesn't collapse.

'Kierkegaard says repetition and recollection are the same movement, only in the opposite direction. What is recollected has been and is repeated backwards. Whereas repetition is always one ahead and is, so to speak, recollected forward. Repetition makes the ordinary man on the treadmill happy. The prospect of consumer goods. Recollection, on the other hand, makes him unhappy. Past experience being what it was – not what he wanted or wants to remember. Unless, of course, he finds in it a pretext for escaping his lot through fantasy. Falsifying memory is an industry too – sugar-coating the past. But soon enough it comes to grief.'

As Tony snoozes he smiles sweetly. The chair has become a part of him. Though buckling under his weight, it is ductile enough to afford scaffolding. Half happy insect, half comfortable furniture. Kafka meets Louis Quatorze. My scrutiny wakes him up.

'I've forgotten something', he announces dopily. 'This sentence is not the same as the previous one.' We laugh.

I see him down the stairs, negotiating the dark on his behalf. He is affectionately amused at himself and at the world, which includes me. Farewells at the door are prolonged, unnecessarily, searching for an appropriate exit line and failing. It does not matter. I think I hear a piano tinkling a Chopin nocturne from the balcony above. Mrs McFee is back?

The small hours of the morning are lightening into day. Talking deep into the night, I tell myself, is a bonus of the Bohemian life, something to cherish. One day I will remember it and feel sad. A night like this is never repeated. But I am content, even happy. I will sleep late. And without dreams.

[13]

AVOIDANCE OF DOUBT

R. O'D. sends me a card. 'What are you up to? You have upset Deila. She made an offer and you turned it down. Renew contact with her and be friendly.' But I am recalcitrant. The Abbey hadn't the guts to reject me outright. I'll make them sweat, I think. But I read over her letter, wondering if I was too hasty. I decide not.

Two months growth of facial hair makes me unrecognisable. I look in the mirror. Something I would not have dreamed of doing before unless absolutely necessary. Did I smoke a pipe to cloud my features? Now I am pleased with the steadfastness of my eyes, my look. Confronting the demons on my own has cured the tic.

The young warrior leads with his jaw, the Remus of the mandible, the Romulus of the maxilla. His victims take it on the chin. Mine was neither prominent like a Habsburg nor receding like a Peewee. It was neither here nor there, a knob at the end of my face. Now with a beard I could both lead and defend myself.

I calculate on a jotter that I have 12,775 days to live and 17 feet 6 inches more hair to grow. By not shaving I will save 44 days for other things. I consider how I will use the time. How many poems could I write in six weeks? At the current rate at least 60.

Let my plays be produced posthumously ('Dead poet leaves theatrical treasure chest. Codicil in will forbids Abbey productions').

I examine my teeth. Still sound, though smoke stained. 'Man has only a certain number of teeth, hair and ideas. A time always comes when he must lose his teeth, hair and ideas.' Voltaire. I think of Weiss's Device, an appliance I saw in the V&A. Fanged clappers to masticate food. Taken out at table, the toothless won't go hungry. I still have a few more years.

'The lower half of Byron's face was a model of beauty.' Faint praise from envious Leigh Hunt. My lower half would remain a secret, my upper half no worse than Byron. Yeats remarked that all great men are owls or scarecrows by the time fame comes. Which would I be? Peering into the future, I see a buzzard.

I mouth vowels to myself. The most common ones uttered by babies are A, M and O. That must be saying something. I roll out the royal Rs of de Musset. 'I await the rapturous kiss of the Countess of Vallombrosa.' My puckered lips engage their image.

I am a young man alone in his bathroom. I can do anything. My pleasure in the beard, jet black and curling like a companion of Ulysses, is not without irony. 'The ensign of wisdom, but also displayed by goats.' Socrates had vanity's number, and mine. I laugh but don't like the look of my teeth. I must guffaw less. Or smoke less. 'The only bacchanalia that's known to man/ is with a pipe. Or so says Pan.' Whatever, if you sport a beard, a pipe is *de rigueur*.

This morning McFee shoved the *Irish Press* under my door. Religiously, he picked up the Saturday edition on his early stroll. We both knew why. My embarrassment was chronic. Four weeks and nothing. I almost binned it, unread.

But an item caught my eye. 'Man Who Drowned Had Run From Fire.' A builder torched the house he was working on. Ran through the village shouting, 'I burnt it. I burnt it.' And threw himself into the river.

I cut out two stories. 'Youth Body Changing Its Role' and

'Playboy Guru Spurned By His Mother'. I was now seeking in-spiration for poems not from other poems but from newspaper headings. I skipped the Derry riots.

On the literary page I was annoyed to see a poem with the same title as one of mine ('An Abdicated Queen of My Acquaintance'). This is really too bad. I must write and complain. Then I saw my name under it and another poem too ('Dolly Price'). My weary brain continued to be outraged for a moment, like an old man obliged to complete a movement because he began it, even if it was no longer necessary. I was runner-up in the Cork Gin Poetry Prize and awarded twenty pounds. The first money I had earned from my Art. That made me a professional.

I scoured the poems ('Dolly Price of Bulldog Lane/ is so thin people can see through her./ But all the same, she's a grandmother of seven'), seeking to read them, not as the author, but as one of the many ordinary readers of the paper (recalling Marcel in Proust finding his first printed piece in *Figaro*, I made a note to reread his lyrical response. Something about the spiritual bread of an early morning newspaper, still hot and damp from the press and the hands of the housemaid). I wrote the poems to enter the competi-tion, adopting a style more like a Northern Ireland poet than my own, wanting to win in order to enhance my reputation with my family. I did not remember what they were 'about'. Lines like 'She won a beauty contest once;/ Miss Sunday Papers 1942./ The victory was by photograph' recalled Mrs Maevis, a neighbour back home. Immortalising her for what, I asked myself. Fame, money, to reassure my mother? I felt uneasy. Was I writing to achieve Art or to succeed in writing?

I had sent three. I dug out the unpublished one, 'Bedfellows'. What was wrong with it, I asked myself. More my sort of poem – vulgar, risky, transmogrifying other people's experience into my own. I wanted to run down to McFee and offer up the three poems to his judgement. But thought better of it. Neither poetry nor the

Three Graces should submit to competitions. I could hear him saying it.

Posing for posterity while nobody is looking, I preen my Bohemian beard. I can't wait to tell McFee. Not Tony, though. He too knows that competitions are transient distractions. Poets are only judged when they are dead. Immortality allows a few poems to enter its dodo race. Hankering for something more immediate is meretricious. But still I am happy this morning.

I start on a mock dialogue with Martin Heidegger. An uppity brio informs my work.

Q. What are poets for in these dark days?
They trace for fellow mortals the way to turn to the light.
Q. On what authority do you deduce this?
My own and the wine gods.
Q. Holderinaminute! Wine gods, who are they?
They inhabit the sphere of intoxication in the heavens.
Q. Where do the poets come in?
They are fugitive wine gods. They seek to escape down to humanity.
Q. Why would they want to do that?
They are lured by the destitution they see down below.
Q. How do they manage to descend?
Fugitive wine gods are divine and have attributes.
Q. Such as?
An eye for the inconspicuous way. They don't miss anything.
Q. How does that help?
They pick up the scent of the track and take it.
Q. How do you know they are poets?
Because they sing as they roll down.
Q Like winos?
Precisely.

As I pause for breath, McFee knocks on the door. 'Your mother.' My mother hated the telephone. She only sent letters. It must be urgent.

'How could you do such a thing? And in the *Irish Press* too. We will be sued.' She upbraids me for exploiting Dolly Price ('a poor soul'), not to mention Mrs Maevis ('She has always been a good neighbour'). I point out that Dolly is illiterate and Mrs Maevis only reads the *Irish Times*. But my mother is inconsolable. I have with my Art intruded into her neighbourly world. 'And God knows what else you have up your sleeve to shame the family.'

Spectres loom before my eyes. Baglady Dolly and the respectable Mrs Maevis on the front pages, the family being dragged through the courts. My windfall winnings wouldn't cover the costs. Ruin. My mother would have to leave her home. All for two poems I did not even approve of, written for gain and notoriety.

'Bad news?' enquires McFee, kindly. 'The worst. I will never write a line of poetry again.' 'Oh! your poem lost? I thought there was a death in the family.' 'No! I won.' The despair in my look must have seemed to McFee like a sudden conversion to the fashionable French philosophy he liked to call the Friends of Failure.

Shame is an unforgiving companion. Mine taunted me for using two harmless old ladies for transient glory and meagre profit. And now a third lady, my mother, was suffering for it. I knew her fears were probably exaggerated. Loss of home and friends was unlikely. But I had betrayed all three. And my Art, misappropriating copy and disguised in a style that deep down I abominated.

That night I burn my Heidegger dialogue in an ashtray. Out of its flames rises a new humility. I write my first Epistle to My Conscience.

The shock of being no longer adolescent makes me timid. I want to contain my new-found antlers, appropriately garlanded, in a flower basket to hang outside my mother's house. Premature jostlings in the field of young manhood shoot the life into space without gravity.

Return to earth is by no means certain. Fear stiffens me against the lure of drugs, sex and rock and roll. I put them beyond reach on the top shelf and bide my time with books and the life of the mind. I lack the courage to rip up the safety net. I distance experience. This is not a sacrifice. It is a challenge.

The young John Ruskin, in a letter to his worried mother, admitted that 'poetry is a shabby pursuit, but . . . my love of it . . . keeps me from the common vices'. I return renewed to my tainted Art. Possibly a better person. A flicker in my eyelid reminds me to write to Deila at the Abbey, who is upset.

[14]

THE DEFENCE OF McFEE

McFee entertains me in his study. Tea is occasioned. 'There is no happiness except in the usual paths.' Mrs McFee's return has heightened his fatalism. 'When Chateaubriand fled the French Revolution to England he travelled under the name of Lasagne. Lasagne, by the way, means chamber pot in Greek. Have a macaroon?'

Mrs McFee's circle is widening. Her new friend Sibyl plays duets. They cancel one another out. After a Chopin or two they stretch out on *chaises longues* on the veranda, frocks and frilly undergarments hitched up like Pavlova cakes, four little pink trotters taking the air. They tinkle more prettily in their merry patter than on the piano. Sibyl teaches ballet to the actors at the Mercury Theatre. McFee calls her Ninette.

He discusses my future. 'Life unfortunately does not present itself as a multiple choice questionnaire. Or if it does, the questions are badly laid out. Our choices have been made for us by grand-parents. Their genes determine ours. Mine were improvid-ent property owners inclined toward theosophy. They married their own, further reducing the gene pool. I inherited my present life from them. My time is theirs, their obsolescence mine. I have no expectations. My only choice is to be content, or not. I choose the contentment.' His cigarette remains unlit.

I wonder when he will get to me.

'Apply my situation to yours and you too will be content.'

Resenting his notion that all I might want is contentment, I challenge him. 'I had four grandparents. All dead. I never knew any of them. A gombeen man, his genteel wife, a jobbing roofer and his peasant woman. I'm told they had nothing in common. My genetic background is a pack of cards. More like the one at the end of *Alice in Wonderland* flung up in the air.'

McFee the Fatalist is more amused than I expected. 'And you're the joker in the pack.' I match his cigarette and think of my verse play being torn into tiny bits and flushed down the toilet in an amateur performance of *The Dumb Waiter*, regretting I can't share its fate with my friend.

Tony rang. 'I hope you don't mind – I gave your address to a chap from the Open University. He is doing an LP with Basil Bunting. Yeats's poems. And Basil Bunting insists on an Irish accent in the studio to keep his brogue on track.'

Alistair arrived that evening unannounced. He whirlpooled in, talking at the rate of knots, defying a superbly controlled stutter (more a drum roll than a speech defect), walking up and down the room, a silk scarf threatening to strangle him. His dark blue silk shirt, brown denims and marching boots seemed like some sort of uniform. I decided avant-garde academic, media corp.

Aware my voice was being auditioned, I said nothing, just smiled and nodded.

He said he knew all about me. A promising young poet. Basil Bunting was a great catch. A major figure. Friend of Ezra Pound and many more famous modernists (he listed them).

There was no stopping Alistair's factual ecstasy. Born with the century. Lake District. Pacifist. Pub brawler. Quaker and earth shaker. Persian scholar. Soho spy. Bestseller book-length poem, 'Briggfatts'. All the young Northern poets in thrall. Some man, some poet. Adding, 'B-by the way, you'll d-do fine.' I had not spoken.

He was gone before I could say more than 'yes', leaving me with a list of poems he wanted boned up on and detailed written instructions on every conceivable aspect of the studio session.

I am at a loose end, prey to any diversion. A well-disposed editor had just returned a batch of poems. 'I liked these as usual. But perhaps it is time for pause. Your prolificy suggests poetic journalism rather than considered work.' David Marcus sent me books to review by way of consolation. *Difficult Questions, Easy Answers* by Robert Graves and *The Strategy of Sex* by A. H. Chapman MD. Having recently seen Trauffaut's *Jules et Jim* at the Gate Cinema, I feel particularly qualified to expatiate on the latter.

Autumn monsoons have set in. So, taking my cue from Dean Swift, I run up and down the stairs for exercise in my socks. I master a 'fleet foot on the corrie' stride, imitating squirrels gliding up trees in Hyde Park. A delegation of McFee tenants – the distressed womenfolk – come out to watch me. Their persistence makes me stop. They want to talk to me.

I am ushered into a basement flat, brocaded and cushioned like a Beatrice Potter nest. Family heirlooms and a posse of older ladies surround me. They cup and plate my hands with tea and ginger biscuits. Phalanxes of hooded standing lamps blind me. I am a prisoner of polite attentiveness. Mrs Usher pours.

The Japanese music student (last seen hanging from the rails) slips in and sits down. His ease amazes me. The ladies take him for granted. He serves himself, old hand. An unsuspected underworld of social life in the McFee ménage reveals itself. How could I have missed it?

Mrs Pond, ex-admiral's wife (photos on the mantelpiece, portrait above it), explains patiently what everybody evidently knows. A chorus of nodding gentlefolk backs her up. 'Mr McFee has been good to us, all of us. Over the years, too many perhaps' (pause for widow's sighs). 'We have come to appreciate his little thoughtfulnesses and judicious interventions in times of' (pause for the *mot juste*) 'of disquiet. As captain of this ship he has been a calm, reassuring presence. He has smoothed many a ripple. In recent months you have been close to him. Books are his life and you are a bookish young man. We have discussed amongst ourselves whether to involve you. After all, you are new here. But Mrs Usher won the day. She believes passionately that you would want to be. So we are appealing to your friendship with Mr McFee and to your discretion.' Mrs Usher interrupts, 'Emma, for goodness sake, get to the point.'

'More tea, everybody?' Mrs Pond takes me aside. 'You have noticed that woman. No, not Eliza McFee. She's a ninny. Grates on my nerves but is no harm. It's that creature Sibyl. She is a cuckoo in the nest, gradually taking over the middle floor. Mr McFee is helpless to prevent – too much of a gentleman. And clearly distressed. We are all worried for him. He is beginning to behave most strangely. Last evening, for instance, when Eva Strong's heritage clock stopped, he refused to give it a look. Almost shouted at poor Eva that time was irrelevant. There are other signs. He goes around everywhere with an unlit cigarette in his hand.'

I become aware that all the ladies nod unanimously while they listen to Mrs Pond. Myrmidons, though of a polite persuasion, I think. The Japanese student is standing up, waving his arms above his head as though flaying a long sword. 'Let's just bump her off.' And sits down, embarrassed.

'Quiet, quiet, Fuji. Mutiny gets you nowhere. What we need is passive resistance. And a Trojan Horse. That's where you come in, Mr Young.'

At the mercy of this cabal of gentility, I'm conscious I haven't shoes on and my socks are beginning to smell. I become acutely aware the heavy curtains are drawn. The world outside – with its dreary rain and ordinary everyday life – is draped off by a tapestry in which tigers with roses in their teeth dance with oriental boys. The trap I'm in holds me more with etiquette than springs. I could get up and walk out ('Bye, ladies. Thanks for the tea'). But I stay put – fear of breaching the *comme il faut* – and hear Mrs Pond out.

'What do you want me to do?' 'We would like you to talk to Mr McFee. Tell him he has friends.' 'Will I give names? A list of signatures would be handy.' 'Mr McFee will know.' 'Is that all?' 'Yes.' 'Why me?' 'We are not known to be acquainted with you. You are, so to speak, the message in the bottle.'

'Why don't you talk to him yourself?' 'We have plans. He may not approve of them.' Fuji and the ladies clamour round me. 'I'll do it.' 'You won't regret it', Mrs Pond whispers as I depart. 'Mr McFee will know how to respond.'

He seems unsurprised when I deliver the message. 'With friends like that who needs enemies?' He changes the subject. 'By any chance is your rent due?' 'How much do you need?' 'I'm doing the rounds of historical clocks. The price of a train ticket to Dover would see me right.'

On his first night away a fire alarm goes off. The distressed ladies are out in the street in a jiffy, assembling an impromptu levée of déshabille and peruques. Fuji appears in a vermilion bathrobe, on his best behaviour. Eliza and Sibyl fluster down – fusty housecoat, man's dressing gown – hairnets askew, pancaked with face cream and more than a suggestion of absent teeth.

The fire brigade turn the house upside-down. I worry about the backpackers on the top floor and the dottle I emptied into the wastepaper basket. But it is a false alarm.

The party atmosphere is rudely curtailed. Sibyl, restored by

fresh air, bosses, 'Back to bed, girls. You have had your fun.'
Round one to the interloper, I think. Though Mrs Pond and her
posse make a better sartorial show. I recall Wallace Stevens's
'Complacencies of the Peignoir'. Poetry is a consolation in an
emergency.

Thus began a sequence of inexplicable events in the House of
McFee.

Sudden power failures, cranking plumbing, pigeons flapping
in panic around the landing, unopened mail dumped in dustbins
and plagues of mice, cockroaches and flying ants. Small disasters
at McFee's were commonplace, but more in a steady trickle than
this fireworks display. The building was being blitzed between
blackouts.

Tenants queued to complain outside the McFee suite. Even the
backpackers joined in. Fuji helped with the language, and encouraged talk of a fault line under the house, subliminal earthquakes
and haunting. Rumours of a stink bomb dropped on the veranda
went unsubstantiated.

Sibyl answers the door. 'Wait until Mr McFee comes back.'
This reasonable put-off with constant repetition wore thin, degen-
erating into shrill rancour. Eliza in the background accompanies it
with sobs. The siege of the cuckoo in the nest and her captive was
wearing them down. The piano duets stopped, no more frolics in
the balcony. A hush of anticipation permeated the silence of the
house. What would happen next?

I kept out of it. My room was disintegrating no more rapidly
than before. I made myself busy, reducing the mountain of paper
I had accumulated in three months to an acceptable molehill. I
carried sackfulls of rejected poems and dead-end drafts down to
the garbage which was not being collected. Nothing mysterious –
the local dustmen's strike had reached the newspapers. 'More pay,
less rubbish', cried their placard in the picket.

I was grateful for an explanation.

When I had cut the pile down to three folders, I boldly labelled them 'Juvenilia', 'New Poems' and 'Prose Asides'. My work was complete, for the time being. Giving my All for Art in Notting Hill Gate had achieved a hundred and eight pages. It was not quite what I wanted – more of less. I could not reproach the time and place for that. What I had to show was not much. But what could I do?

McFee is back. Everything is working again as before – more by chance than design. Tenants back in their boxes, community action a thing of the past, Fuji strums his Beatle toccatas, the distressed gentlefolk fade into anonymity and backpackers are invisible. The house is strangely empty.

Sibyl has disappeared. And Eliza too.

'The Salisbury clock is slower than the one in Dover. Of course it's older. I put a stopwatch on them. By the way, the damn thing isn't in Dover. It is up the road in the Science Museum. On permanent loan. My guide book is an antique.' I steer him gently to the vanished pair. He is disappointingly nonchalant. 'Mrs McFee will be back soon enough. One can only live on love and bean sprouts for so long.'

I do not mention the poltergeists. Or see Sibyl again.

[15]

READING TOO MUCH INTO

The events in the previous chapter may seem way out. Perceived by a young poet with heightened sensitivity, too much time on his hands and a reluctance to ask leading questions for fear of boring answers, actuality is optional. Augustus wants life stirred up and his immediate circumstances is the pot.

His relation to the brew of excitement is songbird to a beaten bush. The bird knows it can flutter off to sing elsewhere but stays – concealed in the thicket – to annoy the dog and enrich its repertoire with the hue and cry of hunts and quests. A mistle-thrush averages a hundred and forty three songs and would outnumber Schubert if it lived as long. Working its territory is a profligate source of profusion.

A transitory presence at the scene of drama, he can like a midwife speed up the action and slip away after the birth, leaving the parents to fight over whose child it is.

Driven by a belief in the uniqueness of the life around him – not wholly wrong: youth also has its wisdom – he defies mendacity with ambiguity, convinced that people will celebrate the exceptional. That is what poets are for. Their prerogative – thank you, Goethe – is to anticipate experience in order to encompass it.

Mrs Pond's, Fuji's and Sibyl's versions of the story would make interesting footnotes to his realisations. But footnotes are for scholars, not him.

Being an exception, his interpretation is diametrically opposed to that of a historian (The Quest) or an investigative journalist (The Hunt). These fixers of the commonplace depend on the collection or extortion of facts in order to distort them as they please. He has the contortions of the imagination.

His secret is not so much to amuse an audience (Scribe) but to amuse himself (de Musset). His last words on the matter are akin to Lady Mary Wortley Montagu's on her death bed. 'It's all been very interesting, it's all been very interesting.' So be it.

Note to self. Have I found a round-about way of accepting 'aboutness' (*pace* Jeff), jettisoning Objectivism? If so, am I still a poet?

I am certainly not a playwright anymore. Deila answered my modest note with a circular letter. 'To all company staff and associates. My work as artistic director of the Abbey Theatre has come to an end. While there is much to regret, I am full of gratitude towards all those of you whose spirit in the common task quickened mine. A dead poet reminds me of the experience. "This long struggle through the deed still doing/ Yet undone, that clogs our eager powers." Success to all your future endeavours.'

My tic goes into spasm.

[16]

BASIL'S WATERBOY

Versey's is the nearest posh restaurant to the BBC. I am meeting Basil Bunting. Nervously early, I wear my Texaco blue jersey (to accentuate Irishness), green corduroy trousers, suede shoes and flowing red scarf with yellow polkas (to signal poet-in-his-own-right).

Although Alistair had reserved the table, his meticulous preparations did not include punctuality – his own. Basil arrives on the dot. His Caesarean entrance could be captioned 'Beware of the Bull in the China Shop'. Long military raincoat, Persian fez. Jimmy Durante nose plumb-lines to a brisk goatée. He surveys the tables, flinty eyes darting a brilliant evocation of exhilarating wickedness. Alert no doubt to the symbolism of my attire, the great man marches towards me, jug-jaw first.

Basil lights a Turkish cigarette and assays me amicably. 'You must be Mr Young. To be young is to suffer.' His rather grand graveley voice is not made for small talk. 'Where's the chap from Auntie?' I feast on his presence.

'A minor poet, not conspicuously dishonest.' Basil's entry in *Who's Who* is wrong on both counts. He looms larger than life – the wondrously bulbous Orson Welles in *F for Fake* crossed with Altamira, the magical quack in *The Elixir of Love* (who sold the hopelessly lovelorn young man, Nemorino, a potion of cheap wine which worked wonders). But in the flesh, Basil's corpulence is more apparent than real, the thin actor playing Falstaff in a Michelin Man suit.

'No drinks on the BBC', Alistair had instructed. Basil is from the North of England and what's more a poet and not to be trusted. My blood is up. If I cannot crack a bottle of fine wine with a friend of Ezra Pound, what is poetry coming to? The licence fee (and poetic licence) my licensed premise, I ignore the injunction and call for a bottle of Bardolino (McFee's advice). I ready myself to recite 'And he who saw in the redness of wine/ the incorruptible rose'.

The semaphoric rigmarole with the cork ends with a flourish and an imperturbable hand decants the wine into a carafe. Its redness is like no other red. Scarlatti! Basil Bunting's beloved composer. Glints of Benvenuto Cellini violets as it is rocked around in the cut glass. Precious though this liquid is, it hints of violence.

The waiter coaxes, coddles, calms the turbulent wine until it is at peace with its meniscus, breathes easily, shows me the bottle and pours to taste. I note the name 'Barolo' and dare not protest. Bardolino turned into Barolo. My tentative pronunciation abbreviated Bard to Bar and olino to olo.

The wrong wine smells of autumn, tobacco and tastes of wild plums, liquorice, chocolate. Nothing wrong with it. I swill it around in my mouth. Basil salutes the Barolo. 'Good wine is a good familiar creature if it's used well.' But declines to taste, sticking to water. So the Yeats quotation will have to wait. I feel as though I'm drinking the Barolo on his behalf.

Alistair shows up, a tumult of papers and blustering apologies. He waves the waiters into action. Checks the label on the wine ('B-Barolo. B-Bussia, 1961. Wow!') as he pours. Out of chaos – orders come. Trolleys of entrées, sides of meat and a folly of desserts appear in orderly succession, at intervals determined by platters licked clean or shamelessly abandoned.

Our director's continuous chatter intrudes on the inchoate communication between Basil and myself. Alistair wants to do a programme on the dream life of animals. Sleep monitors in London Zoo reveal that 'Elephants d-dream all the time, b-birds dream now and then, but reptiles d-don't dream at all'. The rest is staccato drum rolls. I am thinking of Basil Bunting.

Here is a man who 'looks at things bigly and kindly and sees the pattern rather than the niggling detail' (William Morris). How tiresome he must find Alistair's drum roll. But it does not show. He avoids drawing on his cigarette until it is about to go out. The exotic tube smoulders in his long thin fingers. Then at the last possible moment he lips it and pulls hard.

'When I dream of my dog, I'm always a young lad. What I'd like to know, am I an old man in his?' Basil sighs.

In the gents, Alistair puzzles. 'B-Basil is not drinking? There must be s-something wrong.' 'It's hardly the wine', I think. In between prolixities our host slurped down most of it. 'Keep an eye on him. I depend on you.'

The bill falls from Alistair's hand. 'Augustus, you have expensive t-taste.' I pick it up. The wine cost more than the rest of the meal. I make a note to congratulate McFee.

Basil struggles to keep up with Alistair's bounding stride on the short walk. I take his arm and complete the Pound couplet with which he greeted me. 'To be young is to suffer./ Be old and be past that.' We laugh at the madman ahead. 'I have drunk wine from the Country of the Young/ and weep because I know all things now.' His R in 'drunk' rolls up Lower Regent Street into the BBC.

A porter with a wooden leg takes us through the grim labyrinth of Broadcasting House. His limp slows up the proceedings sufficiently to get our breath back. Acres and acres of grey corridors and rickety stairways – the descent to the studio is a game of snakes and ladders.

I mention meeting George Barker. 'Fine when drunk and

forgets his own interests.' Basil has a kind word for everybody. And Vernon. 'The best left hook in poetry today.' He is enjoying himself. Alistair, always on the alert for indecorous behaviour, hears our merry prattle. 'What's th-that?' he calls back anxiously. 'Nothing that needs to be repeated.' Basil is defending our privacy. I feel privileged. 'I am an octopus in love with God', he whispers to me.

Seeing my baffled alarm, he adds sadly, 'Delmore Schwartz. Did I meet him once or just read about it?'

Waiting outside the studio – the previous recording has overrun – Alistair reviews the troops, bouncing up and down and waving papers. His extreme deference to Basil is charged with hysteria. It could easily rebound into extreme abuse. He skirts around the obvious so niftily it is like dancing on air. The blunt Northerner feigns bemusement until his buckleaping courtier falls on his face.

'So you'd like me to sing "The Rose Tree" to the tune of "The Sally Gardens". Well, fancy that.' 'N-No! you've got the wrong end of th-the stick . . .' 'What kind of stick?' Basil is merciless. 'A blackthorn stick?' I titter. Alistair swings round, hissing *sotto voce*. 'Sh-shut up, you. You're f-fat help.' Controlling his stutter admirably. 'No, that wouldn't do at all. The political situation in Northern Ireland . . .'

Basil begins to croon the rebel song, ' "O words are lightly spoken",/ Said Pearse to Connolly'. When he reaches ' "It needs to be but watered",/ James Connolly replied,/ "To make the green come out again/ And spread on every side"', a functionary emerges from the studio. 'Shush, the green light is on.'

As the recording crew streams out, a frail dejected little man follows behind. His despair suddenly relieves itself in a smiling handshake. 'On the razzle, Basil?' Waving his hands at the diabolical irony of things, he disappears in a cackle of laughter. 'Who was that?' I ask. Alistair is impressed. 'Lewis Rickworth, th-the musicologist.'

Basil's head rocks back into neck, a man with his memories. 'I recall from my critic days his famous dictum, "It is time to consider how Domenico Scarlatti condensed so much music into so few bars." He was the toast of Soho. We knew that had Scarlatti frequented as many bars as most musicians he would not have completed his five hundred and fifty sonatas without repeating himself.'

If you know something, you know something else. Rickworth's dictum made a guest appearance in a key passage of 'Briggflatts', Bunting's masterwork. I wonder at BBC scheduling and its serendipity. Basil's secret is safe with me.

Alistair plays an archive recording of Yeats intoning poems everybody knows. I am astonished. A vowel-varying Sligo brogue rolls through his ponderous renditions, cementing the crackling soundtrack. 'Inisfree' is dubbed the 'Leak Isle'. The waterworks motif undulates through long drawn out lines. 'O Oi shayle haff sum piss dayre, fur piss cums droorawping slo-ow,/ droorawping fum d'veils o' d'morhning to whayre d'creakette shings.'

Yeats expounds on his declamatory delivery. 'I'm going to read my poems with great emphasis on their rhythm and that may seem strange if you are not used to it. I remember the great English poet, William Morris, coming in a rage from some lecture hall where somebody recited a passage out of his "Earthly Paradise". "It gave me the devil of a lot of trouble", said William Morris, "to get that thing into verse." It gave me a devil of a lot of trouble to get into verse the poems I'm going to read and that is why I won't read them as if they are prose.'

Basil prepares to perform 'The Cat and the Moon'. But the cat's name is giving him trouble. He pronounces 'Minnaloushe, Minnaloushe' with great gusto, shifting the emphasis between syllables and vowels like gears on a bicycle until his voice falls off. Alistair's deference is sorely tried. I offer a hesitant translation. 'Velvety velocity. A glossy-coated speedy creature.'

Basil is away, out-Yeatsing Yeats in broody declamation. Crushing a loose page in his fist, he creates his own background crackles. He does not need a prompt. Knows the poem off by heart, loving every line to life.

> Minnaloushe runs in the grass
> Lifting her delicate feet.
> Do you dance, Minnaloushe, do you dance?

The sleek creature has found her feet.

A happy Basil recounts Yeats explaining his reading style to a women's poetry club in America. 'I recite my poems as poems have been recited since the time of Homer.' A pert questioner asks, 'How can you presume to know how poems were spoken in classical times?' Yeats dismisses her. 'The ability of the man justifies the assumption.'

'You met Yeats in the 1930s in Rapallo. He called you "one of Ezra's more savage disciples".' (Basil raises his jaw to the moon, stroking his goatée upwards. Then levers it back down into his neck until it disappears. He looks like a seal.) 'What was W. B. like?'

'An umbrella left behind at a picnic. George Moore's description is definitive. He must have been the same age as I am now. Young men bothered him, and the sunshine. He remarked my resemblance to Lenin, a dandified version, and quoted his friend Santayana. "The young man who has not wept is savage." He might have completed the quotation. "The old man who will not laugh is a fool." Yeats was laughing at me. He was no fool.'

His eyes tear over. Alistair allows a minute's silence. Then intrudes, 'Why was he in Rapallo if he d–didn't like th–the weather?' Basil is back. 'To be near Pound. Rejuvenation with animal serum gave him Malta fever, an infection known only to goats. Georgie bought him a flat on the Gulf of Genoa. He needed an injection of Ezra's energy. It worked for the *Last Poems* – more mad Lear than youth regained, and all the better for it. But the heart grew old, gave up. Augustus, read something. All this talking dulls my ears.'

Alistair had specified an early Yeats romance – 'Brown Penny' – to warm up the studio. I had different ideas, the late 'Meru'. Inspired by the archive recording and Basil, I launch into a howl of vaulting vowels, with a patter of Minnaloushe consonants running through them, as though my life depends on it.

> Civilisation is hooped together, brought
> Under a rule, under the semblance of peace
> By manifold illusion.

When I reach 'Egypt and Greece, goodbye, and goodbye, Rome' my voice falters. How my father loved that line. Only Shelley's 'Another Athens will arise' meant more to him. Basil, realising I have lost it, jumps in, 'Hermits upon Mount Meru or Everest', and completes the poem in a single breath: 'know/ That day brings round the night, that before dawn/ His glory and his monuments are gone.'

He is exultant. 'You were Gibbon to my crabbed hermit. The two sides of Yeats's coin. Next time' (he turns on Alistair) 'give Augustus the green light.' My reading was not being recorded.

Our director is joined by a buxom woman in caftan and hairy hat with a feather. She looks like a madame in a seraglio. He introduces her. 'B-Basil, th-this is Meg Windblag, th-the s-series producer.' But Basil is not impressed. He is the Chief Yeoman of the Tower of London spitting out decapitations. 'Blasted foolish time to turn off the sound, that.' Meg conjures up her official smile. 'Sorry, Basil, but I'm sure you realise we have limited air time.' 'Time', says my hero, 'is irrelevant.' His Rs roll with rage.

Meg takes Basil aside, chattering lightly, lolling towards him.

Far from being fazed by his anger, she is roused by it. He is soothed, charmed and strokes his goatée. I would not be surprised if Meg sat on his lap. His gallantry in the face of her gross flirtatiousness appalls me. A technician behind me whistles softly: 'Our lips shouldn't touch./ Move over, darling./ I love you too much./ Move over, darling.' But Meg Windblag is more Catherine the Great than Doris Day.

When Basil resumes he declaims to Meg. It is shameless.

> None other knows what pleasures man
> At table or in bed.
> What shall I do for pretty girls
> Now my old bawd is dead.

His stress on 'do' is obscene. Romancing a middle-aged woman with Crazy Jane poems strikes me as counterproductive. Desperation is off-putting, particularly when it is attributed to the love object. But Meg sits there, in pleasure dome decreed, lapping it up.

Alistair is well satisfied. Basil not only captures the musical subversions of the English language that the vintage Yeats records, but is word perfect, and that means single takes. In addition, a melodic line has materialised out of thin air. Yeats was tone deaf. Basil has perfect pitch. His intonation defies W. B.'s vatic drone. A florid twelve-note range replaces the Doric plod. The poems of Yeats sing.

But the director's satisfaction does not extend to Meg. There is something between them that is not just professional. I saw them first as a couple. They seem separate from everybody else in the studio, in an arbour together.

They touch one another casually when talking. His stutter gets worse in her presence. And their clothes are colour coordinated. Meg's caftan matches Alistair's blue silk shirt and her hairy hat his brown corduroys. Her feather is peacock like his neck scarf.

Alistair's propensity for fidgeting with papers and studio apparatus (to the technicians' dismay) worsens. All the same, his agitation does not stop him keeping an eagle eye on Meg. As Basil addresses her with 'How can I, that girl standing there,/ My attention fix', in the final couplet he flings his arms wide, 'But O that I were young again/ And held her in my arms!', knocking over the microphone. Alistair utters an expletive. Then leaps to untangle the wires to distract, I decide, the studio from his jealousy.

When I read between rests for Basil, the light remains red. He has lost interest in my cause, chats to Meg while I stumble through 'Long Legged Fly' or 'Ribh at the Tomb of Baile and Aillinn'. My demoralisation is complete. That exotic creature with a hat shaped like a wig has taken away the defender of my right to record. The fate of Leda is too good for her. Replace the swan with an old goat, I say.

Alistair, sidelined by Meg, warms to me. Stopping for refreshments – Basil is still on water – he is friendly. 'Your "Meru" wasn't at all b-bad. Have a go at "A Faery S-Song". You're next.'

I read it over and see my chance. It is a spell sung over two doomed lovers, Diarmuid and Grania. When a boar wounds Diarmuid on a hunt, his rival allows the healing water to slip between his fingers as he brings it from a well. Grania means 'the ugly one' in Gaelic, I spitefully note.

The spirit of all the unrequited loves that dogged Yeats's life enters me. My voice amplifies to fill the studio with his authentic chant, a high-pitched monotone in slow motion. Meg and Basil, in nonchalant tête-à-tête, are startled. I fix them with my eye.

> We who are old, old and gay,
> O so old!
> Thousands of years, thousands of years,
> If all were told.

The spirit rounds the vowels and prolongs the words until it seems there is no end to the poem. I am inspired, not a syllable missed. A spell is being cast. And it is working. Basil and Meg are transfixed before me, two doomed lovers. I will carry the water from the well and let it slip through my fingers.

As I repeat the incantatio, 'O so old/ Thousands of years' for the last time, my eye catches the studio monitor. The green light is on.

Basil stops imitating Yeats. In his flat Northern accent 'Sailing to Byzantium' becomes the ramblings of an old salt buttonholing lone drinkers in a public house. Though the studio is stuffy, he has put on his overcoat. This paean to mortality is muttered to nobody in particular. Meg is no longer around.

I have tried over the years to understand what happened next.

Basil, paltry old man, tattered coat upon a stick, is an arthritic artisan. He catches the sensual music of life – seasons, generations, the death of self. 'Consume my heart away; sick with desire/ And fastened to a dying animal/ It knows not what it is.' He is dying in animal obscurity. But clings to a vision of an after-life – informed by his redundant occupation – gold leaf beaten into an immortal object.

He is hammering out his death like a double-bass solo in an orchestral interlude.

Reincarnation into an ornamental singing bird to entertain some fabulous court earths all that is most precious to him. More functional Benvenuto Cellini than abstract Grecian goldsmith, he will live on as a tick-tack nightingale, a wondrous toy. Classical symbolic survival means nothing to him. Basil, the poet-makar, through the medium of Yeats, is crafting his epitaph.

Alistair stops fidgeting. The technicians are attentive. Great poetry, performed by a man connected both historically and intimately with its source, fills the air. Listeners breathe evenly, in harmony with a rare event. The poem and the man become one.

The words are Yeats's but Basil makes them his own. Images and

ideas converted by his alchemy into humane music. The golden bird of
his after-life sings. Basil's anatomy, shrouded in a long raincoat, is a
collapsed deckchair. His chin recedes into the collar.

Alistair looks at his watch. 'We have underrun by th-thirty
minutes. Well d-done everybody.' (Noticing his star turn's
exhaustion) 'I'll s-see you to your taxi. Augustus will accompany
you to King's Cross.'

Sitting beside him in the spacious back seat, my thoughts are dark.
I separate the man from the poet in my mind. A great poet – at
least by proxy – but the double negatives in his *Who's Who* entry
should have warned me he is not to be trusted. As his minder, this
is well to know – final task to see him off safely to Newcastle.

Traffic is at a standstill outside Centre Point. A tap on the
window. Basil rolls it down. Bald Buddhist youths press a flower
into Basil's hand. 'Hare Krishna', they chant. He leans out and
speaks to them in Tibetan. But the Oxford Street Buddhists are
from High Wycombe. Peace signs exchanged, they frolic off ringing bells. 'I like the youth of today. They are open to everything.
Nothing embarrasses them.' My response is to blush.

Was he getting at me? I had better find out, I decide. Youth
welcomes judgements if favourable. But worries about resentment
based on uncertainty and a bitter old age. 'Organised religion
embarrasses me. Free will is closed down.' He looks at me
amicably and laughs. 'Don't look so gloomy. You have your whole
life before you.' He is thinking of himself, I realise. The High
Wycombes (and myself) make him feel his age. This satisfies me.

Basil's revival is sudden. 'Wait here, ten minutes. I have some
unfinished business.' I follow him into Soho. 'The girls are gone
and sex shops open. What a world. Nothing is sacred. All things
become secondhand.' Keeping up with him is no joke. He sweeps
into a public house which clearly prides itself on its ancient
squalor. 'What will you have?' I order a half of best bitter. Basil

('I've done well by water') settles for a sherry. I delight in the thought that his reputation as a drinker is a cover for serious abstemiousness. (My perverse belief at the time was that William Burroughs of *Junkie* fame wouldn't touch an aspirin. He'd live to eighty. And that Lou Reed was as straight as Rock Hudson.)

'Scene of my youth. Lord Berners, Constant Lambert, E. J. Moeran and all the minor composers drank here. I learned that you only compose when you couldn't think of anything better to do. Thanks to them I have lived variously and written a few things.'

I confide my struggle between poetry and real life. I am drawn to the normal cycle of things – career, family, a contribution to society. The life of the poet in a garret is self-indulgent. I tell him these things unabashed. Poetry, like children, would be a bonus. I think as I talk of the poets I have met recently. They form a pathetic frieze of pretensions, an identity parade of shame.

Basil listens attentively. My outburst climaxes. 'I see myself as a socially useful human being but with a harmless secret. When I die some poems will be discovered. If any are good enough, they will survive. If not, so be it.'

He puts his hand on my arm. 'There is, Augustus, a lot to be said for just being useful. Now back to the taxi. The coffers of the BBC are only so deep.'

At a Schelling lecture in Berlin the young Kierkegaard's heart leapt every time the term 'reality' was uttered. He had found the magic word to open his ideal. 'Useful' has the same effect on me. It makes me feel alive, hopeful, knowing where my life is going. Useful, useful. I am on the way to becoming a useful person, in a small way.

I help Basil along the platform. He is an old man again, needing my arm. I hoist him up into the carriage. He waves from the window. I wait until the train leaves. The empty track is a long goodbye, undulating behind the tail-coach from London to Newcastle. I will not see him again.

Alistair subtracted the price of the Barolo from my bill for the taxi. I owe the BBC forty pounds. In the LP of the broadcast my mediated rendition of 'We who are old' comes between the ersatz Yeats and Basil's apotheosis. I like to think it was the catalyst. The sleeve-jacket does not give me or the spirit a credit. I am not bothered. Acute listeners will hear a ghost voice and wonder.

Basil lived for another sixteen years. 'I have done well by water', I can hear him intone. May my reply bounce back, 'And by land too.'

[17]
LET THE SLIME FIND
ITS OWN CESSPOOL

Eliza McFee is a broken reed. Her gallivant with Sibyl to Faken-
ham in Norfolk ended in influenza and heartbreak. Conditions on
the commune were basic. Mantra humming and free-range dancing by the campfire insufficiently compensated for insanitary
sleeping and eating arrangements. The younger members seemed
immune to illness and boredom. They smoked aromatic rollups
and composed acoustic guitar riffs. Sibyl evacuated to a fringe
event at the Edinburgh Festival after a week. Eliza was too weak to
face the uncertainties of the accommodation. Sleeping on the floor
of Monica's flat was mentioned. Who is Monica?

McFee told me all this, manner of fact, without a trace of
triumph. We talk about her renewed piano playing. Marathons
that continued late into the night. I can hear it still.

She spent her time practising the very last Schubert sonata, known
as the posthumous. The verandah was a funeral parlour. Franz's hope-
less hesitancies chime with her state of mind (unassuaged pain, loss,
indigestion). The tentative melody recurrently curtailed as it hit the
same single note, plangently repeated without expression until released
into a dizzy rush of tuneless phrases, swarming unhappily, dissipating
into listlessness. If a scherzo, it was the laughter of clowns. The joke
was heard, two hands picking out the same single note. Chords would be

a consolation. Here there was none. Only a descending scale, descending
in scale till both hands were dead.

'Time is suspended.' McFee's judgement is flaccid, without
bones. No mention of its 'irrelevance'. Labouring the point would
be to insult. I am flattered. This man's feelings, I think, are buried
so deep, no dog could dig them up. But still, in his way, he is looking after his wife.

'Everything that goes around, come around. Which brings me to
you.' I tell him about Basil and Alistair and Meg and my utilitarian
ideal. 'I could do with somebody useful around here. Seriously, I
think he is right. You are not at ease with yourself in the Bohemian
life, which is essentially a discreditable club for thick-skinned
opportunists who think only of themselves. Thoreau says, "It is a
great Art to saunter." You scuttle along too fast.'

We both know that Scotland, the land of practical inventions
where the climate does not encourage standing still, beckons. That
in a week's time I will be on the Waverley train, excited by a future
that offers prospects which, if not secure, promise a measure of
useful endeavour. I am walking into it. No wonder my pace is
hurried.

I dramatise my abrogation from Art with a quatrain, 'Farewell
to Poetry'.

> So it's goodbye, my precious,
> The many hours I spent with you
> Have not been wasted. That's my message.
> I make way for poets new.

I must work on the last rhyme.

[18]

A FIT CONCLUSION

A note from Alma takes me aback. Assuming I was written out of the plot, I shelved the book. So be it. Now I dust it down and look for dog-ears to find where I left off. Tony's revelation about the invitation. The letter – chaste white envelope, urgent hand, my name spelt in full – revives hopes for a foolish moment (Alma has come to her senses and sees my worth).

'Come round on Saturday at three o'clock. Something terrible has happened.' Unsigned. The postmark is Kew.

I descend into the District Line with a heavy heart. I don't really like Alma, only the idea of her. McFee's contention suits my mood. Does she even like the idea of me, I ask? But still an invitation to an English person's home is not to be turned down.

The Saturday afternoon Tube is almost empty. Reasonable enough in an Indian summer. But absence of people makes me anxious. Have they been tipped off? I search the faces of fellow lost souls. Not a clue. We are hurtling towards impending disaster. The absent wag a crooked finger. 'You should read the papers, keep your ear to the ground.' 'Told you so, told you so.' The train chugs in conspiracy.

Kew Gardens returns me to life. Crowds of families are out taking the last sun. The missing faces are here. Overtime, shopping, pints with mates down the pub, visits to granny – all abandoned to take the children to the park. Normal life is going on as usual.

Aeroplanes descending into Heathrow boom over the pleasure gardens. The world is badly organised. Nobody seems bothered. Ordinary life accepts such intrusions as inevitable. Parents share intimate nothings and get closer for a few hours. Children run wild on the grass, tip the sky with swings, queue for ice cream, circle round on bicycles. Ordinary life, not so ordinary.

Old people on benches watch. They've seen it all and want to see it again before it disappears. I sit with the old people.

The sensible writer ignores the divide between Art and Life. Stéphane Mallarmé managed. A job, wife, children. And poetry flourished between the cracks. An honourable compromise, not too comfortable. Enough to keep the wolf from the door and make Madame Mallarmé want more.

He did not despise his job. A conscientious but uninspiring teacher, he withdrew into compiling educational textbooks with dogged zest. For forty years this useful labour was the ballast that allowed him to keep his feet on the ground while pottering in strange territories of the mind and spirit.

When Stéphane's expanding female family needed their mittens and ruffs, he moonlighted in fashion journalism to pay for their modes, putting his eye and pen to use without irony or resentment. The ladies were pleased and allowed him to entertain a ragbag of admirers with tobacco and rum in the conjugal home every Tuesday evening.

Winning this concession to waste a little of what was hard-earned made him feel sufficiently free to stray from suburban ways. Not too far (a lady with long red hair who lived two doors down and a houseboat on the Seine), but as far as a poet can go. He embarked on the impossible, dedicating his spare time to writing the Book of Life.

The author of 'A Dice Thrown Thrice' did not gamble.

Certainly not with his life. He was as happy as an artist could be, and a useful citizen. Posterity has been kind to him. The work that appeared between the cracks endures. As an exemplar I could do much worse. He embraced the practical and lived a useful life.

By the time I reach Alma's gate my mind is made up.

Concrete keeps the garden under control. Not a tree or shrub in sight, let alone a blade of grass. The unnatural nakedness is emphasised by a cluster of potted plants flaunting tiger lilies and a sentimental mock-marble sculpture – nymphs in a stream. The brick path would be dangerous in high heels.

The doorbell's dulcet double tinkle reminds me of something. Alma hushes me in ('Quiet please. My father is entertaining'). Swann visiting Marcel's family in Proust, yes. The kitchen is so aseptic – all white fittings, tiled floor and walls – it is difficult to believe anyone cooks. Decor designed to highlight blood and dirt. The perfect place to commit a murder, I think.

She looks different (as usual). All brightly painted like a restaurant just open under new management. But with nobody yet inside. I accept lemonade but not the Dubonnet. I feel like a health and safety inspector, averting my eyes as she leads me into the back garden. I cannot help noticing a neat patch of greens and leeks. We take our drinks into a Wendy House ('my hidey hole') and sit on children's stools. A lace cloth embroidered with the words 'All Her Roses Burst Into Bloom One Morning And Fell Apart That Afternoon' is nailed to the wall.

As long as I look at Alma's face I do not have to talk. Mary Quant holds her expression together for small talk. Glad to be back home, easier now that her father is in a settled relationship. Raymond is a sweetie. Cooks, cleans and does the garden. Waits hand and foot. Talks and walks with father. A visit to mother. Living with friends. Pippin's song, all's right with the world. Why am I here?

'And Angus?' I ask. A crack shows in the cosmetics. 'Very well thank you, as far as I know.' Alma is in pain but being brave. But I learn as her skin crumbles that her boss has left her for his wife. That she is on long-term sick leave. 'How can I go to the office and take dictation? Life is impossible.' I cannot bear to look as tears crease her face like lava down a mountainside. So I talk.

Respecting her B Phil (hons, 2nd class) in Philosophy I take the Boethian line. Nothing is wretched except thinking makes it so. Stop dwelling on the riches you have lost. Move on to appreciate the preciousness of your true friends. (I am not unaware that my words irritate Alma. But I persist.) Life is a comedy for those that think, a tragedy for those that feel. Think more, feel less, and you'll end up laughing with your friends. What was that all about? Male moans and hormones. Two fingers to the monster inside us all. Two fingers down the throat.

Her indignation erupts. 'What do you know about love? Your ideas come from books. Your poems are little better. You are just a little boy pressing his nose against the glass of other people's lives. Could anything be more unbearably smug? Keeping a safe distance. Birth, love and death close up are messy. The trouble with you, Augustus, is you think you're clever.' I bristle, remembering Jeff. 'Don't underestimate cleverness. Without it we would be still in the Stone Age.' Alma hits back. 'Says the emotionally-stupid caveman whose feelings are all bottled up and labelled "Do not touch".'

Then it happens. Alma goes limp, complexion blanching, blue veins show through. She slumps on the stool, a stricken victim of Pompeii. I feel like a child before a statue made of wax. Touch her and she will melt over you. I sit petrified for over a minute. Her eyes open, a frail smile flickers. 'Augustus, is that you?' Her voice is otherworldly, triumphant.

'What was that?' Alma is up on her feet. 'Just *petit mal*. I can't do *grand mal* anymore.' I remember her boast in the pub ('I can induce an epileptic fit at will'). The performance frightened me.

No frothing mouth, tongue biting, flipping around, but the stillness was a little death. 'I'm not going to ask for an encore.' She laughs, happily. 'It's nice sometimes just to let yourself go.'

Passing through the kitchen, we meet a dapper, bow-tied David Niven look-alike. 'Come here, Alma, you're a mess.' He squeezes a towel and wipes her face clean of make-up. She is a little girl again with her father. 'Where is Raymond?' she pouts. 'Who's Raymond? Your mother is due any minute. Go upstairs and get ready. I'll see your friend out.'

'You are Augustus? I'm amazed you exist. Alma has this problem with imaginary friends.' We talk at the gate. 'Her mother and I worry whenever she goes out. Her therapist encourages it. Calls it psychic socialisation. You must come round again when she is feeling better.' I enquire about her work. 'My brother, Angus, has been very good. Allows her into the office to type and make tea.'

The families and old people in Kew Gardens have been replaced by courting couples. In the realm of the imagination the poet is not king.

[19]

WHY POETRY IS IMPOSSIBLE

I bury myself in Kierkegaard's famous passage 'What is a Poet' in *Either/Or*. McFee wants to use it in his thesis but is dissatisfied with available translations. 'All by divines and lacking vim. Have a go, Augustus. It will be your swan song.' Not knowing Danish is an advantage. I just take an average reading of the various versions and distort it as I please. I have no qualms. *Either/Or*'s epigraph is an unfaithful French translation of a verse from the eighteenth century English poem, 'Night Thoughts on Life, Death and Immortality' (which should be retitled 'Dark Thoughts', I think). Edward Young's plea for the passions is perverted for Kierkegaardian purposes.

Worldly goods packed in two suitcases under the bed, my Bohemian days are numbered. A new life starts in Scotland next week. Poetry put on the back-burner, the flame turned down. It will flicker in the twilight between earning daily bread and the enjoyment of night life.

I phone my mother. The line crackles with static. 'You're giving up what?' 'Poetry, mammy', I shout. 'You call me long distance to tell me that?' I use up my coins convincing her it is not the opposite, that I'm giving up work. Cut off and coinless, I start a letter. But my intention is contradicted by a litany of recent successes, and you don't confide to your mother, 'Writing for me is an act of love. To be paid for it is prostitution.' I tear it up.

'Never in my wordland/ are there ways/ to reveal/ in a phrase/ what I feel.' My favourite Cole Porter rings hollow. I lack the courage to admit that giving All to my Art makes me feel useless. I need to walk on my own two feet and prove myself in practical ways. Flapping wings and giving flight to poetry is an airy nothing. Nevertheless, her advice buzzes in my ears. 'The job comes first, but keep poetry on as a hobby. You'll regret it later if you don't.' It weakens my resolve.

McFee's lack of resolve is heroic. 'One step forward, two back. That is the dance of life. Sibyl told Eliza that. She could have choreographed me.' I accompany him on his early morning walk. Sleeplessness has its rewards. ('Day break' is a silly expression. It should be 'day make'. Dawn puts the world together after night's dissemblings and peoples it. We are part of the making.) 'But I thought you didn't like Sibyl.' 'Not at all. I had hopes of a *ménage à trois*. But it was not to be.'

Bohemian life has many dawns and this is my last one, I think.

The smell of doughnuts from a café by Bayswater Tube station stops us. 'Home in heaven.' McFee sniffs the air. Fresh coffee. The lure is irresistible. An Italian padrone behind the counter prepares breakfast snacks for passing commuters. Too early yet for office trade. Only a few left-behinds from last night crouch behind the tables at the back. No ladies of the night with their pimps, as I had hoped, or tramps who slept in the park. Men in crumpled suits, serious gamblers perhaps from the clubs, counting their losses.

McFee wolfs a jam doughnut like a boy. Castor sugar rings his mouth, hot raspberry sticks to his teeth. 'I sleep less and read more as I grow old. I remember better than I understand. So I make sure that it is something substantial like Dr Johnson. He understood what he wrote and that is enough for me. My mind is a reservoir of random quotations like a table book full of numbers. As grey matter declines, these clusters begin to evaporate. I lose a word or two. The quotations become garbled, more my own. A sort of wisdom will be achieved when all the wise words are replaced by mine. I look forward to old age. I will find out what a fool thinks. Books are the greatest plaything ever invented to make fun of people.'

I tell him about Alma to cheer him up. 'You shouldn't be so hard on her. The mad are blessed.' Her life, I realise, is an unwelcome interruption. McFee is impatient. 'Last night I read *Rasselas* in your honour. The chapter about the poet.'

'I saw everything with a purpose. No detail was unuseful. A mountain range or a molehill, an ocean or a trickling stream, the beautiful or the dreadful, animal, vegetable and mineral. Nothing was useless. I stored in my mind an inexhaustible variety. The Prince stopped him. Too much observation, constant distraction. You couldn't see the wood for the trees.

'Not so, said the poet. My business was to examine the species in order to generalise. I did not number the streaks in the tulip or describe the thousand shades of green. The details of nature were only part of my job. I acquainted myself with all human life – happiness, misery, the passions in all their combinations, and traced the changes in the human mind from the sprightliness of infants to the despondency of decrepitude.

'I divested myself of the prejudices of my age and country. Regarded right and wrong from every possible angle. I ignored fashion. Concentrated the mind on higher truths. Contenting myself with obscurity, abrogating applause and committing all to the justice of posterity.

'My task was to interpret nature, legislate on behalf of mankind, preside over the thoughts and manners of future generations and to be superior to time and place. To this purpose, I had to learn many languages, know all the sciences. And so my style be worthy of my thoughts, I had to incessantly practise every delicacy of speech and grace of harmony.

'Enough, said the Prince. No human being can be a poet.'

'Augustus, be that a consolation in your new useful life.'

I am humbled, but sufficiently confident in my failure to posit, 'Is there any virtue in doing badly what has not been done before?' No, of course not. No answer necessary. I wait for one. McFee fingers residual jam from my plate.

'And if that fails, try Shakespeare.'

[20]

LAST NIGHT IN BOHEMIA

The arrogance of youth requires life-changing decisions to be taken in isolation from advice. Once made, lonely soul-searching is supplanted by promiscuous boasting to dispel doubts. Elders, bound by the caution which governed their own lives, will question the uncompromising, reckless and extreme. Coevals may blanch or envy your foolhardiness, but they respect your decision ('Way out').

You seek out the company of those who offer dispensation. Risks are celebrated. Mistakes don't exist. Everything can be rectified. Nothing is fatal. Correct them with another mistake. OK is the word. Our peers confirm the rightness of the next step in a dramatic transition. No need to tremble on the threshold.

I meet with Tony for a drink on my last evening. I am a paragon of practicality, bragging shamelessly about the skills acquired because my widowed mother begged me to get a qualification. I can set up retorts, calibrate pipettes, mix chemical solutions for the betterment of humanity and get good money for it.

My friend remembers a year drudging in a travel agency because he knew foreign languages and shudders. 'It must be done with the hands' – I cite Tolstoy. His commune echoed early Jewish *mores*. Rabbis were required to master manual as well as intellectual skills.

Tony is not impressed. 'There is an end but no way. The rest is shilly-shallying.' He knows his Kafka. So do I. 'Still, he held down a well-paid job in an insurance claims office. Dr Franz wasn't killing time in the industrial accidents department.' 'He did it to please his father. It almost killed him. Only TB got him early retirement or there would have been no novels. Whom are you doing it for?'

Furious with my generation's lack of understanding, sleep comes hard. Whom are you doing it for? Myself, my mother, the rest of humanity, myself. The permutations go round in a circle until I'm dizzy. Maybe I should investigate *what* am I doing it for? To give my life ballast, to earn a secure living, to pursue in science the Agassian ideal ('Trust no evidence, not even your own'), to embrace the biomedical utopia of Virchow ('Medicine is a social science, and politics nothing else but medicine on a large scale') or to cure my tic? Strange I had not mentioned the Abbey to McFee, Tony. Not telling my mother I could understand.

I open Shakespeare, McFee's last resort. Wrapped in a blanket on the roof with a torch, I commune with the Swan of Avon. 'The lunatic, the lover and the poet are of the imagination all compact.' I separate the three and mediate on each.

'The lunatic sees more devils than vast hell can hold.' I think of mine, the legacy of my moral masters. How I made a pact with my demons. Proud of my arm-wrestling with them, they became my secret, my literary life. But I betrayed that secret to McFee and then to half of London. The demons increased and multiplied. And now they have come to claim my mind. *But it isn't there.*

'The lover sees Helen's beauty in a brow of Egypt.' For Helen read Alma. Named after a battle or a demure Egyptian dancing girl. She fought and danced for me. I was too defeated to be charmed. And now she comes to claim my body. *But it isn't there.*

'The poet's eye, in a fine frenzy rolling, doth glance from heaven to earth, from earth to heaven. And, as the imagination bodies forth the forms of things unknown, the poet's pen turns them to shapes that in the night (reveal) how easy is a bush suppos'd to be a bear.'

I know that trick of light by which a bush becomes a *bonne bouche*, titbits to coax a bear to dance with its shadow. Call it poetry. But people who 'bodied forth' from the Bohemian life for me to imagine and shape – McFee, Eliza, distressed gentlefolk, Fuji, Sibyl, Basil, Alistair, Alma, sundry poets and hangers-on – come to claim their reality. *But it isn't there.*

I stay on the roof in the evening chill, hugging myself. I need to harden myself against the future. Mad poets love themselves. Night, my keeper, watches over me with unblinking stars. I am confined in the city's hum.

I hear the piano below. Stop, start, bang, crash. Eliza and a tenor are practising. The song sounds like Delius, words vaguely famil-iar. 'Women are so seasonable./ We don't know where their spring is.' McFee is rehearsing my chorale.

I retire to my bed, not to sleep, but to rewrite the Kierkegaard passage. Poetry is a state of panic where some poor souls suffer for a time before they go to prose.

'What is a poet?

'An unhappy man who turns his pain into pretty tunes.

'His fate is to be stuffed by a butcher into the belly of a mad bull put to skewer over hot coals. The cries of the poet are sweet music to his tormentor. Customers, far from being put off, salivate at the sizzling, and crowd around congratulating the butcher on his meat preparation. "That beast did not die in vain. Keep turning the carcass and what is inside it. Our dinner is on song."

'Roasting flesh and interior music delights the crowd. The cry of the poet may sound human, but hungry men are deaf. They throw on fresh coals and inflict new miseries. Their tastebuds sharpened by the crackling sounds of cooking, which happens to include tortured cries.

'The bull is drawn and quartered until nothing remains except the poet. "Third degree burns", observes the butcher, displaying the nicely blistered skin. The poet is swelling up before their eyes. The customers' approval says, "Sing for us again."

'A bystander comes forward. "I'm glad to note that everything has been done by the book. The rules of aesthetics have been observed. Well done, butcher. Keep your spirits up, poet, you are not finished yet."

'He is a critic and resembles the poet to a hair – nankeen trousers, smoking jacket, straggling beard, long thin fingers, untrimmed nails. But he has never experienced pain, only knows its consequences. Moreover, the critic is tone deaf and does not have the capacity (or the need) to cry out. The poet waits for his next bull.

'Moral: better to be an abattoir worker understood by the pigs than a poet misunderstood by men.'

Dawn comes up on dirty windows all over London. Sickly suggestions streak the grey pall. The light is not needed to read my Kierkegaard. I turn it off. The travesty could be a prose poem. I perish the thought and put it in an envelope for McFee. I fall asleep (as befits my last night in Bohemia) with my clothes on.

A downpour wakes me. Trimming my beard for the first time, I am putting on my best face. Deadly pale around the fringes, the visage of a doomed prisoner. My employers will be satisfied that they have taken on a serious person.

Restoring my watch to my wrist, I see the time. Past midday. A suitcase under each arm, I rush down the stairs. McFee calls from his study. 'What's the hurry? Sneaking off?'

'I want to be in time for my train.' 'Time, Augustus, is irrelevant. You've already gone.'

EPILOGUE

Some months later in Dundee, the capital city of broken glass, I receive a newspaper cutting from my mother. I scan it while waiting for a rice rat to bleach to bone in the laboratory sink, a process that delights me. The casting off of his Afro-fur and sad flesh resurrects in ghostly solidity, numinous white knuckles. My caged beast, reduced to his indestructible elements, does not need to prove anything. His pure, mineral perfection is sufficiently itself to be about nothing else.

R. O'D. had written a piece entitled 'He the Pursuing Pursued', a fulsome resumé of 'Augustus Young's prolific and original literary career so far'. I feel as though I'm reading my obituary.

'The sonorous *nom de plume* masks a son of the city, donned not by a *fin de siècle* Swinburnean aesthete but by an extremely dark boney young man, rather like a Bantry fisherman, with druidic eyes and a dangerously druidic mouth. He evokes the malicious darting tongues of the early Gaelic bards and the overall flavour of the adolescent animal-boy.'

I put the cutting aside. This has nothing to do with me. My kindly mentor is making up for our failed venture with the Abbey. I have other work to do.

My experiment complete, I forcep the tiny skeleton and hold it up. It refracts the light. Defiance of flesh and blood, clear, un-ambiguous. Strands of someone else's poem thread through my contemplation.

The bleached beast is a constant, my life the flow, the contradic-tion. What is the harm in that? I put it in a plastic bag for analysis. It will prove nothing. That will please Agassis, keeper of the null hypothesis.

Between ten and eleven tonight when the pubs are out I will hear from my room breaking glass and the cries of humanity at war.

I am happy in my work.

PART THREE
REQUIESCAT IN PACE

For my grandparents whom I never met

[1]

TREE RING

The family tree is spread out on the carpet. I kneel on it to flatten the greaseproof paper. My youngest brother put the tree together two decades ago. But why greaseproof – unwieldy, crackling in my hands and hard on the knees? 'It was the nearest to parchment I could find.' Now it needs updating. New births, marriages and deaths. I buy Stephen's ink and a fountain pen. My brother's hand is neat and tidy. After all, he was writing for posterity.

The entries are a pyramid with hieroglyphics, the names and dates. At the pinnacle is Edmund Hogan, my great-great-great-grandfather (born 1713), a Catholic farmer in the bleakest province in Ireland. Cromwell banished the native gentry there – 'to hell or Connaught'. After ethnic cleansing, ethnic conflict. The dispossessed scrambled for land. Edmund's father came up with good land in a barren county. The family motto is 'Fulminis Instar' ('Like Lightning').

I scan for patterns. In the eighteenth and nineteenth centuries, one member in each generation has a large family. Usually the eldest son who inherited the land. Occasionally the daughter – marrying a local farmer. In Penal times Catholic families had no access to the professions. So the rest of the children had the choice between a new life in America or an ecclesiastical career.

The majority went for the Church, where the family did well on the Continent (founders of seminaries, confessors to princesses, reverend mothers). The American few disappeared into the modest middle class or lower. Zane Grey in his Westerns often chose the name Hogan for ignominious hangers-on.

Catholic Emancipation offered the Law as an alternative. Usually the eldest son took it up but only as a sideline. My grandfather exemplified this, becoming the Chief Inspector in Parnell's Land League. He returned absentee estates to the native Irish.

His sons and daughters emerged, an educated elite from the bogs. They took the National University by storm. Idealists, intellectuals, sportsmen and cultured hostesses. The secularisation of the family came with them and the new Free State. Five large families resulted and the diaspora began. Later than most – the family had stayed put and together despite famines. Their children and their children's children secured a wide base of offspring, spread over four continents. The pyramid's collapse into the splits continues.

Tagging the tree for the next generation is disheartening. So many branches have twigs that disappear into nothing, lost to a larger world. It is like visiting a cemetery of unmarked graves. I revert to calculating life spans. Is there a trend? Spinsters and bachelors were long-lived, married males died young. I clutch my heart.

Numbers reoccur. *My grandfather was twenty-four when his father died. He died at forty-five, my father was twenty-one. I was twenty-one when my father died. That was twenty-four years ago.* Twenty-four year circles loop the generations. Has the cycle been broken? I do not have a son.

Playing with numbers is a game of impatience. I force imperatives on the past with opportunistic sums. I want to see the back of it. Number up. Line ended. Full stop.

The antithesis to numbers is ideas. I meditate upon the pattern of the hieroglyphics. What is a pyramid? An apex sloping to a polygonal base, a burial pile for royal stock. Redundant now. My generation is urban middle class. Our lives and ashes scattered to the four winds in four continents, unconfined. My ancestors are dust immured in a pyramid of calligraphy. The family motto 'Like Lightning' – flash!

Family trees only have significance when related to land. And land for us is limited to the gardens around our houses. The snakes and ladders of life's extremities – birth and death (marriage is no longer an immutable) – patterned before me is a game for dodos. The collapsed pyramid has been paved over by a patio.

I fold the document into a jiffy bag. Something is wrong. *If it is not already obvious to the reader I am forgiven.* My family tree, for what it is worth, has been split in half. One half – my father's – is branched with nametags budding births, flowering marriages and berrying deaths. The other half – my mother's – lacking records, is in invisible ink. Which makes it a tree you can hang anything you like on. Gifts from oral memory, dreams and historical possibilities. Turn on the lights.

Spanish sailors from the Armada shipwrecked off Kinsale. Bodies are swept on to the rocks. The locals have heard portents of princes rising from the sea with bags of sovereigns on their backs. They look on – helpless till the storm dies down. Then they assemble the corpses on the beach, stripping them of gold and other valuables. Till they come upon the Galician. Alive. He flickers a smile.

Sheltering Spaniards means death by the spike. He is just a boy, but smart – when they whisper 'Imirt bas' he played dead. The Redcoats watch as he is carried ashore covered in kelp and dumped in the cart with the dead. But on the blind side. When the cart jolts off, the Gallego is caped into a cabin. 'Who are you?' the woman of the house asks. 'Yo soy Gallego.' He is taken care of.

Gallegos are the Celts of Spain, small, dark, sharp, and hard working. They travel well. In no time the boy becomes one of them. Speaks their language, finds his place. They call him Gal Ghaoithe (Blast of Warm Wind). Half a Gaelic transliteration of his tribe. Half a tribute to the gale that threw him up. In time he will prosper as a tanner, his father's trade.

Thirteen years later the Great O'Neill marches from Ulster to Kinsale. Over three hundred miles. The Spanish expeditionary force lead by Don Juan del Aquila has arrived. But is under siege in Kinsale (Gal makes himself useful as an interpreter between the town and the Don). The British are one step ahead. Something O'Neill in his pride and contempt overlooks. He attacks Mountjoy's army in the wrong place at the wrong time and is routed. And retreats north ignominiously.

A little girl becomes separated from the O'Neill straggle. Gal spots her weeping in a ditch. She is the daughter of a dead soldier. Gives her name as Una O'Neill. He puts Una under his protection. Takes her to his workshop. Looks after her. Marries her. Assumes her name. Gal O'Neill.

Centuries later in Orense I sat in a café watching the youngsters sucking their milkshakes. A dark determined little lady with corrugated jet black hair, practical hands and a remote look took my order. It was my mother. During my month in Galicia I met my mother many times in various guises. I was home.

Some soldiers from Aquila's force remain on. Mostly from the Celtic North. Stone masons, carpenters, men with trades that built the great cathedrals of the north-east of Spain. Salamanca, Santiago de Compostela. They see in Kinsale the makings of a Spanish town, a pocket Vigo. The headland descends into narrow winding arched lanes on a hilly plateau. Ochre earth, red slate and the ocean beyond.

These men of Galicia helped shape the only Spanish town in Ireland today.

The Gallego O'Neills graft a tolerable living in Kinsale. Skilful people. When the tannery falls foul of the occupying British – fearful of sabotage, imported their own artisans – the O'Neills turn their hand to building granaries for local farmers. Their style is distinctive, based on the Galician horreo. Mushroom-like stores raised on stone platforms to protect the grain from rats. When bailiffs, fearful of sabotage, increasingly employ army craftsmen they turn to thatching cabins. A thatched cabin is a cottage, a status symbol for tenant farmers. Calls for thatching lessened with the famines of the mid-nineteenth century. The O'Neills moonlight as migrant workers on conacres.

These tenant cooperatives offer a seasonal living for hordes of willing hands in hard times. All the same, thatching is a skill that survived into this century. My mother's father was the last in line. *The sixth child in thatchers' families are born with a sixth finger on their left hand.* That is the legend. Watching my mother putting up a light bulb or climbing through a skylight, I knew she was a thatcher's daughter.

The Gallego O'Neills never tenanted land for long. They were too honest to cheat the rent collectors. When the Land League came their hopes were high. But a local gombeen man duped them of their due. This was not uncommon. My mother's father did not live long enough to see things otherwise. Providing for eleven children through farm labouring and thatching is hard. One year he diversified into cramming turkeys for Christmas. My mother coming home from school saw them perched in the barnyard trees. The birds could not be coaxed down. The turkey dream came to nothing. My maternal grandfather died in his forties. He never thatched his own cabin.

The eldest sister took over the family. Already she was in a position of some prestige, the parish priest's housekeeper. Most of the brothers emigrated and lived decent lives in jobs requiring manual skills.

My mother was seen as the daughter most likely to marry into land. Petite, olive skinned. Darkly pretty. Quick at school. Strong legs and hands. At sixteen the priest found her a job in a city guesthouse. Here she would learn nice, domestic ways to increase her eligibility. My father, a bachelor professor, took rooms with service.

He is attempting to teach the landlady's boy the rudiments of arithmetic. My mother knocks and enters, sees the bemusement of the boy. Tells my father off and explains vulgar fractions in simple terms. The boy understands.

He approached the parish priest and offered to finance my mother's renewed education. She was sent to the nuns in Fermoy. The eldest sister, disappointed in her plans, declared the girl a kept woman and cut her off. That was that. My mother's mother met her secretly from time to time. It was a great sorrow for her and the other siblings. She was excluded from her mother's deathbed.

My mother's father's brother was a musician and took life easy. He lived to see his children prosper. Owning not only land (through my mother's younger sister's marriage), but the local garage, pub and shop. Recently an unmarried grandson opened a gourmet restaurant. Meals cooked by hand, his own. Most of my generation and their children still live in Kinsale. My mother's Gallego looks survive in two of her children, my younger brother and second sister. The Gal O'Neill line is fertile. I look at the hands of the grandchildren. Artisan potential, a sixth finger?

This is the other half of the tree as told to me.

Gal Ghaoithe meets Fulminis Instar. Lightning strikes, warm winds balm.

[2]

DROPPED LOOPS AND
BIRTHDAY BOYS

The year of birth is wrong on my birth certificate. An emergency baptism on a premature baby delivery by Caesarean is not the cause. My father carried the registration form around in his pocket for a month. It was retrieved from the drycleaners, smudged with tobacco shreds and damp. A bored copy clerk in the City Hall, transcribing proof of my existence, dropped the bottom loop in a 3. It became 2 and I gained a year.

The discrepancy caused me bother only once. In Porto Velho on the border between Brazil, Columbia and Bolivia. An impassive customs official, with the usual drooping *bigote* and well-filled uniform, looked at my papers and then at me. Tapping his fingers together, he pronounced, 'No regular'. I had been waiting all my life for this moment. I congratulated him on his perfect English and uncanny powers of observation, tipping him lavishly, but discretely, in dollars. It was enough. I was let through. Escaping a police record in the hottest drugs spot in South America made me feel a year younger.

The day of my birth is correct. July the 8th has no feast day. It is the day families move out of town for the holidays. A day to try the patience of a saint – armies and large families should stay at home.

My inconvenient birthday was rarely anticipated. Parental visits to town, harbingering presents, were unlikely. A last minute flurry in the village shop was the best to be expected and parties a pipe dream. Arranging them in transit was unthinkable. Anyway other children were not around. I never had a party in my growing years. In adult life I have never given one. Self-celebrations embarrass me. They're absurd. But perhaps in this I am commemorating my childhood birthdays in their own idiom.

I understood why my birthday could not be otherwise. It's easier to understand than to accept. A lesson I learned young – the best time. The most I could hope was that my birthday would not be forgotten. I was all ears for my mother's eleventh hour preparations, urgently whispered to sisters. It always moved me. She had so much to do. I viewed their reluctant cooperation with sibling wryness. Excited by something else – the seaside. I understood but did not accept. They had properly planned birthdays and parties. It was not fair. I measured from year to year the number of minutes in the eleventh hour before the flurry. A good year was five past the hour. Despair set in at quarter to twelve.

On my sixth birthday the holiday hullabaloo is complicated by music exams. Once again my mother does not forget. But it is five to twelve. A trip to the village is not possible. My sisters are in town. I am hanging round the yard outside the kitchen. 'I haven't forgotten your birthday.' My mother gives me a balloon and a promise of something else later.

The balloon is in a floral envelope. With a crayon sketch of a boy kicking a football on the vellum. My mother pauses on the step, smiling helplessly. She says my name and goes back in.

The big move tomorrow, no help at hand – I understand. Ungratefulness would be to my shame. I can accept. Taking the balloon and the promise beyond the long hedge where things grow wild, I sit down in the raspberry bushes and begin to blow up the balloon.

I see barren apple trees with weeds entwining their twisted flanks, a white sticky moss where the fruit should have been, long grass strangling the gooseberry bushes, a thick rusty grove of decaying palms, a smouldering fire where rubbish was burnt that morning. People have been here. I cannot control my breathing. When the balloon inflates larger than my hand, it slips my mouth and the air is lost. Poor breathing is a prelude to tears. I harden myself against them and think of the fuss made of my brother's birthday. Fluffy buns and lemonade with his friends. The highlight a gramophone record of the Hindenburg Disaster. Pop goes the balloon – flipping noisily into the gooseberries. I leave it there.

The recently stripped raspberry beds are unencumbered with overgrowth. Face down, I crawl amongst the stalks, picking out stray berries lurking under leaves. Each one perfectly ripe and larger than I expect. I gobble them down, the afterglow a happy memory. In the criss-cross of the stalks hard little raspberries nestle. I eat them slowly. They taste salty like tears until the pulp explodes in juice and the sweetness is the sweetest sweetness ever. The aftertaste is smokey like autumn. The last of the raspberries foretell the fall of leaves, the first frost.

I forget my birthday. Slip through a hole in the hedge. And wander down to the Atlantic pond. Boys wading in muddy water are netting freshwater shrimps. They show me how the shrimps disappear in the hand – pink against pink. Fey fabulous creatures dropped in jam jars full of water. I watch them for hours.

Returning home, I am sent to the bathroom to wash my face. Red blotches of raspberry juice show in the mirror. The boys must have thought I was an Indian. At tea a town cake with six lighted candles appears. My sisters' surprise. I blow the candles out. My breathing is back. Everybody applauds and 'Happy Birthday' is sung with mock hearty zest, as it should. The cake, the candles and the song do not make me happy. I am happy already.

On the way back from the pond I uncrumpled the envelope in my pocket. The boy kicking the football is me. The drawing is by my mother. And she never ever draws.

It was my best birthday.

[3]

THE SPELL

A whirling bird fluttered above his pram, the crest like a lily, the feathers blue as the sky. He smiled but did not chortle – an infant's delight in the world is silent. Later he came to know the crest was a wimple, the downy blue a habit. His first flamingo had appeared as a Bon Secours nun.

Bon Secours? The bell beat of the phrase became a childhood charm. When told it meant charity, he did not believe it. Charity went with faith and hope, words strung out like beads on the treadmill of prayer. He did not understand prayers. They were what you said.

Years later, taught to spell, he accepted the word succour. It was a good word thought it sounded noisier, more fleshly than a nun, and had pleasurable connotations. But it was only the half of it. The 'Bon' remained a mystery word, a sweet one. Children are suckers for bonbons. Understood that.

The charm survived the joke. He still secretly believed if he repeated 'Bon Secours' often and fast enough, it would propel him into flight. Tried it once. It did not work. Put it down to lack of faith or hope or charity.

His mother had her hysterectomy in the Bon Secours hospital. Visiting her, she sent him down to the local grocer to buy a miniature brandy. He was honoured to be entrusted with this task. But alarmed. As a pre-med student, worried about the effect of capillary expansion on the stitches. As an adolescent prig, feared for his mother's reputation.

Returning with the brandy, she rustled it under the pillow and smiled. Just in time. A wimpled nun in surgical blue waddled through the ward, seeing everything. More goose than flamingo, he decided. A domestic one, not much flight in her.

Bon Secours, the spell broke.

Those days post-operative pain was considered good for recovery. She slipped him a ten shilling note, and smiled again. Come back tomorrow at the same time.

When he arrived with the miniature, his mother was gone. The bed was made up. It seemed to him, like a body laid out. A Bon Secours nun, possibly the same one, sat him down on a low stool. Feared the worst.

Instead, she began to lecture him about his irresponsible mother. 'A bad patient. What will Mr Corkery, the surgeon, say? Three days after his operation too. All that skill gone to waste. The ungrateful patient. She just took flight.'

The kitchen light was on. He could see his father inside. His father was rarely in the kitchen. Could see through the window his father was making tea. He never made tea. Then he saw his mother. Missing her because she never sat down in the kitchen. But there she was, pale as a dove, perched on a stool in the corner.

Through the bars of the window, it looked as though she was in a cage.

[4]

BLESSED DONALD CROWHURST

I never could make a raft float. The garage door redeemed from a rubbish dump and trollied down to the Atlantic pond sank. Wading around the mud-stuck wreckage I salvaged a cheese sandwich. My brother had read about the Kon Tiki expedition and he was my handbook. You cut down middle-aged pine trees, rope the trunks together and load up empty oil cans, survival rations and home exercise books. All these components of raft adventure were near at hand in the neighbourhood, but there were always parents lurking around the corner to pounce and ask questions.

My brother had settled for a conceptual journey. He knew the books and the ropes, and mocked at my ignorance and ineptitude. For instance, I thought a compass was some sort of lasso. I knew about radios. I could turn on the wireless. But it needed to be plugged in. My brother laughed. He had assembled a crystal set and listened to Radio Caroline in bed.

As I worked on another door in the waste lot behind the back garden, he sat reading in a deckchair, keeping watch and offering advice. I never knew when he was serious, but I was desperate to make a raft float and he liked constructing trolleys with pram wheels.

He cheered me off on my last fatal voyage with a toy periscope. I did not get the joke. He guessed correctly that my craft would end up at the bottom of the pond. But not that I would be attacked by a swan, and rescued from the hissing bone-cruncher by my father. My punishment was not the drenching in the pond or the shock of a bird turning Hitchcock. It was the shame, not of failure itself – I accepted that – but failure observed by my parents. I could not see why they should be amused by my humiliation.

Thirty years later Donald Crowhurst, the round-the-world solo yachtsman, took on the five oceans in a makeshift boat. Becalmed between the Bahamas and the Azores, he sent fake radio signals and fooled everybody, except himself, that he was passing the Cape of Good Hope, rounding the Antipodes and going flat out for the Falklands. This deception continued for several months, while he edged his craft towards England. Unable to face being found out as a fraud, Crowhurst disappeared forever into the Atlantic, which he had never left.

Crowhurst's voyage into certain failure, and its dénouement in self-effacement, still strikes me as one of the most heroic ventures in maritime history. Drifting nowhere into the biggest lie any sailor could entertain, his realisation of the truth grew day by day until it dissipated his shame into the welcoming mists of oblivion. I rest his case for sanity, if not sanctity.

[5]

DRAM, DUGGAN AND
LOVE DARCY

I was a dunce at school, scarcely able to read the *Beano*. My back-wardness was tolerated at home. By a stroke of luck, the retired professor of medicine, a friend of the family, attended my christening. He was a master of the spot diagnosis and took my father aside to confide a disorder of the pineal gland. Be gentle with the boy. He will not be long for this life. My parents were at a loss as to the meaning of this prognostication but they believed it. Descartes insists that the soul resides in the pineal gland. This my father, a scholarly man, knew. He must have decided that like animals I had a defective soul, and he liked animals.

My mother was instructed not to 'push' me. My infant sluggish-ness was allowed to develop into mental laziness. I grew out of baby dresses and bootees to become a brutish boy, given to run-ning around all the time in circles. I discovered sport and that gave my running a purpose. I excelled in the playground and paid school as little attention as possible. My mother, who was sceptical of Dr Dram's diagnosis but went along with it for peace's sake, relented when she saw my complexion turn to puce in the heat of ball games. She noticed also that afterwards I did not sweat. Instead I steamed. She decided that this was something pineal.

What my mother did not know was that I made up for a lack of natural aptitude in sports with fierce ambition and played games in a state of blind temper. This cut no ice with other little boys but it helped to protect me from being 'pushed' and I grew up in ignorance. My younger brother learned to read before me and passed me out in school. When I was eight years old my parents panicked. Dram's prophecy was coming true but it was my mind that was not growing, not my body. I was taken to see another family friend who specialised in mental retardation.

Despite my running and steaming I was a quiet child. I did not say much, not because I was shy, but there was not much to be said. Dr Duggan, however, made me shy. My embarrassed mother told him that I could not read properly because of 'lazy eyes'. There is nothing wrong with his brain. I listened, thinking I must be really stupid because I am not aware of anything being wrong. I knew I did not pay attention in class and that the serious books that I was expected to read did not catch my fancy. If that is being a retard, well, so be it.

Dr Duggan asked to see me alone. I expected a vigorous examination with the heavy metal instrument that hung around his neck, but he just asked me about school. He was a tiny man, no taller than most boys in the under-twelve football team, but he was as wide as he was tall without being fat. His eyes jiggered behind rimless glasses. I was glad to be amusing without having to try and answered his questions honestly.

I told him I did not like to sit down, that sitting down was a waste of time in my opinion. Legs were intended to be stood on and made to move. This was not fluently imparted. Being shy with the doctor I did not want to talk. But I forced myself and I was surprised by what came out, and the thought that I probably liked him. That is why I am saying what I mean, I thought.

I cannot recall everything we discussed but I remember he asked if I got headaches in class (Do the nuns give you headaches? is how he put it). I said, sometimes. He asked me what I thought about in class. I replied, nothing. I was not going to admit to daydreaming of kicking a football. That would be going too far. He laughed, this time with his mouth. You must think of something. What do you think of when you have headaches? I think of the headache, I conceded. Dr Duggan now began to laugh with his voice. He chuckled with controlled glee. That's more than most doctors do, he remarked, regaining a semblance of seriousness. We don't think enough of headaches.

The guffaw that followed must have alarmed my mother. She rushed into the room and stood before the doctor's desk. Is he saying stupid things? He does that sometimes to annoy people. He does not mean it. Dr Duggan looked at her kindly. Calm yourself, Mary. He is behaving himself perfectly. In fact there is nothing wrong with the boy. He is just bored. Take him away from the nuns. They are boring him out of his skull. Send him to the National School for a year or two. It will toughen him up. That's all he needs. Something to struggle against.

The doctor laughed and my mother nervously joined in. Two grown adults laughing together over a backward boy is not a pretty sight, I thought. All those teeth! As we left, Dr Duggan asked me what books did they give me to read that I couldn't read. I remembered one with particular hate. *Black Beauty*. He let go a final laugh which ended with the words 'No wonder'.

My mother held my hand like I was a toddler as we walked home. She was not displeased. I was vaguely aware that my charmed life was over. I was not a pineal defective after all. Being brought to a doctor to see if my brain was all right was no joke, except for my brother. I was relieved to disappoint him. Though I was worried. My days of quietness were over. I would be expected to say something. I would be spoken to. I would have to listen. But my worst fears did not materialise. Whether from habit or lingering doubts, when I got indifferent results at school my parents merely sighed and neglected to punish me, as they would the other children. Expectations continued to be low. I was free to run and steam as before. My retard status was assured.

I changed from the nuns to the National School on Dr Duggan's advice. It was the first of a string of schools I was to attend. The headmaster, Mr O'Brain, beat the village children from ignorance to knowledge with willowy canes cut from the ash trees that surrounded the school. The cane ruled this demented man as much as his poor pupils. He did not even spare the girls. The experience did not harden me, however, as was hoped.

The school was a short walk from home. I collected a puny infant called Love Darcy on my way. He had been assigned to me by Mr O'Brain. I was usually early, or else everybody else was late, because I remember many a morning standing outside the wrought-iron gate praying no-one else would turn up. The smell of lilac from a tree that entwined the gate is still redolent for me of the violence running through that sorry school. It must have been pollenised in my nostrils in the summer term that ended my year there.

It was not always summer in the National School. I remember with nausea the smell of milk spilt from the lunch bottles on the steaming radiators. And playing a game named cat and mouse with knobbly sticks and round stones in the schoolyard, to keep chilblained hands warm. And the ceremony of laying, lighting and stoking the school fire in a capacious hearth, a short happy moment when it blazed. Favoured pupils, and I was one, were allowed to tend the fire.

One boy came in a wheelchair. He had a bright smile for everybody and invariably wore a suit. His cleanliness was exceptional. A doting mother prepared him every day for school. He and myself were the only children not regularly beaten by O'Brain and his swarthy female assistant, Mrs Hodson. I was not beaten because O'Brain had been a student of my father and held him in high esteem. The boy in the wheelchair was not beaten because of his ailing health. Not being beaten was a stigma which made us objects of contempt amongst our classmates. However, to their credit they did not bully me. The cripple protected me from that. Also Love Darcy had big brothers.

I was taken away from the National School that summer. The impending arrival of Aunt Hana prompted the decision. She was my father's eldest sister, and as the arbiter of what was right and proper in the family had decreed it was not seemly for the son of a professional person to attend the State school, even to toughen him up. At the time I thought it was my tales of cane abuse and the fact I was permitted to mark myself in the school exams. I thought the latter so unfair that uncharacteristically I confided in my mother. She did not believe me, I learnt later. In September I was to go to a pay school, run by Christian Brothers for the better-off families in the town.

I was relieved, but experienced a qualm of conscience when I saw the delicate Love Darcy in the village. Who would accompany him to school now? I recall his pathetic attempts to slip his nervous little hand into mine on our walks to the National School and my brutal repulses. He lived in a shack behind the village with innumerable brothers and sisters. His father, a wiry little man famously dissociated from his brood, was the local spare-hand, useful to have around when off the drink. I still wonder what happened to Love Darcy.

Every story has a happy ending. A few years ago I was mulling over the Dram diagnosis with my mother. The retired professor's mission in life was to finger neonates with a putative pineal defect and to counsel the parents on how to handle its hopelessness. Several mothers in the town were living in constant fear of their child's imminent collapse. My mother found this out through the accident of gossip. One family called Corrigan were not so fortunate in finding a Dr Duggan to reverse the diagnosis. The boy in question ran away to sea when he was seventeen and died healthy in Accra from a stab wound.

Nowadays the pineal gland is called the pineal body. It is believed to be the vestige of the third eye and in certain reptiles and primitive mammals it is sufficiently exposed to the surface to receive light. It is possibly the origin of the Cyclops, hitherto regarded as a mythical monster. In man it is the mystery gland, hardening into a little bone about the time of puberty. This helps doctors to detect brain tumours with X-rays. It also has lead to speculation that the pineal has something to do with sexual development. This gives me pause for doubts. Could Dram have been right? A little nasty voice says, am I woman in a man's body or a failed fish? I do not feel like either. Every story has a happy ending or is happy to end.

Professor Dram, a brilliant man in other respects, was convinced that his intervention was a service to humanity. My parents neither thanked nor blamed him for it. Nevertheless, Dram was the only visitor I recall being thrown out of our house. Apparently he offended my father's gentleman's code by relating something vicious a mutual friend said behind his back. A bewildered Dram was shown the door. Hearing raised voices, my brother and I watched from the banisters in our pyjamas. There was our father, in a controlled rage, guiding a distressed old man out of the house. He firmly shut the front door. We sped to our bedroom window and watched my Nostradamus on the crazy paving, flaying his arm around in frustration and slamming the garden gate decisively as he stomped off. He didn't look back. I felt sorry for him.

[6]

WHEN THE VOICE BREAKS

My brother Michael exploited the ladies of the village with his winning ways. His Harpo curls and knitted suits did the rounds with spinsters and widows. In return for sweet cake and three-penny bits this incarnation of Cupid was theirs.

He compromised my reputation to ingratiate himself. I was the bullying older brother. Tales of persecution never failed. One kind woman bought him a popgun to protect himself, another roller-skates. Older brothers give younger brothers a hard time to prepare them for the world. I would have been softer on him had I known.

We shared a bedroom. The appearance of these new toys taunted me. But Michael was nimble, slippery in the chase. I rarely landed a punch. He got away with a tale to tell. He won.

Michael's ladies cherished their Cupid as a unique visitation. They did not like to talk about it. So his reputation in the village as a promiscuous child was safe from the family. It was only when Miss Austin spotted him emerge from Mrs O'Brian's cottage scoffing a cream bun and an hour later saw him in Miss Payne's front room enjoying afternoon tea that my mother found out. Our son is a cuckoo. My father was amused.

The spanner in Michael's *la ronde* was jealousy. It stopped the merry-go-round. All unchaperoned visits were banned, except to Mrs Flossy Scott. She was lonely from the recent loss of a son. My mother trusted her.

Weary of juggling his round of biddies, Michael took it well. Flossy was his most generous patron. He was also feeling his age. Freddie Bartholomew days were numbered. Time to settle down and submit to crew cuts and corduroys. His good grace disappointed me. All the same, a normal brother was a relief.

Little Lord Fauntleroy roughened himself into Tom Brown. But his ways did not change. He visited Flossy every day and the gifts mounted. Their macho nature perplexed me – dumb-bells, light weights and baseball bats. Only when Flossy Scott complained to my mother about my bullying did I realise what was happening. I was aggrieved. I'd barely touched him.

I decided the best tactic was to rile Michael into attack. Retaliation would not be countenanced but understood. Work his anger, stick your jaw out and say, hit me there. The aggressor must be punished. All the spinsters and widows of the village thought I was a monster. I would show them.

It was the boxing gloves that did it. Big, *pink* American gloves. I caught him sparring before the mirror, more Sal Mineo than Paul Newman in *Somebody Up There Likes Me*. 'Flossy's boy has pinkie mitts.' I punched his nose in the mirror. Michael came clomping after me in new boxing boots. I led him a merry dance

The house was a maze of extensions, built on as the family increased. I positioned myself under the stairs, opposite the study and watched Michael clodhop through the open door. I peeped in and saw him land a kick plum on the pants of a figure bent over the wastepaper basket. I absorbed the shock. It was my father, who did not flinch, preoccupied with retrieving some vital scrap. Michael ricocheted past me like a hunted hare. He was not seen again that afternoon.

I couldn't help but admire his hit and run technique.

Later I overheard my parents. 'A strange thing while I was bending.' 'It must have been one of the boys.' 'They're beginning to kick me now.' His wry tone was touched with self-pity, as though remembering some real slight in the past.

It was the first time that I had been mistaken for a man.

I recruited Michael for the school under seven stone rugby team.

[7]

LUCAS A NON LUCENDA

'A grove is a light because it does not shine'

Each Easter I received a blue airmail letter postmarked USA. The handwriting was like barbed wire and cut both ways. I opened the letter as a prisoner on death row would a doomed reprieve, careful not to miss a word by tearing a margin. I already knew its likely contents. There would be inside information on American domestic politics, a palm frond to be burned and blessed for Ash Wednesday and a special request, invariably too impractical to achieve. Why my father's eldest sister, an important nun, chose me as correspondent struck me as doubly incongruous. Aunt Hana was a glamorous figure within the family. She was reputed to have escaped from a prisoner of war camp in the Philippines during the Second World War and was now her order's prime fund-raiser in the States. Since I was a dunce at school, replying must have been a traumatic experience. I cannot remember writing one. My mother's determination that her eldest son would not let the family down undoubtedly meant innumerable drafts and much knuckle-slapping, which memory in its kindness has suppressed.

One year the envelope contained a sachet of yellow seeds. I must have been nine because it was sealed with an 'I Like Ike' sticker. Aunt Hana's barbed hand scratched exacting instructions about how to sow and nurture portulaca garnered from the convent hothouse. Its flowers would be a little bit of American flamboyance amid the greenness of an Irish garden. I noted the dry, chaff-like seeds and had my doubts. Moreover, flowers in my world were strictly for trampling on when no-one was looking. Still, I knew it was a sacred duty. That April afternoon I raked the portulaca seeds into a sunny spot in the rockery and thinned out all signs of growing things in its vicinity. Earthing them, my hoe hand did not tremble, shaman-like. This was a bad omen. I constructed a twine fence around the seedbed, and looked to the sky for birds. There were none to be seen but without doubt they were waiting patiently in the evergreen trees for a swoop and a peck.

I watched the patch for a few weeks. Three little leaves would signal a portulaca had taken root. Aunt Hana's instructions were precise. The three-leaf seedlings were to be transplanted once they appeared. But nothing came up. A few familiar weeds sprouted and I uprooted them with pleasure. I was not at home with growing things or with waiting. Nothing showed and it was June. I lost interest. A boy has more important things to do than scouring the earth, except for something edible.

Breakfast was bad news that summer. First, there was the morning when a policeman called with a telegraph. Uncle Michael had died suddenly in Dublin. He was the only member of the family I had never met, my father's youngest brother, the reckless one. In the thirties this crack horseman taught himself to be an air pilot. On a flight to Iceland he scorned the standard protective wear and contracted frostbite. In the heart, I was told. Not bothering with the pills and living the life of an entrepreneur with the Irish Sweepstake, he paid for his enduring dedication to wild oats with a massive cardiac failure. I was his godchild.

When the bad news sunk in I did not think of his wife, the wonderful and willful Mary Barry. I did not think of his five children. Or my mother who loved this handsome, strapping, humorous man. Or my father who felt responsible for him and could do nothing about it. I could only think of the large package I received that spring. I had been waiting for almost a decade for a godfatherly gift, for a sign that he acknowledged me as his god-child. I opened it, knowing it must be from him, only to find another parcel inside it. I continued to unwrap this Chinese box of diminishing parcels until I found in the last one, no larger than my hand, a note from my sisters. 'April Fool, April Fool.'

Mary Barry was the merriest of widows. Not even the cancer that killed her the following year prevented her arriving at our house in a purple Ford car, throwing all routines – even my father's – into chaos as she organised trips to the seaside, race-courses and Big Houses with ornamental gardens. I adored this large, outgoing, chain-smoking, flask-swilling aunt by marriage, with her knowledge of horses and horse sense and boundless capacity for fun. Mary Barry was a whirlwind of a woman who never knew her place because all her life she was on the move, drawing an awestruck entourage of friends, family and besotted admirers behind her.

When Mary Barry came to visit she went out of her way to make up for Uncle Michael's neglect, teasing me unmercifully to draw me out. I derived much silent pleasure from this. I was too flat-tered to talk. I had something to say to her, but I hadn't the words. I wanted to celebrate her, to declare my love and admiration. My shyness drove her to wilder and wilder excesses. On one occasion she even stopped the car on the bump bridge outside Cloyne, telling this dumb, blushing boy 'to talk his way home. It will make an orator of you.' Of course she picked me up a couple of minutes later, backing her florid Ford at racing speed. I crowned her delight by saying nothing, getting into the seat beside her and looking to the road. I was conscious of sustaining her joke and she laughed through her cigarette until she coughed unpleasantly, threw the newly lighted fag out the window and chortled with a sigh, 'You'll be the death of me.' I basked in Mary Barry's largeness.

The second bad news at breakfast came with porridge, a blue airmail letter addressed to my mother. In the dying days of August lumpy, loathed porridge appeared to herald the end of summer. There was a chill in the air. Carefree days of sun and sea and endless idleness were numbered. The porridge was peremptory. School was starting again.

Letters in August were not always bad news. The previous year one arrived to tell us of a delayed school start (due to a polio epidemic) and an unexpected Indian summer was our delight. This time the letter was from Aunt Hana. I recognised the clawlike hand. My mother read it, biting her lips until they distorted. The news was clearly not welcome. She put the letter aside and continued her exhortations – eat your porridge – with renewed venom. At the end of the meal she announced, 'Aunt Hana is coming to stay next month.' Her tone was neutral.

Children are the surface of the family. Ideally they should mirror tranquil skies above. But what went on before or happens behind their backs – or is simply beyond their egocentric understanding – sullies the surface, making it murky. The mirror is clouded from below. Adult undertows create currents that threaten to drag them down. The news excited me as it did my siblings. A family legend, my father's big sister, was coming to stay. I saw in my mind's eye an outsized female warrior of Christ disguised as the nun's Barnum, and forgot completely about the awful airmail letters. When she came there surely would be fruitcake and honeycombs for tea every day. After the announcement my mother seemed to recover her usual fighting spirit and pounced on my inane expression. 'Why are you looking so pleased with yourself? Aunt Hana, I will have you know, is asking after your portulaca.' Everyone laughed. I dryly swallowed the lump of bread in my mouth and could not wait to get out of the house.

There was nothing in the portulaca patch except some frayed sedge. The crudely fenced-off square foot was a microcosm of a desert wilderness. I wanted to dig it up with my bare fingers to get to the yellow grains. But I did not dare. The earth dedicated to the sacred seed was not to be disturbed. Something might still happen. 'Most terrible is the bite of enraged necessity', says Montaigne, who was an amateur gardener, 'and belief is its teeth.' I really believed for a moment – faith before reason – that if I left the patch alone a bedful of scarlet flowers would spring up. Though dusty autumnal soil, which flaked when I touched it, did not augur well for miracles.

Later, when my mother asked me how the flowers were doing, my reply was a look and the look was evasive. 'I hope you tended them properly', was her only comment. I knew she knew the worst and was waiting to see how I would negotiate the consequences.

I considered prayer. But my mind wandered. I saw an ocean liner capsize in a hurricane. Nowadays it would be called a disaster movie. Aunt Hana was sailing in the Mauritania. Some years later I was to come across Gerald Manley Hopkins's 'The Wreck of the Deutschland', about five nuns drowned on the Atlantic. My daydream was a premonition. 'Sister, a sister calling/ A master, her master and mine! – And the inboard seas run swirling and hawling;/ The rash smart sloggering brine/ Blinds her.' It is less a boy's poem than a grown-up's poem by a boy. I echoed without knowing it Hopkins's cry of despair at nature, the avenger with God's blessing. 'But ah! but O! Thou terrible/ Why wouldst Thou Rude on me.' I knew my dream was a dead loss.

Better to hope for a man-made disaster. I was aware – from a passage my father read out from a book about Hiroshima and the Bomb – that the day after an atomic explosion the bulbs and seeds in the earth multiplied madly and flowers sprang up all over the place. I willed an H-bomb. Portulaca flourishing beyond my wildest dreams and a radioactive Aunt Hana saying, 'Well done.'

Standing over the dead patch, I experienced a renewed desire to scratch the soil with my fingernails and stir up some growth which would, in time, make a satisfactory wreath for Aunt Hana. I did not really believe in sins of thought. Deeds, yes. So I did not defile the earth and accepted its barrenness as my fate. In every indolent boy there is a budding Buddhist. Drained of all hope, I knelt on the ground. I did not levitate.

My sisters took an unexpected interest in my patch. One of them sprinkled milk, flicking it with the backs of two fingers like the priest dispensing holy water at benediction. The other tried chanting over it. I took a sporting interest and joined them in what was a cynical game. None of us had any faith in a miracle. I stole a thimbleful from my father's brandy-flask, hidden amongst Rennies in the medicine chest, and soaked it into the soil, humming a mantra. Plates of glass I found in the village quarry were turned into a hothouse wigwam placed over the plot. I lit a fire beside it and scorched the glass with smoke, telling my sisters that smoked glass attracted moonlight and moonlight had magical growth properties. All it needed was a full moon. My sisters declared me stark staring mad, having lost interest in the game. Oddly enough, a day or two later some weeds sprouted up. One sister looked up their names in her *Everything in Nature* annual. Speedwell and pimpernel. Aunt Hana's arrival was the day following. I was bizarrely confident. She might know about Japs and wealthy Yanks, but native American flowers when transplanted into Irish soil? What did she know about these?

September was well advanced when Aunt Hana arrived. She suddenly appeared ahead of schedule in a taxi. This caused shockwaves, particularly in the kitchen. The day maid, Kitty, stopped whistling, like a bird before the storm. My mother was the eye in that storm, making her manners to Aunt Hana with a creepily constrained mien. What outsiders might mistake as servility we knew to be barely suppressed rage at being caught on the hop. The house was not ready for Aunt Hana. Neither were the children. Only my father took it in his stride. He changed for nobody.

I was just back from school. My shop-fresh uniform – black blazer with red and yellow braiding, grey flannels – was scruffy from my first tussle with a new rust-haired boy called Maurice. I had decided he was to be my friend and had introduced myself with my fists, as was the custom. My mother pushed me out the back door and told me to wait in the garage until Kitty had time to bring a bowl and soap. The garage had a store of apples wrapped for the winter in newspaper. I plundered a large yellow fruit, unfolded a deckchair and waited to be cleaned up. It was pleasant to be left alone and I stretched out, hands behind my head, savouring the moment.

Aunt Hana turned out to be a tough old nun masquerading as a living relic. Her blue frosty habit and matching veil were a tribute to starch. The habit encased a stout build like a suit of armour, and the veil was more like a helmet than a halo. The white brow-band that strapped in her superior forehead, a family characteristic I did not share, was so stiff it hurt to look at it. Her manner with everyone was the same, a starchy seriousness advertising an unbending will. Children were neither seen nor heard in her presence, and grateful for that. But we soon discovered her weakness.

She nibbled like a mystic at my mother's meals. Gargantuan labours in the kitchen were to little avail. Seeing the piles of untouched food dumped in the garbage was an offence to my boy's stomach. I did not consider my mother's feelings. The least she could have done, I maintained to myself, was to redistribute the leavings amongst the hungry and that meant me. I was always hungry. It never occurred to me that throwing away the good food, something she never did, was a statement. Compounding waste with waste appeased her rage.

Children learn more about house guests from examining their wastepaper baskets than meeting them. This my sisters knew.

Empty cans of American food were found – stuffed vine leaves, squid in their own ink, and tuna and crab, her favourites. The gastronomic education in those ravaged tins served us well for dinner parties in later years. It soon became apparent that Aunt Hana did her serious eating in her room, and she ate well.

Meals with Aunt Hana were nervous events. It was not merely that she did not eat. She liked to argue others into indigestion. When my father ate with the family it was worse. Aunt Hana went all out, haggling high-minded, abstruse theological notions. It was easy for her, not having to concentrate on food. There was no room for doubt in her world. My father, with his fine socratic turn of mind, was given to honest doubt. The clash of wills echoed sibling cymbals from childhoods so distant that a prehistoric gnosticism prevailed. Aunt Hana froze further into herself as she angered.

My father's amusement – getting a rise out of his eldest sister – brought out a cruel extrovert quality, unseen by us before. He was normally a gentle, thoughtful man, slow to enter the fray and always fair-minded. His usual diffidence being replaced by a near triumphant glee made me unpleasantly aware that it was our presence as children that gave him the upper hand. It was not that Aunt Hana was outnumbered. We gave him a symbolic advantage.

Hana's polemical sallies degenerated into pious truisms. My father treated them like profound theories, analysing their inanity to break them into little bits. Even a child could see this was fluff. His legalistic mind overstretched itself. Youthful radicalism, long in the past, surfaced. My mother was more annoyed by this than by Aunt Hana's disdain of her cooking. She too felt mocked by his unnecessary fireworks. All for Hecuba. All for Aunt Hana. It was unedifying to witness a superior mind engage in trivial pursuits. The object of his intellectual pickiness defended herself by disappearing into her habit. We children, confronting the ancient battle taking place before us – refereed erratically by our mother – were confused, almost to the unheard-of extent of losing our appetites. There were two pickinesses in the air. I preferred Aunt Hana's more visceral one of food – the most important thing in my life at the time.

The difference between the God of the Old and New Testaments is that in the Old Testament God spoke to mankind, but in the New He listened. Aunt Hana, like Jehovah, spoke but did not listen. Whether the wireless was on for the news or a J. B. Priestley play she talked over it. There was no rest for mankind. The wireless was turned off. When my mother tried card games like whist or snap, Aunt Hana did not hear the call of other hands, made her own rules and the game was a farce. This diversion was soon dropped and serious conversation resumed, mainly monologues on the Everest expeditions, earthquakes in the Ionian Islands, Stalin's death. All news we had heard on the radio, months ago. This news of the news she made sound as monotonous as recurrent decimals. She ended with a dogmatic recital on what the Pope thought and went off to her room to rest.

Mercifully, Aunt Hana brought a plague on the house. In the first week of October my second sister, and Aunt Hana's namesake, went down with scarlet fever. Little Hana was isolated in the nursery, the most remote room. The hoped-for calamity had occurred. We were withdrawn from school. As in all plagues the weather was perfect. An Indian summer, my father intoned. He liked the phrase. But it sounded unhealthy to me. India in boys' annuals was all rickshaws and rickets.

The house was surrounded by trees and the leaves were turning vivid browns and reds. The sun shining through them was pure alchemy. The gold made me squint like a miser in heaven. Though confined to the house and garden, we were released and not just from school. We were free from all received routines and waited with an inner hush for our doom or the appearance of a rash. When the leaves turn from dusky green into brilliant metallic hues it augurs their fall. We too, blotched with the wild game pigments of high spirits and long hours in the sun, were in the prelude of a free fall, passing the time before hitting the ground, cutting patterns in large potatoes to make primitive prints on white wrapping paper from the invalid's presents. That was the nearest allowed to my sick second sister. We were happy and saw Aunt Hana's coming as the agent of this happiness. Our feelings towards her began to change.

During the quarantine my mother lost control of the household. Aunt Hana, with her prisoner of war experiences to the fore, organised the offensive. The family was manoeuvred into action. Directives, proclamations and health and safety precautions were issued at all hours. Prophylactic diets, baths and family prayers were introduced. It was martial law laid down by a remote religious figurehead. Both our parents toed the line, my mother in particular. The plague and Aunt Hana had two things in common. They inspired fear and obedience. Fortunately for us children fresh air was considered the best remedy against scarlatina. She always called it that.

Aunt Hana's commanding response to the family emergency brought us closer to our father. Reduced to the ranks, he exuded the craven eagerness of a new recruit. The lowest of the low are cynical of authority, to gain favour with the less downtrodden. Our father sought complicity. Behind Hana's back he was one of us. I had expected him to establish a rival regime. But with family sickness he was out of his depth. That was my mother's sphere, and now that she had been supplanted he was somewhat at sea.

Being in the same boat with him was a new experience. Revering a father is easy. Sharing indignities with him is difficult. True, it lessened our own sense of unworthiness, but in pre-Dr Spock days that made us insecure. Our place at the bottom of the pile was being usurped. This whispering, subversive new recruit was not to be trusted. Even when he complained, with a twinkle in his eye, 'we're all eating out of Aunt Hana's hands,' and added, 'if not her tins,' The joke was on us. Our discovery had moved upstairs. Moreover, we couldn't help noticing he managed to elude the tougher sanctions. When the family rosary was restored by decree, Aunt Hana led the sorrowful mysteries and our father was absent.

It was the reign of vitamin tablets and holy pictures. The tablets were an American substitute for cod liver oil. Twice a day they were handed out to the troops. Unlike cod liver oil, the vitamins tasted like nothing. It seemed a waste of spit to swallow them. Holy pictures appeared all over the house like propaganda leaflets from an airdrop. There were sub-Murillo blue and white virgins standing on snakes, priests in purple vestments raising the communion host to choirs of cherubs taunting Baby Jesus in His basket, St Teresa, the Little Flower, clutching roses and a cross to her saintly bosom and pleading with Hollywood eyes 'to plant the Cross in every Pagan Land'. These were scattered throughout the house, save the toilet, for instant edification. A holy picture of St George was slipped into my missal by a mystery hand. He was the patron saint of plagues, as well as England, my mother explained.

After the rosary *Les Misérables* was read aloud in the drawing room, large, sparsely furnished, and rarely used. Aunt Hana stage-managed the gathering, opening all the windows and placing people in chairs as far as possible from one another. 'Nobody within coughing distance' was her edict. I would not have been surprised if gas masks had been issued at these aseptic occasions. Or posters unfurled from the ceiling glorifying The Leader with slogans and curfews, and a giant representation of Aunt Hana with her finger in the air.

My mother read Victor Hugo's sombre tale in her best voice. Her empathy with the characters surprised us. She was not usually given to sentiment. The delivery was strong and clear, though conversational. Aunt Hana clearly approved. She conducted the performance with little nods of her head like a Punch and Judy show. My mother could have been an actress. When moved to tears by a particularly pathetic passage, instead of blubbing she stopped for ten seconds. Then resumed with voice restored to its full strength. In the dramatic interval it was we who blubbed. We blubbed for her, and for our sick sister.

Only Aunt Hana and my mother ever saw her, the sacred mascot of the regime. Aunt Hana's room was adjacent to the nursery. This enhanced her power. She was the Matron to the invalid. My mother was relegated to being the Kitchen Orderly, a position she accepted without question. We wondered about this. How long would it last? And about Little Hana. She was said to have a complexion like a cartoon toadstool. Red, white and blue spots. In retrospect I wonder at the coincidence. My sick sister was showing the colours of the American flag.

The extended holiday and the change in balance of power suited me. I began to court Aunt Hana's attention. I hung around her, hoping to be useful. And I was, fetching writing pads and umbrellas. I was a good runner. Now I ran for the house dictator. I was not merely a lackey of power. I became Aunt Hana's houseboy because I was grateful to her for forgetting about the portulaca. It had been at the back of my mind since she came. Relief made me a willing slave.

I was also on a secret mission. Every other day after lunch Aunt Hana engaged me to run down to the village chemist with a letter. I escaped from the garden through a hole in the hedge. Mr Purvis took the note into the dispensary and returned with a brown paper parcel. 'Handle with care', he observed, dryly. The mystery medicine squelched in its container as I ran. Aunt Hana waited in the back garden, meandering by the gap with her missal for cover. She slipped the parcel into her commodious sleeve, snapping her teeth together in a squad-drill. 'This will do Hana the world of good.' And disappeared up to her room.

I was flattered in the knowledge that this formidable woman

relied on my discretion. All the same, the covert operation bothered me. If my mother found out, would she be pleased? Qualms about feeding strange drugs to my sister did not enter my mind. I knew enough about family doctors to trust that Aunt Hana, with her wartime experience in the Far East, understood better what fevers needed. But I believed my little deceit was her way of removing yet another responsibility from my mother, and was uneasy at being party to her downgrading.

Aunt Hana went out of her way to show me public favour. At table I was called on to pass the pepper when she deigned to assay a morsel. This was the nod of official approval. Other important tasks like fetching an item of fruit or putting out crumbs for the birds were now my domain. I was clearly to be trusted. The family noted this and began to see me with new eyes. My mother consulted me from time to time on Aunt Hana's behalf. Did I think she would like her eggs boiled or poached? Would she be likely to sit out in the sun or the shade? As Aunt Hana's emissary I was making crucial decisions. I dispatched them capriciously. Power corrupts and I was aware of mine. Being the go-between even gave me a modicum of power over Aunt Hana.

But it also had disadvantages. My brothers and my elder sister ganged up. 'Auntie Hana's pet' was their taunt. I reacted stupidly to teasing. Instead of remaining coldly indifferent, I flushed and lashed out. Girls fight dirty. Hitting them is considered cowardly. Something to do with babies. This they know. My sister delighted in my tantrum and danced around me. 'Auntie Hana's pet, Auntie Hana's pet.' My brothers, being little and spry, eluded my blows and hid behind my sister. I retired to the back garden and shed tears of frustration in the cabbage bed.

There is nothing like a lonely cry to purge self-pity in a boy. But Aunt Hana, to my horror, was sitting on a log nearby, reading her office. She had observed my distress and came over, hesitating on whether to give me succour or a row. She decided, not unkindly, to ignore my state and instead changed the subject. 'What happened to those flowers you were going to grow for me?' At that very moment my rampant sister with my brothers in her wake came bounding out of a derelict raspberry patch. 'Caught you, caught you. Auntie Hana's pet!' Seeing Aunt Hana, they stopped short. Then ran off in confusion. I followed them at pace.

My father turned day into night. He worked in his study till dawn and slept all day. Wrangling at table was in the past. Aunt Hana reigned supreme, bestriding the floorboards on stilts of righteousness. Her clanking did not respect his sleep, upsetting my mother who took to going to Mass each morning at the convent and pausing at the nuns' graveyard on the way home. My parents' capitulation coincided with my elevation. As Aunt Hana's side-kick, I was second in command. Nevertheless, I tiptoed around during the day, not to disturb my father's sleep. Foolish the victor who drives the defeated to despair. I knew that Aunt Hana's régime would not last forever (it was sanctioned by a plague). I also knew whom I would meet on the way down.

Summer endured with golden days but the evenings were chilly. The plague had not spread and the victim was getting better. Her resourcefulness in captivity was acclaimed. Sketches of the garden from her window and stories with a mystical turn were displayed in the drawing room like flowers. Little Hana's plucky sojourn in the nursery assumed legendary status. Isolated from our friends and the local swimming pool we, on the other hand, were bored. It was difficult to hide – children at a loose end are an eyesore. The creative energy from the sick room put us to shame.

My mother and Aunt Hana agreed on one thing. Boredom in idleness was a sin. Compendiums of games lay fallow with over-play. We were bored, and the grown-ups too, with sallies into the undergrowth of the imagination and coming up with truffles of excitement. What was known as 'going on adventures'. In the early days of the quarantine the adults delighted in our sudden disappearances and sudden returns, garlanded with tales to tell.

Now nobody knew what we were up to, secrets hermetically sealed by lack of interest, our own and theirs. We were building a collapsible wigwam from branches and fallen leaves in the woodland that skirted the garden, kindling forbidden fires from dry twigs to roast potatoes and channeling the smoke into the road outside through a roll of lino. We were in the clandestine jungle of childhood, surviving on our wits to overcome the demons by making ourselves invisible. Only a call from Aunt Hana to run a message could break the spell.

The game was up when our mother discovered the hideout, passing the hedge by the road with my father who was suffering from insomnia and needed a walk. Smoke from the lino was the tell-tale sign. We were told to stamp out the smouldering site immediately. All games after that were to be out in the open. Luckily, we invented one which exhausted our surplus energies. Hedge clippings were set up as jumps on the front lawn and we played human horses, leaping over them, fence-knocking and time faults giving it competitive edge. Hours on end were spent improvising our own Aga Khan Cup. Another diversion, a quieter one, was watching our parents become closer together in their defeat. During summer holidays by the sea we had noticed something similar. It was not whispering or holding hands or anything mushy. We noticed they were in step when they went out for a walk and still in step coming back.

Aunt Hana's regime was predictable and peremptory, but there were a few surprises. After spiriting the brown paper parcel up to her room, she rested. At four the family gathered in the front garden for the house briefing. It was the least militaristic of the régime's rituals. Grown-ups reclined in deckchairs and children sprawled on the grass. Our leader on these occasions was more Mussolini than Hitler. She was not always on time. Her entrance was dramatic. A certain light-heartedness in her gait was complemented by a smile, more self-satisfied than regal. The siesta clearly agreed with her. She dilly-dallied and made heavy-handed assays at play with children. These flutters of friendliness came to nothing, disappearing into thin air. Her attention was else-where or all over the place or on higher things. It was not for us to speculate.

Once settled in her deckchair, the briefing began. Reporting on the progress of the gallant little invalid, the mood was rhapsodic and the method anecdotal. Then there were old rules to renew and offerings of sage advice to all and sundry. The benignity of it all was alarming at first, but as it became the daily pattern we found it even agreeable.

One such afternoon when I was setting up her deckchair, Aunt Hana stopped me in my tracks. You must get an umbrella. The sun is catching my glasses.' She swayed around a little as if to mime what she was saying. Indeed the slanting sun was low in the sky and I hurtled off to fetch the brolly from the garden shed. Out in the back garden I glimpsed black clouds, the first for weeks, accumulating above. I decided – power corrupts – not to alert her to the break in the weather. When I returned she was inspecting my sister's daisy chains and at the same time perform-ing the elaborate manoeuvre of settling herself in the deckchair. I moved to help and she turned to me suddenly, just as she sunk her haunches into the seat. 'By the way, remember those seedlings . . .' The deckchair collapsed. It seemed to happen quite slowly, a tender embrace between her hind-parts and the soft grass of the lawn. I realised that in my haste, the notches of the deckchair had not been secured. Aunt Hana lay there, the epitome of the prostrate in a holy pageant, only the wrong way up. More like a saint, in fact, on a cenotaph. The impact – she was gravid of rump – must have been less gentle than it appeared. Her spectacles were displaced and one eyeglass was cracked like a spider's web. I bent down. She smelt of medicine. Her bulk was beyond my strength. I caught my mother's eye. Amusement danced in it. I had no time to reflect, for at that moment the heavens opened.

I ran into the house for assistance, still carrying the brolly in my hand. Kitty, the maid, roused from her afternoon slump, and my mother raised Hana to her feet. She was still muttering something about seeds but it was lost in the excitement. With Kitty and my mother each supporting an arm, she was escorted into the house, a crusade of children propping up the rear. The rain poured down like an overflow from a chute. I held the umbrella over the fallen aunt's cortège. It was only wide enough to protect my patron. The rest of us were drenched to the skin.

Aunt Hana was placed in an armchair with legs resting on a footstool. White worsted stockings and a can-can of lacy slips showed under her starched habit. The grin on her face was the rictus of shock. She jabbered feverishly. The accident was not commensurate with this transmogrification. No bones were broken. Her ravings were difficult to catch. But I knew what she was saying. Aunt Hana was repeating her last words before the fall. 'Remember those, remember those . . .' My mother spooned brandy into her mouth. She took it without making a face, licking her lips. The curtains were drawn. Aunt Hana was asleep.

I was pleased, despite the continuing downpour, to be sent down to the village. Beside the chemist there was an eyeglass maker. The spider's web was replaced and a new frame fitted on the spot. Returning to the house my feet dragged. The rain had stopped and sun shafted through the avenue trees to make mantilla patterns on the tar road. 'Remember those seeds, remember those seeds' kept ringing in my ears. I opened the garden gate with a heavy heart. My fate was awaiting me. Aunt Hana would wake refreshed and finish the sentence – the sentence was mine. I scurried into the woodland for a moment's respite and perched on the bifurcation of a Japanese cherry tree. The hour of the portulaca had come. Someone would descend and call me to account. I did not despair. I did not cry. I was resigned.

Some months before Little Hana deliberated on which members of the family 'had character'. We were astride this self-same tree, with my brothers and some friends. One of her conclusions was that if I had 'character', it was weak. I had a small head, a low brow and a weak chin. But now I felt I had real 'character'. I could face my fate with the best.

I opened the spectacle case and tried on the glasses. They fitted me perfectly. My cranium was as big as Aunt Hana's. I rolled my head back and around like an idiot. The sensation was agreeable. The russet-green leaves of the tree above were like aeroplanes in a movie with tracer bullets shooting them down. I was the camera-man who decided what appeared on screen. It was my movie. Round and around went my head and the optical dazzle made me dizzy.

The movie was *Objective Burma*. The only real boy's movie I had seen. All the others were holy ones, approved by the nuns or Christian Brothers. There were usually donkeys, saintly peasants and miracles in them. Though Aunt Mary once took me to *Boys' Town*, with Spencer Tracy as a priest who said, 'There is no such thing as a bad boy.' Kitty the maid was in love with Spencer Tracy. In love with a priest? I was in vertigo from rolling my head. I took the glasses off. The frames were the same as my father's. This gave me an idea.

I sneaked into the house. Everybody was in the drawing room. I could hear the passionate strains of Ferguson's bagatelle. My sister was playing for Aunt Hana. Kitty appeared from the pantry carrying a bottle of sherry. 'Quite a party they are having', she said. Her lower lip was wet from a swig. I took off my soggy boots and slipped up to my father's room. The rolling waves of the piano echoed through the house. I can hear them still. If McDowell out-chopined Chopin, Ferguson out-chopined McDowell. The door was ajar. No wonder, I thought, the noise was always waking him. I could hear my father breathing. Its evenness reassuring, as was the darkness. I found my way to his bedside table. There would be a book on it and his spectacles inside as bookmark. I swapped Aunt Hana's glasses for his.

In the drawing room she was alone, seated by the window. 'They're all out saving the washing', she chortled. 'It's soaked.' Her mood was mischievous and her accent strangely American. I noticed a small glass in her hand and the bottle of sherry in the other. I handed her the spectacle case. 'I feel great', she said. 'Let's see the sights.' Putting on the spectacles, Aunt Hana looked around the room as though she did not know where she was. 'Great to have the eyes back. All I need's my feet.' Gallantly I helped her up. 'Well, my boy, where are you taking me?' The tone was flirtatious. I knew exactly what she meant. But I pretended puzzlement. She allowed herself to be guided out the front door into the garden. The rain had stopped. There was a rainbow. All was sweetness and light.

Aunt Hana and I were the same height. This gave me confidence and courage. She lent on my arm. 'Where are you taking me?' I did not answer. The sun caught the glass plates in the flowerbed. The rain steamed off them. The elements are with me, I thought. We stopped before the patch with its makeshift cordon. 'What are you showing me?' she demanded, with some of her old dignity, but not all of it. 'That's them.' I pointed at the weeds and the miasmic frame. 'The portulaca.' Aunt Hana looked closer and shook her head. 'What portulaca? That is not portulaca. It's phlox.' Then she laughed, an out of control cackle that alarmed me more than I can tell. 'I must have sent you the wrong seeds.'

She lost interest and was looking vaguely around the garden. 'Everything seems so strange after the rain, bright as underwater. I don't feel well.' That moment Aunt Hana lost her balance for a second time. It was more a glide earthwards than a proper collapse.

I broke her fall and she hung briefly from my shoulders. Then slowly subsided. She sat on the ground. Took off the spectacles. I whipped them from her, always the willing helper, and careered off into the house, shouting for help. I didn't dare look back at the crumpled pile of starched habit.

My mother was coming in from the back garden with a basket of clothes. She dropped it and made for Aunt Hana. I rushed upstairs to my father's room and replaced his spectacles, retrieving Aunt Hana's. My father woke up. 'I'm sorry', I bawled, 'but I think Aunt Hana has had a seizure. Mammy said to come down.'

In the garden my mother was telling her, 'You shouldn't have come out. The ground is so slippy.' My aunt was smiling benignly. Without her glasses she looked quite helpless. My mother grabbed the spectacles from me and handed them to Aunt Hana. 'Nice to have them back. Thank you, Mary.' 'Going out without your glasses?' my mother tut-tutted. 'You really are a one.' They both laughed. The first laugh I had seen them share. 'Mary, I do believe that is your James running for President.' I looked round. My father was shooting out of the house, dressed, or nearly dressed, in a fashion that might suggest a Bombay beggar, a collarless shirt half-tucked into his pyjamas, his great mane of white hair wild on his head. The slippers he wore did not dignify his progression up the crazy paving, nor the fact that he had forgotten his glasses. He landed in the flowerbed beyond Aunt Hana. 'Come to see the flowers', she commented and even my father laughed.

I made myself scarce, watching from a distance my mother and father shouldering a hobbling Hana into the house. It was happy sight. Next day the starch reasserted itself in Aunt Hana and my mother respected it, for form's sake. Mutual first names were now used. That was the main change we noticed. The other one was that my father appeared again at dinner sometimes. Dangerous subjects were avoided, by both.

The Indian summer was coming to an end. There were frosts in the morning. The visit was ending too. The prospect made us warmer towards Aunt Hana. Not least because her departure meant the return to school could no longer be delayed. The plague was past. My sister would shortly be returned to family life. I was not asked again to run down to Mr Purvis for the medicine.

[8]

MESSIAH

'The Immaculate Conception was a phantom pregnancy'

We crowd around Tom Mach in the bike shed. He pontificates, being the only shaver. Tom initiated us into white clay pipes. A sweet shop next to the North Infirmary stocks penny pipes, sixpence each. Old women having babies smoke them under the blanket. Birth is a mystery. Happens in a cloud. We puff tea leaves.

He croons, 'Watching smoke rise/ clouding your eyes/ I see your face forming out of the blue.' His father makes tombstones. Plays trumpet with the Dixie Blue Band.

Macher says, 'Die in this town and your wife goes to my father. He'll tootle "When the Saints" and offer a choice of inscriptions – Fats Waller or Jack Teagarden. Take your pick.

'"They took the fragrance out of the dew/ and sprinkled roses all over you./ Like a garden you're a heavenly thing."

'Or, "In reverie, sweet memory/ takes me back to the days that we knew./ We were happy. Now I'm alone/ with smoke dreams of you."

'Or, "The graveyard is a mean ole place./ They throw you down the hole and dump earth in your face."

'Or what about, "You can't keep a good man down."'

Nobody dies in our town without a haggle.

He sings, 'In the twilight gloom/ of my lonely room/ I light a cigarette./ First of all a glow/ then the ashes grow./Just like a banished love I can't forget.

'"Paradise lost./ Think what it cost./ There's no escaping the things that I do./ I'll be haunted all my life through/ with smoke dreams of you."'

The Holy Ghost was the phantom and he left his mark.

Tom Mach died of lung cancer last year. This is his epitaph.

[9]

SUMMER LIGHTNING

The jungle that boys inhabit is Darwinian, the survival of those who fit in best. And Masonic – the lodge divides into snobs who decide the excluded, and yobs who bump them out. Shane O'Shea is the snob in chief. Gang leaders always are. The included are his chosen nobs (who also act as bouncers).

The chief chooses himself. Not because he is bigger and better looking. But because he takes the snobbery seriously. Boys who go along with him are embarrassed to find themselves honorary snobs by association. But being in the gang means shelter from the weak and smelly and proximity to the bevy of girls who follow the leader.

The gang roves around the beaches on the off-chance that men with boats will take them out fishing. SOS, his preferred title, curses his chosen for not being rich, Protestant and boat owners. Social snobs are pathetic. SOS, with his breezy aplomb, is not. His pretensions amuse: I am not a snob – I'm a social climber. Get on my back if you want to get to the top.

We horse around. Sons of auctioneers, drapers, butchers, grocers, dentists, doctors, lawyers, insurance men and turf accountants are confident of their status in a merchant city. The families of grain merchants and factory owners are absentee citizens. But

269

SOS, whose father owns a garage with ambitions, selling Opels in a Ford town, is rather too fond of his bantering airs.

Out fishing at sea is a levelling experience. Particularly when the shoals are in. Factory workers turn fishermen and commandeer rowboats with outboard engines. Extra hands are needed to harvest the sea. The gang enlist – intent on impressing the men and each other.

Feel the hair bristle of myriad sprats over the sides. When they dart and spark and shrieking seagulls hang their fuselage overhead, mackerel are about to break from the water like hovercrafts. And we have something to prove. Lines alive and hauled in. Slap-happy catch to be stunned, fingers through the throat, unhook with a knife. Fish flapping and flying everywhere. Boys after them in pairs. Stun, finger throat, slit and dump in orange crates. Loaded into Ford vans and sold on the streets tomorrow. A shilling each, good money.

This is a firecracker of a summer – everyone and everything burnt. What is rain, we ask? The men live in tents above the cliff, smoking pipes, raiding farms for chickens and vegetables. Always a billycan of soup on the fire outside their bivouac. Ford workers who after their two-week holiday threw up jobs and stayed for the summer. Hard men all with hearts of gold. But we are romancing. The men keep changing. They are shift workers moonlighting. Wives and children hawk the fish in town while they rotate assembly lines with the seaside.

Back on shore Shane becomes SOS again. He befriends me, straggling behind the gang, hand on my arm. He confides he knows my father is a member of Sundays Well tennis club. The membership is closed. SOS's ambition is to enter the junior tournament in Rushbrooke. Rushbrooke is where the families of the grain merchants and factory owners play. But he needs to practise on grass courts. I agree to invite him as my guest. In return he offers me the pick of the bevy.

I feel power and reflected glory.

The best way to spend time with yourself is in a crowd. The perfect crowd is at unifying events like Eucharistic processions or football finals, and the funfair in summer by the sea. There boys in gangs hunt out girls. Three or four hang around the merry-go-rounds, mocking the swingers and eyeing the talent. Giving the impression they would rather be in the shooting gallery, but their money is spent.

Shane stands out in such company. The tilt of his seal-like head, the shrug of his shoulder swaggers: I am the prow and here are my galleys. All looks alight on him. The cynosure of all eyes. I disappear down into myself. The heat of the day is stagnant in the air. He is joshing the loud frizzy redhead whose hoopla skirt globes out, showing more than a leg. Her quieter companion, little Angela Ryan, in shorts, the backs of her legs gripping the undercarriage, all knees, clinging for dear life. I settle for Angela Ryan as my dream girl. She also does not stand out in a crowd.

Returning by the cliff path, Primula clings to Shane. Angela walks stiffly beside me. It is low tide. Subdued sob-like cries echo from the rocks. Gulls, I say, gulls with insomnia. Angela does not laugh. We are thinking of Mrs O'Dea who leaped to her death. A theatrical fall from Shane breaks the unease. I tumble over him. The two girls laugh. Primula hoots, Angela tinkles.

The moon is full. White horses comb the locks of the sea. We walk together, bumping along.

'Are you one of *the* Ryans or just a Ryan?' (Shane)

'Snob. Shane's a snob.' (Primula)

'Snob? Me? I just need to know if I can expect free samples.'

Everyone has a place in the firmament, says the Madman of the Old Head. Hers is O'Ryan. O-r-i-o-n. The moon on the water is too bright to see the stars. I feel Angela stiffening against Shane. She does not like him. I am happy. Orion. The hunter who got the

271

girl and ended up a transfer in the heavens. I try to piece together
the legend. The moon is too bright.

In a field hedged with fuchsia we scrouch. Primula and Shane
smoke while I talk, recounting the plot of the film *The Long Hot
Summer*. It is getting chilly. Angela removes the sweater from
around her waist and puts it on. She reminds me of Lee Remick.
Not the plangent smile – I haven't seen her smile – but the neat-
ness of body and stillness. That's why I'm boring everyone with
the plot summary of a feud movie. Lee Remick is the tender shoot
in the roughlands of white trash country. I am Paul Newman.

Shane partners the Major at Sundays Well tennis club. Major
Connors owns Blarney Mills and serves like Monsieur Hulot. He
does not like to run. I partner Moke, the town furrier. He tips me
off. Lob it up to the Major or volley to the baseline. No drop shots.
Easy for Moke, a touch player. I can only play flat out. Smash, slice
and first serve.

The grounds flank a river fast flowing to a weir, which sounds
like a crowd in a distant stadium. The immaculate court is grass-
less with the heatwave, and Shane exploits the high bounce when
playing to me. I can't resist the smash. The Major lets it go.
Moke's look tells me, you've blown it, the free drink. Shane snig-
gers. Afterwards the Major gives Shane his card and ignores me. I
won't be asked to play again.

We sit by the river sharing a Guinness. Shane remarks, 'She
fancies you, I think.' *A salmon leaps in the air.* 'Primula', he adds.
Flops back. The water breaks and smoothes. I am taken aback. 'Go
way.' 'She says she likes your Elvis sideburns.' I'm flattered that
this feisty girl would give me a second look and imagine Barbara
Stanwyck in *They Clash by Night* kicking me around a seedy
water-hole. But why only my sideburns? My most modish feature.
What's wrong with the rest of me? Nevertheless, I entertain the
notion of Primula. A large-boned piece with pointy breasts. But
Shane is always hovering in the background. What is this,

Peyton Place? I'll share grass courts and stout with him, but not his girl.

I see Angela Ryan crouching over a rock pool scouring for cowries. So gently made in comparison. Periwinkle mouth, no slash of lipstick. Containable in a pullover as the shell in her palm. I only want to talk to her but she doesn't talk much.

Observing someone from a distance is a dream perspective. Approach closer and the point of intrusion is reached. Then you wake. I had found the perfect distance to watch Angela. The edge of the cliff overlooking the Blue Pool. Closer would mean clear air and a plunge to certain death.

I am reading a book about Orion. The legend seems as remote as the constellation but not as bright. I piece it together as a Hollywood Western. The picture is clear. *Rancher barters daughter to buffalo hunter in return for ridding his lands of vermin. Welches on the deal, gouging out hunter's eyes instead. Brothel madame's remedy restores hunter's sight. All daughters will henceforth fall for him. The rest is revenge seductions, posses, decoys, a crazy virgin with a deadly shot, love after death, Wanted signs in the sky, heavenly choirs of bereft daughters.* My cast includes Kirk Douglas, Orson Welles, Virginia Mayo, Olivia de Havilland, Eli Wallach, Raymond Massey, Walter Huston, Walter Brennan, with cameos for Doris Day in gun-toting mode and Marlene Dietrich as the mystical madame.

The legend needs a treatment or it dies. What's allegorical transmutes nicely into the film industry.

Angela is now in swimming togs. Someone is with her. A man in a town suit wearing a soft hat. It is my father. His imperious bearing contrasts with her shy stance, one leg snaking around the other. There is a quiet solemnity between them. The two are talking man to man.

Later my father mentions his pleasant chat with Ryan's youngest, a serious girl. '*The* Ryans or a Ryan?' my mother asks. '*The*', my father laughs. 'What did you talk about?' 'Tennis.'

The last few weeks of the summer is the end of a world. Families return to town, gangs break up and half-heartedly reform. Shane seems only interested in Rushbrooke. He practises at Sundays Well, a guest of other members. The seaside becomes a fishing village again. Houses boarded up, beaches deserted, a touch of autumn stings the air. My parents will stay on to enjoy the Indian summer. The last dance is tonight. I dress up but change my mind. My cliff top eyrie draws me. Stretching out to watch the sea. Tide is full out, the shore a waste land. I see two people leap-stepping along the rocks, hand in hand. My dream of lovers at exactly the right distance. They approach closer and recognition intrudes. Shane in flannel pants and Angela Ryan in a frock. I wake up.

Days later I meet up with Shane and Angela, friends, old friends. I take them to my cliff top scrouch. We lie around talking about Rushbrooke and nothing. It is pleasant, watching the tide come in and turn again. *The sun is a pickle above the skyline, just about to sink into its jar, preserved for another day.* Shane smokes, blowing rings. Angela tickles his chin. They snuggle up. I look away. And see my parents on the path behind. They overlook the long spiky vegetation, my father pointing out something beyond.

I whisper, 'Down, down, my parents.' Angela giggles. I throw myself between them, arms around both. 'Please, shush.' They lie face down in my embrace, holding their breath. My parents' voices can be heard. My father is explaining the sunset. *The celestial pickle drops into its container, and the sea ambers. Something lost, something gained. Yellowing clouds billow where the sun was. Night and its mysteries, days and their discoveries. Nothing definitive, everything unsure.* I feel a surge of gratefulness towards the two – for what I do not know. We lie together for a few moments. Complete harmony. Friends. Shane passes round a cigarette. Darkness comes.

The sky lights up like day again. We get up and untangle ourselves. Summer lightning. Thunder. Rain. *Great big blobs.* The first for months. *Titan's tears.* Huddling together, drenched to the skin, taking our time going home.

Shane was beaten in the first round of Rushbrooke. Angela married a Sisk. I lost contact. Years later I learnt that Shane took over the business, expanded it too much and ran off to the West Indies to escape debts. I bumped into Primula in town. She recognised me. The years had built a fortress round the large boned frame, her pointy breasts now cannons. She boasted five children and no husband. 'And no loss. You remember him. I think you once were friends. Shane, Shane the snob. The nobs nobbled him. And now he is . . .' She waved her powerful arm westwards and twiddled it. 'Do you remember my Elvis sideburns?' A wild shot to bring down her tragic limb. Primula looked at me. I was not there. And dropped her arm.

I knew if I looked up Shane would impose himself on the sky.

Where are you, Angela Ryan?

[10]

IN PRAISE OF PRIVET

Privet is the hedge equivalent to lawned grass. Gardeners are mostly puritans who regard nature as something to be cut back. Privet's topiary is short back and sides, making it the box tree of suburbia. It is the most orderly of evergreens, blossoming mother-of-pearl in July, harvesting shiny black berries in the autumn. The shrub is dense enough to afford privacy without drawing attention to itself.

Untrained it is a different matter, a tree trapped in the body of a shrub. Wild privet flourishes outside his window. Wraiths of disparate branches sprawl up at all angles like giraffes in a hall of mirrors. The base is a knot of huddled clumps which ivy embraces but cannot penetrate. An introspective world of insects hums within. The upper reaches outreach themselves.

Only when the privet flowers is it released.

On sweltering midsummer evenings the smell of the blossom is as delicate as any orchid. A tough woody underscent draws the moths, which bump around the table lamp. The aroma asks for the light to be turned off. He complies. Take in my fragrance and my down-to-earthness, it says. Moths fold into corners, inert as petals stuck to glass.

The smell is an antidote to clamminess. It says, *lie down – sleep.*

And he does. The word privet suggests a private place, a place of retreat. The garden he grew up in had a clump of privet. In the autumn the mystery betrayed by the leaves was retained in its thicket. He smoked a pipe to help him study in his last year of school. As long as the pipe stayed alight he could concentrate. Smoking in the house is forbidden. He took his books into the garden. When the first chill of winter came, he hollowed out a grotto in the privet undergrowth, large enough to sit in. There he smoked and attended to his books.

The privet outside my window is green and bosky. Unlike the shrubs of my youth which were gold and fresh of hue. In my old age the privet will be dark and sere. I will sit in my arbour puffing. And wait for the blossom.

11

SAPLINGS AND DEAD WOOD

The college gardener gave my parents a wedding present. A hundred saplings. Planted, they made a tidy hedge around the half-acre garden. The saplings took root and flourished into trees. Some soaring to a hundred feet. A rare hybrid cypress we called the palms. Five children grew up in the shadow of these giant evergreens.

The palms were my father's pride and joy. Nobody could touch them. Not even Mr Bonus, the ancient gardener. *His shears ache to prune adventitious branches. Respect for my father.* Allow them to grow. *The good gardener suffers in restraint.*

They cut the house off from the outside world. Confined the garden to a coop for children's play. Sun-starved, shrubs were the life and the soul. *Laurels, lonicera, privet, broom, holly, hawthorns, olearia haastii (with its ghostly snow bloom).* Sacred names in the family lexicon. Flowers grew on thorn, *brief show, long droop. The light discourages. Tough little blossoms peep out of rock gardens and return to the earth.*

A stunted mountain ash despite the palms *berries every year. A large laburnum up against the front of the house receives the sun through the gap of the gate. Each Easter its hanging vines blaze with yellow.*

The sheltered garden satisfied the imagination of young children. *Shady nooks. Places to hide.* Soon aware that invisible strangers passing by could look in and see our world, we were on the look out. Adolescent alienation arrived one day looking through the palms from the road outside. *Brothers and sisters playing in the wood. They could not see me. A strange feeling. Being free to watch myself at play in a recent life. But in a cloister, my father officiating. Gloomy. Saddening.*

The torment in my father's love of the palms was the birds that colonised them. Working in his study at night, going to bed at daybreak, avant-sleep was disturbed by the dawn chorus. He slept fitfully through the day. The household tiptoed around his struggle. The thoughtless child running up stairs was punished with beatings and bed, a rare event. I remember bringing food on a tray (my mother's temper was short-lived) to a whimpering brother, still smarting with shame at what he had done.

Only in the dead of winter did my father sleep well.

The palms in autumn were possessed by wildlife. Spiders spun webs in under-branches. Shake a bough and midges fill the air. In thundery weather tree-flies invade the house. A ceiling darkened with constellations. The room was cordoned off, windows secured. Straggles of sticky tape hung from every lightshade. But the invasion prevailed, a black static pall on the ceiling, the house unbearably hot. Then suddenly, mysteriously as it came, the plague of flies disappeared.

Photo shot through open french window. My father in his study. Head inclines towards the writing pad on his knees. He sits in his armchair, aware of the intrusion – a hand to his hair. The great brow at work. Superimposed on the portrait is the reflection from a side window. Two sweaty summer boys in short pants, braces and no shirts. My brother and me. Standing to attention. Watching the take. The other window reflects a jag of palms.

A childhood ritual. *Being taken out on the lawn to venerate the black-bird that sings from the topmost perch on the tallest palm. Early*

evening, late spring. My father recites, 'Stop, stop and listen for the
bough top/ is whistling . . .' The blackbird is the nightingale of early
Irish poetry. The glee from its bright, yellow bill – pecked into a pot of
gold in a magic cave – thrilled the monks. For me it makes the palm
tree sway without wind. There is only one way of looking at a blackbird
in full voice. The red barked trunk knots upwards, verdant branches
recede in waves until the palm tree twists free in a single tender vane.
A black lyric dot tops it.

My father vibrates with the trills. Tells us that Mozart tran-
scribed one of his finest melodies from a blackbird in a Bavarian
garden. Our delight is impure compared to his. Looking up, we see
him conjure a packet of Rolos from his sleeve. Each child gets a
segment. For being true to the spirit of the occasion. The bathos
does not elude him. We are told that Macpherson rendered a line
in Ossian's *Temora*, 'The heart of the aged beats over you.' It
should have been 'My heart leaping as a blackbird'.

I grew up to the accompaniment of the palms. The slightest
breeze made them stir. A hundred trees alive with the wind, their
sway whispering to the house. *As a child their sounds lulls me to*
sleep. Background music to my dreams. Sonorous or stormy, the palms
are a comfort – the house their cradle and I am in it. Rocking gently.

The palms were reeds in a gale, compliant to winds trying to
strangle themselves in their whiplash. Eerie sighs whistled through
the branches. Safe in bed, we knew they would not break (the more
the boles bent, the stronger the recoil).

In adolescence they keep me awake. The rustling of the palms
intimate alien possibilities. The world beyond the house. *Past*
worlds from books suggest petticoats and furbelows, the lure of sensa-
tions only known in words and illustrations. I sit by the window
unable to read.

Present worlds intrude.

A car coming up the hill. Flashing headlights. Guffaw of an engine
changing gear. Roar of power skidding round the bend at the summit.

Throb of motor receding into the distance. Silence. The palms stunned. Their silence. But whispering returns. Slowly, surely. Sensation coming back after shock.

Or youths from the village coming home from a dance. Loud groups reassure. *I will be amongst them one day.* 'He-festivals, blackguard gibes, ironical licence, bull-dancing, drinking, laughter' (Walt Whitman).

Or quiet couples. They are different. Disturb. So similar to the trees. *Whispers and embraces.* I close the window but still hear. Palms or lovers. I did not know which. I bury my head in the pillow. Silence by force the whispers or embraces.

In their twentieth year the palms began to decline. The bright green feather-like leaves rusted at the edges. Whole branches browned. Mr Bonus had warned of a deep chalky subsoil, unkind to cypresses. The roots had reached the chalk. My brother and I pruned discreetly, using a saw to amputate dead limbs. The palms were losing their pyramidal shape.

Storms became family crises. The rifle-crack of snapping branches. My mother would send for the Maggs from the village. They arrive with axes, ropes and ladders. Wiry, red-headed lads lead by spry old Maggs. *The apex of a falling tree is lassoed, the bole cracks as they tug and crashes down, away from the house.*

My brother and I watch from our window. *The men and the palms and the great winds.* Caps flying from ladders, scaled to axe off recalcitrant trunks. The Maggs tribe – Goliaths in shirtsleeves, worsted pants, ropes coiled round their waists. Taming wild horses in the movies is child's play.

At the tail of the tug-of-war, behind old Maggs, our mother.

In his study my father continues working. The Maggs are the storm troopers, not him. *But still the family knew that each branch torn from a palm was like a limb to him, each bole a life.* His suffering more terrible than my mother's fears for the house.

The aftermath of a storm meant helping the Maggs clear the maim. *The smell of freshly bleeding trees and their torn white flesh is human.* Our clothes and hair embalmed in the fragrance of tree resin for days.

Fallen branches were chopped up and carted away. Detritus to be dumped in mudflats marked out for land reclaim. I stood with my mother at the gate. She was happy.

The winter of my first year at college, storms uprooted whole palms. The new year was arctic. March saw the first frost-free morning. A large kaiser pear tree in full bloom fell overnight. *In all its finery spread-eagled on the raspberry patch, a bride abandoned at the altar.* Last autumn it had fruited prolifically. We stood around, distressed. The ground giving under us.

My father took to his bed that June. The doctor said, 'Only nerves.' The bed was brought downstairs. In the drawing room, the brightest room in the house, he lay in inner darkness. All summer, his favourite time of the year, tennis and swimming. We knew it was serious.

The blight had reached the sap. My brother and I started work. All summer cutting the palms down. Going at them with animal fury. But systematically. Chopping off branches, chain-sawing trunks and steering to earth with pulley ropes. *The crack and crash in the felling of a tree is strangely satisfying.* Blistered, splintered, dust in every pore, ecstasy of controlled destruction. I still have a scar on the instep of my left calf from a saw that slipped.

Two palms untouched by the blight were left. In the front and back gardens. We kept the devastation from him. But he had lost interest.

In September marrow cancer was diagnosed. *All summer his bones breaking one by one.* Submitting graciously to dependence, he was less the self I knew. The mercy of dying is this wearing away of the familiar person. Death made more bearable for those who remain. The bones encasing my father's brain were also fracturing, his unrelentingly logical mind giving way to a keenness for the immediate.

I spent more time with him in his last month than in my entire life. At his request I smoked the pipe he couldn't. 'Not an unknown custom amongst civilised people.' He read my first poems while I proxy-smoked. Moving his lips with the words. Propped up on pillows – head larger than usual, body dwindled to a mere suggestion – he intoned one phrase. '"Beyond the cliff ten thousand years of trees." That's a good line. You will write more.'

I listened to his guttering breathing. Decaying palms in a storm. *I was twenty one and my father was dying.* He clutched to the last details of living – the move of a hand, the sip of water from a sponge. The life of an intellectual refined to the grabblings of the new-born. The circle from cradle to grave complete.

I went out into the night. He loved the stars, and Shelley. 'I am the eye with which the universe beholds itself and sees itself sublime.' *In the dark the absence of the palms was the loss of the garden's flesh, the bare bones of the house exposed to the world.*

The mourners waited on the lawn for the removal of the body. University colleagues amusing themselves as though at a garden party. Worst enemies chatting amicably with favoured friends. October sunlight saturated the scene. Looking out, my mother said, 'It is so bright outside.' Tears welled up, her first for several days. 'Oh! the trees.' She cried for her husband, my father and the palms. Mixed feelings resolved in the outward sign of grief. The funeral would appease.

12

THE HANDSHAKE

The blind vulture turns up for the funeral mass. His aide-de-camp steers him up the aisle. The mourners gape. The only man my father hated. A dark, abstract hate.

They fought on opposite sides of the Civil War. The vulture was not blind then. Leader of the Irregulars, he lay low. My father intercepted intelligence on the vulture's whereabouts. Assassinations were not Free State policy. He sent a warning message. The walking stick used in his last illness was a thank you gift.

My father regretted his intervention. Irregulars assassinated Free State leaders, friends. The vulture took power within the decade and kept it for thirty years. Praised in a public debate for his long reign. My father rejoins, 'Stalin too held power for three decades and is now gone to his reward.'

Further gifts, an embarrassment. What he wanted. Funding for learned institutes, journals. The vulture's sentimental streak rippled a regard for scholarship. Now guided to the front pew. Shake hands with the next of kin.

My father remarked at the powerful old bird's official appearances at funerals. 'Adds another terror to death.' I remember this, and more. Wartime neutrality, withdrawal from the Commonwealth, backward-looking economics, patriotic humbug, challenges to the autonomy of universities, conspiracies of silence at emigration figures, power-mongering while the country became a miserable backwater, condoned by the Church in return for its grip on education and the faithfuls' fears.

I refuse his handshake. The aide hurries him on. A boy preoccupied with his grief. My mother more gracious, accepts his touch. Seeing the hated man close up. Head bowed, long back bent, old father time at work, murmuring conventional condolences. Just an old man being ushered along, believing the performance of his duties is a comfort.

The withdrawal of my hand, hardly a gesture – no-one noticed. I want to cry out. Traitor, mountebank, survivor. Half meaning myself. His dignity, my lack of it. The free man shakes hands with the devil.

What is a handshake? A symbol. The blind vulture swore by symbols. Started a civil war because of a symbolic oath. Fight symbols with symbols. Hand to hand. I should have.

Shame. A senile devil descending into a blind alley. Not noticing more than a stutter in the ritual, a stumble in beneficence.

My father a symbol of the blind vulture's survival. And of mine.

[13]

SHARKER'S BLEMISH

Sharker's blemish was barely noticeable. You had to look twice. The philtrum above the cupid's bow of the mouth was slightly pinched. A vertical indent threaded from lip to nostril, not unlike the mark of a heavy pen on an under-page. The skin snaggled before he smiled – a fleeting snake. He had yet to learn to merge it into a sudden grin. We were in play school. I stared until I saw.

Thirty years later, when I met him for the last time, the snub nose wriggled into action but the cleft had disappeared. His eyes, though sunken, were the same eager peepers, but not seeing me as *I was,* his boyhood friend. Shake hands, practised smile. I had to look twice to see the ghost of a desecrated totem, no miracle of surgery. The thread between us had vanished.

Hometown gossip had made him a glamorous figure, a B movie gangster. I could recognise that – the sheeny shoes and trophied fingers. But the screen was opaque, flat, one-dimensional.

Three decades ago he stood against a blue sky energised by the pylon of the power station behind him, glorying in his blemish. Nothing to hide – a sliver of unwanted flesh between friends from childhood is nothing. There, and then gone. I thought of Faustian pacts, walking away.

Sharker's harelip was the story of his life. A successful life, by all appearances. He was a war baby. *Actress mother playing Hecuba in suburban repertory fled the stage to marry handsome army officer.* Blackouts on furloughs afforded Captain O'Sharkey circumstantial mystery during their brief courtship. Killing children as Priam's wife to empty houses and ending up a dog decided it. In grateful memory Ruth named their first and only child Hector.

The Captain's secure presence mollified the Blitz. But he was neither young nor dashing. Stray shrapnel from friendly fire – conscripts – assured him a pension. Old before his time and going nowhere, he retired to Ireland. Housebound, he dozed the years away reading military history. Ruth's actorly skills, it was said, kept the marriage in amiable quiescence. Teaching drama in private boarding schools got her out and about. She kept herself young dashing around in a resolute morris minor.

Hector grew up between a dark, couchant man sunk in silence and Napoleon tomes and an absent mother who ruled by remote control. Nevertheless his unflinching existence was the bolt that kept the home together. Ruth raged around the countryside like a Sibyl dislodging the mighty within her bosom for Hector's sake. He was her pivot. The Captain was as little trouble as possible – to allow the pivot free wheel. Smiling to himself at Hector's lack of interest in soldiers, he left the boy alone. Visitors to the house marvelled at the whirlwind of the mother, the slippers of the father and the calm hold Hector had on both.

Other boys observed and wondered, uneasy at the tables being turned. Children want others to be like themselves – at a disadvantage to adults. All the same, to my surprise my parents approved of him. Highly intelligent, they said. Hector is a highly intelligent boy. Hating and fearing the expression, I felt stupid.

Ruth's friendship with my mother threw us together and Hector seemed eager to challenge me as though we were equals. That staggered me. 'Call me Sharker.' He hit my funny bone. 'Hector is a stage name.' Knuckles and heels were shown and in a flurry – legs and fists – we became friends.

That's how things are at seven. Seven is easy.

I no longer saw his fleeting snake. But I heard it in his speech. Harelip hoots the voice like a blocked nose. His cousin Trevor Roberts was 'Twevhor Wobber'. Sharker learned to roll his Rs like Orson Welles, roaring out the fricative lisp. Friends take each other's defects for granted, but I couldn't help noticing.

He was his mother's best pupil, winning a verse speaking competition. A child part in a local play – *The Curse of Blessed Martin* – followed. Hector, blacked-up as the infant Martin de Porres, strutting the boards, made me proud. He sounded so loud. After the first interval he joined us in the stalls. His make-up was cracking with sweat and the snake showed for a moment. Then disappeared into the sludge. This thread of recognition was invisible on stage.

Several years later I was his understudy as Hamlet's father's ghost in the school play. I learnt the lines intently, spouting them even in my sleep. 'I am thy father's ghost/ Doomed to walk the night.' My younger brother fled screaming from the bedroom. My father downstairs in his study heard nothing. But my mother did.

The O'Sharkeys lived in a bungalow. Ruth was taking us through the lines, the doors to adjacent rooms left open. 'A thespian superstition', she explained. 'Always leave the door ajar at rehearsals. You never know what will walk in.' Our voices echoed through the house. This is Bohemia, I thought, the artistic life.

Sharker had not prepared. I prompted him. Soon we were reciting in unison, 'Remember me. Swear', my pipsqueak to his rolling basso profundo. Ruth recognised the dramatic potential. 'The dissonance creates an otherworldly resonance. It heightens the scene. Spooky. Tyrone Guthrie would approve.'

While we stuffed ourselves with mince pies she expatiated.

Hamlet's father's ghost's last three words, 'Remember me. Swear' are the McGuffin, the key to the play's ending. HFG was not saying, 'Remember me as I am, nothing extenuate or set down in malice.' Unlike Othello, he wasn't about to kill himself. Already dead, he was saying, 'Forget me, but not my murder. I want everybody dead.' A cry for blood rather than for someone to write his obituary. The last act bears this out.

The Captain blundered in with a pile of books in his arms, spun around with unexpected aplomb, muttered 'Sorry' and exited like a marching bear. Sharker murmured, 'And I to sulphurous flames/ must render up myself.' We all laughed.

I never did get to tiptoe across the creaking boards of a darkening stage draped in candlelit sheets. 'Pity me not, but lend thy serious ear to what I will unfold.' But Ruth persuaded Joe Soap, the producer, to countenance the duet. For three nights I was the upper register warbling from the wings. Hector's dependence on me for his spectral triumph was its own reward.

Our double act changed at university. I became his echo. Tenor sax to his bass. Talking like him. As though I had taken the operation for a sympathetic cleft. If Sharker jumped lectures, I jumped them too. He believed in books rather than pedants. Had worked things out for himself.

Maxim One: there are only two things you can do at the same time – enjoy yourself and make a fool of yourself. I enjoyed being his fool.

His mother respected his freedom. English people do, unlike us. We are freedom fighters. We fight freedom. Such were my thoughts. She lent him the morris for trips to the Red Forest or the Old Head of Kinsale. I echoed his enthusiasm for prehistory and lost battles.

Maxim Two: put off girls till you push off. If a local girl loses her virginity someone is bound to pick it up and hand it back to her mother. It is a trap. College hops were skipped for night strolls in winter by the seashore, preferably in high winds at high tide, the icy spume washing the face.

Maxim Three: beer is a waste of money when you can have free ether from the Atlantic Ocean. The pallor of the moon was ours. A bracing swig from the whiskey flask back in the car got us talking about God and fathers, fathers and God. God's failure, fathers' failures. Supplant the tyrant impostures.

I could not see myself supplant my father. Sharker already had supplanted his. Easy for him. My father was a tortured intellectual who sweated blood at the state of the world. His was a complacent militarist who, having spent his life teaching people how to kill, retired to another world, one peopled by ghosts. I said nothing. I knew I was not fair.

Blasphemy was our heroin. Our dice with body and soul. The cosh to destroy the seeds of inevitability in our lives. Fathers must die. I was not up to Sharker's high standards in starting again, becoming your own father, the first man. I had a secret altar in my heart, not to be shared. Sharker's father was his personal football and God the game he played.

Maxim Four: I swear by Fasnet Rock and the birds and boats that shatter on it that I will be a millionaire by the age of thirty. I did not join him in this aspiration but I was awed. I believed him. Sharker, I said, if you are not God, you are Steven McQueen. He knocked me down.

He had begun to dress like Steve McOueen, the marine in *The Honeymoon Machine*. Sleeveless turtle-necked sweaters, fawn cord pants, horribly tight. Sharker shared with McQueen a capacity for dramatic weight changes. His body shape swung from athletic to adipose within months, and back again. The increase came and went with religion. In fat phases he was to be seen with his parents at Mass, demonstratively pious in the front pew. Religion and weight gain inspired obsessive studying. Months would go by. Then Sharker would bounce back, keen for blasphemy trips.

Pounds fell off him like a cartoon character in a heat wave. As he became skinny the thread resurfaced. It snaked once more in moments of high emotion. He was my Sharker again.

One by one he began to break his own maxims. One: he stopped fooling around when enjoying himself. His orotund delivery – prone to pomposity – solidified into a downbeat gravitas. He smiled but did not laugh. Two: he began dating the Bullet – a tiny, busty local girl with an explosive walk. Three: on the bus home from a rugby trip to Skibbereen, he spouted bawdy songs, threw beer bottles out the window and got drunk with the boys. Blasphemy trips were replaced by student binges.

Only Maxim Four was not discarded.

While I struggled with exams, he sailed through, graduating with honours six months ahead. Ruth invited me to his graduation ceremony. I still have the photo. Sharker, fulsome in gown and mortar, grinning fiercely, flanked by his parents. Ruth the proud mother. The Captain anxious at losing the bolt that keeps the family together. Off-focus, and with an arm missing, I slunk. The thread is not apparent. Not a happy group.

Several years passed before I heard from Sharker. I was trying to keep a job down in Welwyn Garden City. My mother sent me news. He had set up a Body Corporate for pharmacists in the North of England, sidelining in cosmetics. By all accounts – and Ruth was truthful – Maxim Four was well on the way. I sat reading the letter in my bedsit. It was stormy outside. I thought of the Old Head. Sharker, his hair standing on end in the gale, tearing a book in two with his hands. It was a childhood diary. 'I am no longer a child. Destroy the past. It's only baggage. To the future.' He threw loose pages to the wind. The frayed petal of a pressed flower stuck to his upper lip.

The phone rang. Sharker. Long distance. His hoot crackled.

'Hector speaking. Just an impulse. I was thinking of you. Talking to my mother a few minutes ago. She mentioned yours and you. Gave me your number. I must come down and see you. Next weekend. We could have one of our walks.' 'Not much seashore around here. Hertfordshire is hopelessly flat and dull. But we could take a trip. The Isle of Dogs! Should I book you a hotel?' 'No. My secretary will.' That was that.

I waited for him. Close to the phone. Waited all weekend. He never came. If I thought of ringing him or writing, I didn't. Sharker, the success, had better things to do. I was just a passing sentiment. And power, sentimentality and brutality go hand in hand. *I recalled how the petal fell off and the thread was revealed, glowing and wriggling for an instant like a worm on a spit.*

The rise of a provincial *arriviste* is Samuel Smiles. His fall is a tale by Stendhal. Sharker's glory days were clouded by an undertow of hearsay. Success lends itself to hometown imaginings and the dividends are excess and its dire consequences. The Smiles stage dies before its time. Stendhal is anticipated by those left behind. It is not just envy. Interest is kept up by rumoured downsides.

I knew from the gossip that Sharkers had achieved Maxim Four. Marriage on the rocks. Arriving home in a Jaguar for his father's funeral with two blondes, one his ex-wife. The tale of two blondes warmed many a hearth fire. Criminal connections were mooted. I laughed. Pharmacy was bound to . . . A millionaire at twenty nine, one year ahead of schedule. And a bastard to boot. Attaboy.

I was pleased for him and Ruth. She could perhaps open a theatre. *Sharker's Follies featuring Two Blondes. Shakespeare in Verona Adapted for Ice.* I amused myself, felt kindly. Should he turn up at my door it would be as before. Hector, Ruth and myself, though without the Captain. His final exit was comic, a fall down the basement stairs.

I would embrace Sharker and murmur Maxim Four. He would mock rant. I would play the fool. I had it all worked out, feeling confident. My own life had turned out better than expected. Nothing glamorous. Solid. I had kept down a steady job, had been promoted, had hopes of being a householder. *Three 'hads' one after another. Who has been had? Sharker and myself predicted such a life for the squareheads we despised. 'All vain tumult and salary.'* Now I was relieved to live it. Even felt Sharker would respect it and me. I would forgive him for the Welwyn stand-up if he did.

My mother forwarded a letter. It was short and to the point. He needed to talk to me. Being troubled on my behalf. I had been mislead. Our friendship was in danger. There were dark forces. But he had seen the light. It was signed S. There was no address. The letter heading was 'Spirit House', entwined in a serpent with two vertical stakes running through it. Not unlike the American dollar sign. The envelope was franked Birmingham South. I rang my mother. Ruth was distraught. She had received a similar letter. I tore mine up.

My mother confirmed Hector was in the keeping of a cult. Sold his ailing business, handed the money over and was now drying out. Ruth had talked to him on the phone. Afterwards she kept repeating, 'Humble, my Hector has gone all humble. He is lost.' My mother was with her when she collapsed. She did not recover.

I wrote to Sharker. A high-minded letter, ignoring his apocalyptic message. Simple enough in style and content for a superior being down in his luck. But life-enhancing. I would bring him back. Witty as of old, to remind him of better days. And of me. I rewrote it innumerable times. Each draft increased the eloquence. *I still have the carbon. Reading it makes me want to disappear. It is all about me – lauding myself, self-deprecatingly. Humble to the humbled.* When he did not reply I was offended. I washed my hands. *My shame in sending it is recent.*

News of his return to life was a matter of interest. Small-town gossip. But also of indifference. He had retired home. Nobody saw him by day. The lights were on in the bungalow all night. Word was, he engaged in smuggling antique furniture across the Ulster border, an improbable venture. There were no visitors. No signs of life.

Nevertheless, regurgitated gossip of his glory days kept the legend alive. The town needed their legend to rise and fall again, an endless circle. Fresh tales of a killing – the Stock Market – vied with the Northern Ireland Troubles.

When I finally met him he was a ghost. I had not expected to see him in daylight and in a busy street. My disappointment at the vanished harelip was compounded – he was like everybody else. A normal, unhealthy middle-aged man with a suit on his back. That he was polite upset me. That he no longer hooted appalled me. I was not ready for ordinary conversation. He was open, even confiding. Only in the brightness of his eyes did I recognise a glimmer of my evil genius. Or was it medication?

He told me the Birmingham business was behind him. The chemist shops fronted a cosmetics factory. Doing well, until he expanded into theatrical make-up. He became supplier to thespian ventures all over the world. Managers don't pay their actors, actors don't pay their suppliers. A vicious circle. And he was weak, the theatre made him weak. Diversified into more and more niches. Cosmetic surgery included. It was his ruin.

But he recovered something. The medicine market was stable and separate. Early retirement. Amuses himself buying and selling knick-knacks. 'I don't have any great thoughts now. I live for the moment.' I watched him recede into the distance – without regret. About to turn away, I saw him stumble and fall. Pick himself up. Disappear into the nearest pub. I walked away.

[14]

DISTRACTION

The Saturday after my father died I spoke at the Union against the motion that 'Columbus went too far'. In the frivolous debating style of the time, I argued he did not go far enough. A shocked silence ricocheted back at me. I did not speak in public again during my college years.

Anger is the young man's despair. Mine wears fatigues. Student against everything. Weapons – sarcasm, righteousness and jokes. Fighting – against injustice and exams. I study modish paperbacks and play violent games. My room is blackened with pipe smoke. I stay up doodling verse until everyone is asleep.

Walk into town. Down in the docklands. Lowlife. Pubs. Drunks, sailors and prostitutes. I am invisible. See girls board ships, scuttling up gangways, vanish into holds. A stevedore on a spree hits the slattern come to fetch him. He goes home docile. This is life. In the Palm Court dance hall shop girls jive with sailors. A Dixie combo backing the local Elvis, clad in a clear plastic mac. 'Heartbreak Hotel' in two-time. Behind the wallflowers, I spot a stray student. We talk Real Life under the power station until dawn.

Coming home once, tipsy in the small hours. Lights still on in my father's study. Put my head in. No questions asked. 'Nice night?' 'Yes, clear skies.' Out on the lawn, looking up. Together.

We talked of America – my father telling me that Christopher Columbus failed in his mission. Wanted to circumnavigate back to Spain. *He believed the world was round, but got distracted.*

The Saturday after my father died I spoke at the Union, and made a fool of myself.

When I look at the stars I see the States.

[15]

THE HILL OF THE DISAPPEARING ORCHARDS

I am walking through an overgrown orchard. The disfigured trees are mouldy with ripe fruit. I try an apple. It rots in my teeth.

A tapestry of golden plovers rises from the raspberry bushes. Rickety stalks all that remain.

I walk on, thinking of nothing in particular. The pellucid husks of freshwater shrimps in a jam jar, the blue angel curled inside a glass marble, a water-ice melting on the sill of a schoolroom window, the whisk of a cloud that is gold for a moment as the sun sinks.

I am a child on a ramble going nowhere in particular.

I realise the orchard has disappeared. I am walking up a sloping field, the declivity below cut off by a hillock. The orchard is my childhood and the hillside my memory of it.

At that point I should wake up. I don't.

The hill descends to a thoroughfare, and climbs again as a tar-road. I run home early from McClinton's party. My run is restricted – knees knitted together splaying pounding feet. I have been caught short. Hoots and shouts resound from across the hill. Don't turn round. You are the main attraction for all the party children. Their entertainment is unmentionable things happening in your pants. Don't turn round. Not being noticed allowed you to play with them. Not being noticed being noticed is all you have left.

An image superimposes on the running boy like a painting on clear glass. His future self fifty years on, twisting upwards on a mountain bike, silver-haired. He sees the McClinton's house turn into a home for paraplegics and the child guests grow up into discreet dinner parties. The boy fades.

My friend Hubert has red frizzy hair. His twin sister Avril's hair is redder and frizzier. She is not my friend. They both have pamper white complexions and auburn eyes. Hubert and Avril do not have a mother. She walked into the river one night when they were little and never came back. Their father has a stoop from trawling the estuary for her. He sails a dinghy, looking over the side a lot. He is bald and kind. The two go together. Gave his hair to the children, the maid says.

I visit my friend's house. He is crying. Tears on a white face topped with a red shock are orange. Avril smirks, pretending to do her homework. Did she pull your hair? I ask. Or hide your yacht? Or break your matchstick galleon? Hubert is obsessed by boats, but doesn't like the water, can't swim.

There is no limit to what Avril would do to see him cry. At first I think it is the orange tears. I ask her straight out and she says 'Phffft!' and makes a face like one of those carvings on a Viking galley. Avril makes Hubert cry so she can pull faces. She has more faces than anyone I ever knew.

Hubert went off to boarding school. At the train station he wept because Avril was there. One orange tear, goodbye – we weren't to be friends again. During the summer holidays I sometimes spotted him in his father's yacht. The tilt of his sailor's cap told me something and I kept away.

His superimposed image is windswept, ruddy with a mop of frizzy white hair. Hubert has sailed the seven seas as an international yachtsman. He married late having, some say, given up hope of finding his mother. Avril became the wife of a maxillo-facial surgeon. Does she leave making faces to her husband? I doubt it.

Jesus was twelve when he went to the Temple. I went to the Bank, the Ulster Bank on the Grand Parade. My interest is not wise men or money. It is Clodagh Goode. Every day after school she arrives with her satchel for a lift home. Her father is the assistant manager. I go to catch a glimpse. Positioned on the blind side of the City Hall bridge, I can hear her trim trot before her self-contained demure-ness comes into sight. Her 1955 winter collection of overcoats and woollen scarves are in my personal movie museum.

I sit next to her in the City Youth Orchestra. I do not feel the need to talk to her. Looking at her profile is enough. I once stopped my bow to listen to her violin. Her playing is neat and tidy, not wonderful. I take care not to show off my virtuosity, and behave like a little gentleman. I wait to be discovered as her one true admirer.

It never happened. I probably existed in the margins of a well-ordered life, a shy boy with a roving eye whose lift home was near hers.

Clodagh Goode vanished without warning, her father posted somewhere else.

Seeing *Picnic* in the Lee cinema a year later brought Clodagh back. The world dubbed Kim Novak a big shy blonde, diffident about her beauty. I saw something more and less. James Wong Howe, the cameraman, found focusing Kim Novak frustrating. At the last minute she always turned away. This is why so much of Kim Novak on screen is in profile.

But when James Wong Howe catches her face full on, delicate shadows play in the contours. Her mien as a country belle is nerv-ous but determined. Fate does not offer a social marionette choices. When her man has to leave town she follows, at a distance. Stoic dutifulness is her small tragedy. A lost girl, lost to herself.

Of course my Clodagh was lost only to me.

Twenty eight years later Kim Novak appeared in *Malibu*. The fragility of her features has solidified. Febrile shadows no longer play about her face. Her walk is the confident lurch of the careful drinker going nowhere. There is less profile, less side. The silhouette has filled out.

I thought of Clodagh at fifty. I wish I hadn't.

In the last year of Kim Novak's life she played a dying woman. The beauty is back, cadaverous shallows perhaps, a last flicker. The close-ups are mostly in profile. Clodagh would be fifty-eight now, the same age as Kim in *Liebestraum*. Still flickering in my mind's eye.

Drownings punctuated our summers. Three months without school, one by the sea. The drownings loom large. A litany of them lingers:

Little Girl from Mayfield drowned in Graball Bay, pray for us
Father of Four from Dunlop's drowned in Myrtleville, pray for us
Pregnant Woman from Belgooly drowned in Fountainstown,
    pray for us
Handicapped Boy from Fota drowned in Crosshaven, pray for us.

I only knew one of the drowned. A boy my age from a rival school. *He swam too far out.* We tussled once in an under-seven stone rugby match. His name was Eoghan or Aoghagan. *And the swell took him.* I glimpsed his body being thumped for life on the beach, the pallor like the skin after tearing off a plaster.

Some of us went to see his grave. A cemetery behind the cliff, facing the sea. The legend on his headstone read, *Ni bas acht a fas.*

Not dead but growing. A fresh load of seaweed fertilises the plot, weeping iodine.

The night of a drowning we scan the horizon. A rock breaks the sea. The afterglow of a life flares. The lighthouse is dark and silenced. A black pearl is stored forever in the seashell.

In summer people drowned and you were carefree.

[16]

MNEMOSYNE:
WARDEN OF THE BRAIN

1. Fond Memory

Memory is necessary for the operation of reason.
But reason is not necessary for the operation of memory.

Geriatric workers have an acid test for first visits. Ask where the money is kept. The client who tells you is mentally infirm. 'Memory believes before knowing remembers.' William Faulkner's gnostic mantra in *Light in August* is elucidated. Knowing what to do with what you remember.

Mentally infirm people in St Jude's have the choice between afternoon devotions and a memory hour. Memory hour is better attended. The occupational therapist is a nun. She laughs, 'Wheelchairs and zimmers no longer tussle for precedence. It brings out the best in them.'

It is the only time in the week that patients are coherent. Their memories are astonishingly clear, as though speaking in tongues. They are considerate towards one another. No-one interrupts. This is because no-one listens to anyone else. Collective responses are for chapel, the discordance of prayers led by the priest. Children reciting the two times table. Here it is a solo voice speaking to itself. When one falls silent another starts up. A litany of reminiscences. In chapel they are herded. In memory hour they are heard.

Women are better at it than men. Not having the release of the pub in the past, they are holding forth for the first time. No one judges them. Even people with profound amnesia show to advantage.

What do they remember? Nothing apocalyptical like births, marriages and deaths. Small things, epiphanies from everyday life. A time spent away from home. Departures, homecomings. The beauty of a sister's hair, enjoyed while combing. The preparation of a meal. Not just recipes. The food can be tasted. Each ingredient given a past, each mouthful a presence. Being a child in a safe world. Holding hands with a bigger brother. The smell of clean bodies, clean sheets. Nothing important, nothing trivial.

The memories make a daisy chain in a world more real than a last resting home. But what is a daisy chain for? It passes the time at a picnic. And is left behind like cut grass.

When the bell rings, confusion returns.

2. False Memory

> *Memories aren't true.*
> *But you can be true to them.*

We are at the mercy of memories. Serendipity lies in wait. A clearing in the mind and in they jump. Is the past falsified or fossilised? Who knows. The validation of memories is a religion with many adherents and no theology. It divides the world. All memories are untrue to their source. There are degrees of mendacity.

A mind surprised by a memory is possessed by a lie. A lie is not the opposite to the truth, truths being absolute, lies relative. The lie, if not deliberate, is white with a tint of rose.

Remembering a dream is impossible without distortion. We

need to tell. No-one is interested. Unless we sketch it into story. Then it is something else. Pinning down this butterfly, so rare only one person can catch it, is not to describe it as it was. Description would need precedents. To convey the unique butterfly, the air flutters with white lies against the rosy backdrop. The teller recognises the necessary colours. The memorialist who knows his own lies is true to himself.

Remembering is the lowest form of truth-seeking. Often it is all we've got. Don't judge too severely. Artifice is integral though relative. There is some truth in this.

A calculating mind manipulates the past to fool others. Inbuilt verifications. These blatant fabrications are false to memory. Deliberate lies – the sorry truth behind bad faith – are not memories. Their paint is poisonous.

Submitting to the fallibilities of memory is to live a dream. Faking memories promotes nightmares. To carry out terrible deeds with a clear conscience (that is, without a conscience) tyrants must forget everything. Memory only exists in abnegation. Stalins do not have memories. They have agendas, the colour of blood.

Memories should be hard on the recipient, benevolent to the donor. The real world mocks the ideal. After the festival of reverie, the memory of debaucheries is forced. The gaudy reds and blacks of penitents an occasion of sin. Onlookers are tempted. Masochists, humping crosses, flagellate themselves in the streets for the pleasure of sadists.

Forgetting one's friends is foolishness. Forgetting one's enemies is to court victimisation. Forgetting oneself is unforgivable. Memory colours our lives.

3. Grandparent Memories

My paternal grandparents led separate lives, according to the daguerreotypes in my father's study. Solo framed portraits.

Michael looks boldly at the hooded eye. Twirling moustache and thumb in waistcoat, posing proudly in a rose bower. Gentleman farmer and lawyer celebrates his prime. Halfway through his adult life. Thirty-two. Thirteen years to go. *A man of the word unsheltered from the dark side.* His obituary emphasised relentless practicality. Perfect for doing business with cattle jobbers, gombeen men, politicians, ecclesiastics. Pluperfect in arbitrating between the landed gentry and tenants, transferring absentee acres. *Man of the people, man of the world.* Trusted by both sides. My father deployed the expression 'all things to all men' disapprovingly. Could he have been shyly sniping at the absent father that an overcrowded short life suggests?

Bridget Glennon outlived him by thirty years. Her portrait, *sitting on a straight-backed chair in the centre of a sweeping lawn,* is a long shot. *A distant Victorian lady – small head, shoulder shawl and gown billowing to the ground, a paragon of gentility.* The perch of her head frightened me as a child. *Nestling birdlike in the nape, face hidden. The lens catches the severe crease of her tight-drawn hair, a cranial suture.* This faceless, fractured grandmother haunted my dreams. My mother reassured me she was a gentle, thoughtful woman. Artistic. Kept her distance. But radiating kindness, particularly in the presence of small children. Your father inherited that. Children up to seven, before the use of reason. She did not patronise children with baby talk and bubbles.

My grandmother owned the house and farm that they lived in. Michael developed his family estate in Bodyke, breeding quality livestock *(one of his horses finished the Grand National)*. But the marital home was Kilrickle. Two hundred acres of fine scenery rather than arable terrain. Bridget was probably loath to move. Her mother was a Jackson. Said to be distantly related to Stonewall of the American Civil War. Unlikely perhaps – General Jackson was a staunch Calvinist. But his death, *mistaken as an enemy by one of his own beloved soldiers,* would accord with the melancholy of my grandmother, a trait continued in my father and surviving still in present generations.

Apart from my maternal grandmother, my grandparents were dead before I was born. She was as good as dead. A family feud excluded her. I missed them. I felt they would explain my parents. I know from Mendel that genes jump a generation. Grandparents would explain me.

Their absence has prepared me for a world where the overlapping of the generations is losing ground. The dispersal of families all over the world means a labyrinthine bagatelle of conflicting traits.

One memory of my grandfather. *A boy returning from Ballinasloe with the newspaper, reading as he walked. An old peasant woman stops him. 'What is the news, garsun?' He was reading about the outbreak of the Serbo-Turkish war, and told her. The woman threw up her hands. 'Shame on them! They won't stop till they've killed one another.' Adding, sadly, 'In my day, poor boy, it was a terrible thing to kill a man'.*

My father passed the memory on. But as a historian he did not believe in a Golden Age. 'In the old woman's time it was not uncommon for local men to kill one another in a hurley match. A team from Gort lead by the Blake brothers was notorious.' Darkly adding, after a pause, 'Death was no stranger to these parts. She would remember the Famine.'

4. My Father's Memories

'Pluck Plaheen was another world.' The phrase evokes the lost forever. 'My childhood ended in 1914. The year Bertrand Russell said the world lost its innocence.' Dryly appending, 'Bertrand meant himself.'

Dineen's Humpty Dumpty of a Dictionary translates Gaelic words promiscuously. Multifarious meanings. Everything and nothing, neither more nor less. Pluck Plaheen is given as *the hill of loneliness, the hill of barrenness, the hill of emptiness or the hill of the unknown.* Alternatively – *kneecap hill, flat hill, bald hill or down hill.* My favourite is down hill.

Pluck Plaheen is bog land, not in the ordnance survey map. Only in summer when the turf dries out is it accessible. Stretching three or four miles beyond the frontier of my grandmother's farm.

One spring, I came to see it – a student hitchhiking in the Easter holidays. Less a hill than an undulating plateau, declivities flooded and the turf too soft to walk on. Pluck's peremptory bleakness reminded me of Finisterre, *the end of the world. Wisps of mist on the horizon.* Watery sunset. *The unwary fall off.*

I camped by a dry stone wall. Waking next morning, the tent was starred with slugs. I had bivouacked in Kilrickle's old grave-yard. *Had the slimy gastropods fed on my ancestors?* Reluctantly I wiped them off.

The house my father grew up in did not disappoint. I saw it from the road. Large, shambling, shabbier than remembered. I crept up the drive through the banking bushes. The grey stone was discoloured with damp, ivy or creeper absent from its dull facade. My cousin and her husband, an auctioneer, lived there. And her bedbound mother. There were no children. *Once it was overrun with children and books. And the endless coming and goings of a large ambitious family.* Now a dereliction of life prevailed, outlying fields going to scrub, not an animal in sight. Cultivation had ceased.

This house could have been my home. My father decided against it. In the mid-1930s his eldest brother was killed in a car crash in Aughrim (where Ireland lost to William of Orange). My uncle, a powerful man in government, was speeding home from Dublin in the small hours. *Consumed with dark forebodings, a characteristic shared by many revolutionaries who saw democracy established over*

*the dead bodies of friends. He had three small daughters and an invalid
wife and lived in fear of coming home to a house on fire.*

My father ceded his inheritance to the widow. *He needed the
memories of this house more than possessing it.* He drove south in a
box Ford – the roof rack overflowing with books and more books –
to the university where he taught. The books slowed him down, an
uncomfortable journey – punctuated by punctures. At his digs, my
father was greeted by the warm licks of two red setters, his hunting
dogs. *Followed him a hundred and twenty miles, a pace behind.* They
were returned to the farm.

He never returned to Kilrickle.

My father had his memories. Only one was shared. 'Pluck Plaheen
was another world.'

*Two boys grouse shooting on a glorious morning in 1910. One of
those days that only comes after a sustained spell of fine weather.
Before daybreak the sky is pearl and green. The sun rises, a cool peach.*

*The firmness of the turf emboldens them to explore beyond Pluck
Plaheen. Hiding their guns in a furze bush, they walk into the
unknown. The blueness of the sky is pure Shelley.* The faint lilac
glow that lines the horizon will not change all day. *Empty hunting
bags flying behind them, the boys run up the slow incline. They scuttle
after rabbits, startle a brisk hare. A plump grouse breaks cover.
Lazily, knowingly, displays its bracken-coloured plumage and red
spotted brow. The disarmed hunters laugh helplessly – so near and yet
so far.*

*Orange-tipped butterflies everywhere. A lone red admiral unfolds
on a nettle. The mossy surface of the dried out bog gives way to richer
vegetation – clover, stubble-grass, a stunted tree shrouded in pale dabs
of dog rose. Down hill at last. Woodland. Several hundred giant oaks
skirted with ash trees.*

*The boys clamour through the underwood – dusky ivy laced with
light lily-like weeds. A copse of aspen choking with brambles. Fallen*

branches, pocked with lichen, rot like corpses in their path. Dying trees give way to a clearing. They stop.

An overgrown orchard. Mouldy apple trees. Humid air, unstirred by life. Stone outhouses collapsed. Musty smell. Desiccated cowpats. Silted pond. Lawn of thistles and ragwort. The derelict mansion sprawls amid the ruins.

They enter the orchard. A snipe clatters out of a bush. Hundreds of pheasants rise in a rainbow phalanx from a tangled bed of raspberry bushes. The wonder of such gravid birds taking flight. The raspberry bed is heavy with fruit. The boys gorge themselves.

Then a little greenhouse. Intact. Peaches on the walls, vines knotted across the roof. The dwarf peaches are curiously bitter, the grapes luscious clusters. They fill their bags.

A tiny woman dressed like a man is standing behind them.

'Very well, keep your plunder, but on one condition: you stay to dinner.' She is smiling. Instinct is to run, the boys shoulder their bags and follow into the house.

'I am your neighbour. Perhaps you have heard of me. Mrs Moore. Bridget Glennon's boys. Don't be shy. I don't often have gentleman callers. Feel welcome.'

The house is neat and tidy, the grand staircase blocked off. Hunting trophies and family portraits crowd the walls. Biddy, a bony wraith-like creature, sidles in to lay the table. Her disgust is evident.

'Today is Saturday', confides Mrs Moore, 'and we shall be sure of a decent dinner, otherwise I wouldn't have invited you.'

Flies swarm on the ceiling. Biddy half-heartedly shoos them with a cloth. They settle on a chandelier. Inconsequentially Mrs Moore remarks, 'The Emperor, Domitian, was much delighted with catching flies.'

Hunger makes a frugal meal a feast. The watery stew, sopped up with soda bread, appeases the boys. Unexpectedly Biddy sits at table. Mrs Moore talks rather than eats. Dinner party patter, an air of timorous and hopeless expectation.

The harridan disappears into the kitchen. 'Don't mind Biddy. In her day she was the life and soul. Danced and sang and had an eye for the young men. Too many eyes. The womenfolk took against her. A witch, they said, and went to the parish priest. Silly man. My husband rescued her. She has been with me since.'

Biddy returns with pastries and the decanter. Pours herself a tumbler and guzzles through wobbling teeth. Mrs Moore plunges from politenesses into sudden confidences and back again. This bothers the boy who was my father. He wants secrets and mysteries, his own explanations.

He thinks she has no friends nor intimates, not because she is isolated or odd, but from choice. Other people only exist as cutlery to play with. Her whole being is turned inward upon herself. The melancholy of this makes him like her.

She speaks of her marriage. Biddy leaves the room. The boys hear, 'Three blissful years and then . . . I thought I should not survive him. I could not even weep. They laid him out in this very room. On this table. I did not stay to watch. Would you believe it, I slept sound that night? Next morning I went to look at him. A summer's day like today, the sunshine lighting up his body from head to foot. It was so bright. I saw one of his eyes was not quite shut and on this eye a fly was crawling . . .'

The boys returned home. The fruit rotted in the sacks, thrown away. They say nothing to their parents. That winter Mrs Moore disappeared into the flooded Pluck Plaheen. Biddy reported the missing person to the police. Village gossips had a field day. The body was not found.

Many years later I read a version of this story in Turgenev's *Sportsman's Sketches*, my father's favourite book. He lived most of his life inside his head. Life was a welcome intrusion, a rare visitor.

I sit by the stream that runs through my grandmother's land. I will camp here tonight. The house before me is a drab, damp dwelling sunk in unworked scrub. I feel dispossessed. Not of property or land. But of a life I might have lived.

Why knock on the door? I am not part of that legend. My

memories of my father's memories, my father's memories of my grandfather's memories. The links in the chain of the past. Broken at my feet.

My happiest memory of my father. Halcyon days waiting in the estuary inlet for the appearance of a kingfisher. *Once or twice each summer a swirl of blue and green is sighted, skimming over the water, smoothing the winds and waves.*

5. Memorabilia

The history department honoured my father's centenary with a commemorative conference. Asked to suggest showcase memorabilia, I came up with:

1. Birth certificate (b. 1898).
2. Diary handwritten during the fight for Independence (illegible, 1920).
3. Photo of plaque listing Free State Directors of Intelligence (position held April to September 1923).
4. Ornate walking stick. De Valera's thanks for intercepting an assassination attempt (1923, not engraved).
5. His Major General's uniform (loan from the city museum, 1922).
6. The script of a memoir read into a dictaphone when seriously ill (1952).
7. Black and white photographs. One in Patrick Street with wife and two boys (late 1940s).
8. The only letter he wrote to me (aged six, 1949).
9. Leather-backed writing pad (doodles on blotting paper, 1932–1963).
10. Bulldog paperweight (piebald bronze, 1926–1963).
11. 78 recording by the Hungarian Quartet (late Beethoven, 1940s).

12. Programme of a concert by Victoria de los Angeles (his beloved, undated).
13. Sample suit (grey, replenished every other year by tailor Coakley, 1935–1963).
14. Grey soft hat (worn while driving, 1958–1963).
15. An austin somerset car (black, circa 1960).
16. Swimming togs (one-piece, 1930s).
17. Tennis racket (usable despite being racked for 35 years).
18. Packet of Rolos and storybook about Pookahs (bedtime treats, 1947–1963).
19. Crayon sketch by child of honeycomb and fruitcake (favourite foods, 1950s).
20. Pipe and Erinmore tobacco (his friend, 1960s).
21. Black telephone with lobster-like receiver (his enemy, 1950s–1960s).
22. My poem on playing tennis with him (year of death, 1963).

The historians decided. Strict scholarly criteria were applied. The glass case finally displayed:

a) Papers with handwritten evidence of exegesis (items 1,2,3,6,8).
b) Two photographs verified by family (item 7).
c) The army uniform. Gold buttons missing. My mother transferred them to a grandchild's jacket (item 5).
d) The pipe. Tooth marks on the stem (item 20).

History disowned my memories. *But the tooth marks were mine.*